A CULTURAL HISTORY
OF WOMEN

VOLUME 6

A Cultural History of Women
General Editor: Linda Kalof

Volume 1
A Cultural History of Women in Antiquity
Edited by Janet H. Tulloch

Volume 2
A Cultural History of Women in the Middle Ages
Edited by Kim M. Phillips

Volume 3
A Cultural History of Women in the Renaissance
Edited by Karen Raber

Volume 4
A Cultural History of Women in the Age of Enlightenment
Edited by Ellen Pollak

Volume 5
A Cultural History of Women in the Age of Empire
Edited by Teresa Mangum

Volume 6
A Cultural History of Women in the Modern Age
Edited by Liz Conor

A CULTURAL HISTORY

OF WOMEN

IN THE
MODERN AGE

Edited by Liz Conor

Bloomsbury Academic
An imprint of Bloomsbury Publishing Plc

BLOOMSBURY
LONDON · OXFORD · NEW YORK · NEW DELHI · SYDNEY

Bloomsbury Academic
An imprint of Bloomsbury Publishing Plc

50 Bedford Square	1385 Broadway
London	New York
WC1B 3DP	NY 10018
UK	USA

www.bloomsbury.com

**BLOOMSBURY and the Diana logo are trademarks of Bloomsbury
Publishing Plc**

Hardback edition first published in 2013 by Bloomsbury Academic
Paperback edition first published in 2016 by Bloomsbury Academic

British Library Cataloguing-in-Publication Data
A catalogue record for this book is available from the British Library.

ISBN: 978-08578-5102-4 (HB)
978-1-8478-8475-6 (HB set)
978-1-3500-0982-0 (PB)
978-1-3500-0984-4 (PB set)

Library of Congress Cataloging-in-Publication Data
A catalog record for this book is available from the Library of Congress.

Series: The Cultural Histories Series

Typeset by Apex CoVantage, LLC, Madison, WI, USA

CONTENTS

SERIES PREFACE

A Cultural History of Women is a six-volume series reviewing the changing cultural construction of women and women's historical experiences throughout history. Each volume follows the same basic structure and begins with an outline account of the major ideas about women in the historical period under consideration. Next, specialists examine aspects of women's history under eight key headings: the life cycle, bodies/sexuality, religion/popular beliefs, medicine/disease, public/private, education/work, power, and artistic representation. Thus, readers can choose a synchronic or a diachronic approach to the material—a single volume can be read to obtain a thorough knowledge of women's history in a given period, or one of the eight themes can be followed through time by reading the relevant chapters of all six volumes, thus providing a thematic understanding of changes and developments over the long term. The six volumes divide the history of women as follows:

Volume 1: A Cultural History of Women in Antiquity (500 B.C.E.–1000 C.E.)
Volume 2: A Cultural History of Women in the Middle Ages (1000–1500)
Volume 3: A Cultural History of Women in the Renaissance (1400–1650)
Volume 4: A Cultural History of Women in the Age of Enlightenment (1650–1800)
Volume 5: A Cultural History of Women in the Age of Empire (1800–1920)
Volume 6: A Cultural History of Women in the Modern Age (1920–2000+)

Linda Kalof, General Editor

LIST OF ILLUSTRATIONS

Introduction

LIZ CONOR

The modern era has again and again been defined not only by innovative ideas, technologies, and modes of production but by the velocity of their circulation and exchange. The ethos of modernity has been characterized as voluble, skittish, fractured, alienated, and inconstant. Informing this sentiment have been the keystone developments of industrialization and mobility along with the primacy of vision. The impacts of all these changes intensified during the twentieth century, as their varied attendant technologies increasingly became part of everyday life, but many have their origins in the nineteenth century and, in a few critical instances such as typography and visual apparatuses, much earlier.[1] Massive migration events took place beginning in the 1850s and throughout the twentieth century, which was crisscrossed by the circulation of people and social movements. They took with them critical ideas, most prominently rationalization, acquisitive-competitive individualism, and the rights discourses of franchise, citizenship, and self-government. These rights discourses were themselves often countered, to the detriment of marginalized peoples, by expansionist imperialism, scientific racism, assimilation, eugenics, and social hygiene. Modern migrants transferred aesthetic visions, amateur ethnologies, and what Tani Barlow has dubbed "vernacular sociologies" to "new worlds."[2] People arrived in foreign worlds via new technologies such as the internal combustion engine and the extension of roads and railways, and they were sometimes equipped with knowledge and skills in energy production, administrative and corporate bureaucracies, leisure forms, syndicated advertising, and mass communications. All were part of the escalating global exchange of the capital-ist world market in the twentieth century. And all were experienced by women according to the various gender regimes they lived within, or within which they found themselves newly situated.

The movement of populations in the nineteenth century had been immense: fifty million Chinese, fifty million Europeans, and thirty million Indians.[3] In western Europe prior to 1914, this movement had been largely unrestricted by passport.[4] But this freedom of movement, as Marilyn Lake and Henry Reyn-olds write, was first restricted by immigration laws in 1855, in Victoria, Aus-tralia. Towards the twentieth century and throughout its first half, immigration restriction became the cornerstone of claims by "white men's countries" to self-government and nation building.[5] The intensification of immigration re-striction reacted to "the most intensive period of human migration in human history," from 1850 to 1930.[6] But migration was not always voluntary and perhaps was mostly under the pressures of economic hardship, or due to the violent upheavals of minority discrimination or religious persecution. Migra-tion had its corollary in the displacement of the indigenous, of racial minori-ties, of peoples uprooted by war, natural and, increasingly, climatic disasters, or extreme weather events. The colonial project of "maximising settler access to land, and converting that land to property,"[7] as Evans et al. succinctly put it, remained central to the expansionist ethos of newly forming nation-states in the early twentieth century. But at each geopolitical and ideational crossroad, women were positioned differently from men.

Women wrought their own relationships to each innovation as the flux of modernity propelled them into unprecedented ways of life. The movement, particularly of Western women, beyond their traditional realm of homemaking provoked anxieties regarding an authentic feminine essence and the unmooring of a dependable idea of womanhood from its static place in the maternal and the domestic. Ideals of familial connection and attachment to homeland were felt to be fractured through industrialization, such that traditional feminine roles were held as the special province of the home. Nostalgia for the "peas-ant" village or "primitive" kinship provided a refuge through tourism and its trinkets from the impersonal market and the disruptions and alienations of modernity. As women stepped over the thresholds of home and homeland, metropolis, workplace, and nation, they carried with them particular skills and knowledge into new domains. They continued to account for the well-being of the people in their care, but no one in the much-altered yet resiliently patriar-chal family was responsible for their care, sometimes exacting a toll of exhaus-tion and compromised physical and mental health. The gender "revolution in the workplace" often entailed corralling women into labor reserves of unskilled and, towards the end of the twentieth century, increasingly less formal work.

Compulsory public schooling had redefined children as family dependents, but their care was increasingly scrutinized by the penetrating gaze of the welfare state or aid and development organizations. Paid work was cruelly segregated from the organization, or lack, of child and aged care, and this divide remains unresolved for working women with caregiving responsibilities. It is most acutely felt by migrant workers who are forced to leave their children to the care of their mothers and other relatives while they travel long distances to work as nannies for affluent Western women. Yet intimate ties, as Gail Finney has argued, were nevertheless critical to new formations of modern subjectivity.[8] In the new domains they made their own, women never ceased to be homemakers, indeed the home itself, set apart from the public realm, was remade under the influence of women's activities beyond its reach. The changing space of home, throughout this period of dispersion and migration, has complicated the meaning of home wherever it was resituated in new, unfamiliar locales, and as it came to be intercepted by labor-saving devices,[9] or maternal and child health reform, or development agencies.

For Western women, as Kathy Peiss has argued, "the development of wage labour, imposition of time discipline by employers, and rationalization of the work process resulted in a new sense of the rhythms of time and cognitively sundered 'work' from 'Life'."[10] But the separation of spheres had welcome outcomes, too. Peiss has extensively documented the ways this distinction created a working-class leisure culture at the turn of the twentieth century that offered autonomous and heterosocial forms of commercialized recreation for young working women beyond the family. Large-scale urbanization focused the sight lines of the modern metropolis on the newfound presence of bourgeois women in the traditionally masculine domain of central business districts— it was assumed that these young women were in the pursuit of leisure and shopping. Rita Felski's influential work has, in many ways, defined the relation of the feminine to the modern. She writes, "The changing economic, legal and cultural history of women encouraged a sense among many that it was they, above all, who epitomized the changing nature of modern life and the spirit of the new."[11]

By the twentieth century, elements of modernization, particularly the presence of expanding corporate markets and global economic interdependence, were present in most countries. Its geographic reach and demographic involvement, and even the resistance it could encounter from each country's brand of political nationalism, however, varied dramatically. Women's participation in these innovations invoked the late nineteenth-century typecasting of the New Woman and the Modern Girl, who, as Alys Eve Weinbaum et al. have recently shown, reappeared around the world. The Modern Girl Around the World research group has documented how international corporate strategies deployed the Modern Girl figure through global circuits of exchange and cultural flows involving commodities and images.[12] U.S.-based corporations such as Max Factor employed local brokers in the Philippines, the Middle East, and Cuba.[13] By demonstrating the diverse locales where the Modern Girl simultaneously emerged, this research group has challenged the conflation of modern with Western, and has actively sought to destabilize the hierarchy of developed and developing countries.

This sixth and final volume of *A Cultural History of Women* has had its own unrealized transnational ambitions. The hope to include a diversity of women's experiences of the modern era has not come to fruition, as the standpoint in the volume is Euro-American or Western, largely because of the linguistic affinities of the contributors. Despite my best efforts, excluded from the remit of this collection are indigenous women's experience of the modern and the quite distinct ways modernity was construed of a narrative of advancement that more often than not demanded their assimilation to imposed Western standards of living, often incompatible with their economies, care responsibilities, and custodianship of homelands. Indeed, what marks indigenous women's experience of the modern is loss of home within their homeland, through removal to training homes, government stations, or mission reserves. Domesticity became a key measure of "progress," and often the site of surveillance, while maternity was disavowed under government policies shaped by eugenics and aiming at biological absorption. Indigenous women's sexuality was encountered by settlers in the half-light of coercion and violence, or disavowed relationships, all vouchsafed by medical science, which accepted white men's access as inevitable and necessary, while it intervened in women's bodies as the purported source of venereal disease. Nevertheless indigenous women toiled to keep their families intact in the face of these dislocations, and the loss of cultural traditions, themselves an important source of identity.

The geopolitical global bloc of the West was in its entirety a "melting pot," despite often violent attempts, as well as legal restrictions along with social coercions, to shore up identity within distinct racial groups, and homogenize populations, particularly in Australia and Canada, as white. Yet just because modernity is characterized by globalization, and has been shown to put in circulation many traits that led to shared experiences of the modern, this should not excuse scholars from attending to the differences between women be they settler or indigenous, as living under communist or fascist regimes, or recently decolonized nation-states or within established industrialized democracies. In fact international collaboration across industry, science, culture, and trade was often Eurocentric, with unidirectional flows from the metropole to the periphery. Yet none of the overarching historical changes of the modern era such as industrialization and nationalism proceeded evenly in each locale.

The chapters in this volume may be able to generalize from some aspects of Western women's experience of the modern, however the limits of the collection need to be set out clearly. These particular studies are each based in Western countries, and most of them are concerned with the impacts of modernity on the lives of white middle-class women. This compromises the reach of the volume but it should not be read as setting the parameters by which women can be considered modern. Indigenous, migrant, and women of color were impacted by the changes described, but very often they were excluded from any benefits, instead being further displaced by urbanization, or megacorporate projects such as mining, and excluded from even compulsory education and national health and welfare schemes, as well as cultural production, or exploited in unskilled labor reserves, the demands of which made the care of their families untenable.

Yet the activities of women also wrought profound changes, perhaps the most important was their increased presence in urban space that forever altered the nature of the modern public sphere. Women's growing public presence shaped modernity's representational and imaginative systems including art, literature and popular culture. The particularly modern representational forms examined by Felski—such as the novel and the display conventions of commodity culture—were decisive in the organization of sexual difference and in its significance to ideas of the modern. The crowds attending the new-found leisure-form of cinema were swelled by women with some disposable income and a degree of autonomy of movement in the city. They challenged the Victorian tradition of separate spheres. Photojournalism, commodity culture, and cinema in Weimar Germany also challenged traditional expressions of sexual difference, spurring attempts to reinstate those earlier expressions.[14] Modernity was marked by the reorganization of sexual difference through representational systems. For Felski modern cultural forms evince a paradigmatic masculinization of the modern values of "rationalisation, productivity,"[15] and repression of the natural world, itself associated with the feminine. In social theory, the modern is wrought by male figures such as Baudelaire's culturally botanising Flaneur, the active technological innovator, the colonial and capitalist empire builder, even the Marxist revolutionary. Moreover, it is characteristic of modernity, as Felski writes, to throw off tradition embodied by the feminine. Yet since gender is an organizing principle of the social field the feminine has been required to mark sexual difference as well as carry its significatory burdens. As this volume hopes to show, this is borne out and implicated within modernity's representational strategies. The feminine developed a prevalent but ambiguous presence in modern visual economies, particularly when predominantly positioned as spectacle. As an object of fascination in modernity's representational fields the feminine became symbolic of modernity because of its newfound exposure in visual culture and through its association with the commodity image.

One of the defining lineaments of modernity was the development of visual technologies and the mass production of imagery. Janell Hobson, in her chapter on artistic representation shows how the precedents for the twentieth century "cinematic framework" were undergirded by photographic technologies that had emerged in concert with Western colonization. Hobson notes that "Not long after their inventions, the earliest photography and motion pictures were utilized both for ethnographic depictions of nonwhites and pornographic spectacles of the female body." Later this "National Geographic aesthetic" was further expanded by the Internet, particularly in Second Life scenarios which enable users to transcend "the limitations of the physical and national body." Hobson details the work of feminist artists critically engaged with these new technologically mediated territories, particularly one artist who documents the IT factories of Southeast Asia where women assemble the hardware that allows increasing numbers of women to take flight from their prosaic identities.

The coincidence of visual technologies with colonial expansion, this "conquest of the world as perspective,"[16] has also been described as a characteristic feature of modernity.[17] It meant that the gaze created under the conditions of colonial modernity was applied to the bodies of women on the frontier with possessive intent. In the eighteenth century the scientific revolution and its extension of the human gaze through ocular apparatuses such as the refracting telescope had unleashed an exploratory, surveying gaze. Martin Jay argues that this "mapping impulse" facilitated "a more active search for controlling and dominating the earth."[18] Stephen Kern notes, "As human consciousness expanded across space people could not help noticing that in different places there were vastly different customs."[19] The fascination in "native" women prompted the inscription of the "racial hierarchies at modernity's heart."[20] The expansion of literacy, the invention of the woodblock, the outreach of transportation and communication through imperial trade routes created new prospects for the dissemination of European accounts of racial difference. As Hobson has detailed in her earlier work this logic of looking underpinned the appraisal of colonized and enslaved women as exotic. It led to the display of Sara Baartman, the "Hottentot Venus" in the exhibition circuits of Europe and finally the display of her genitals in a jar of formaldehyde at the Musee de l'homme in Paris until the late twentieth century.[21] This circulation of images of exotic and sexualized women depended on the industrialization and commercialization of imagery through the invention of the half-tone block, enabling the reproduction of photographs in print media[22] as well as in the picture postcard format[23] and within picture atlases. For example the emergence of the dry-plate in the mid-1880s allowed Australian photographers such as J. W. Lindt and Nicolas Caire to abandon their studios and travel on photographic expeditions as far afield as New Guinea and the South Pacific.[24] Their work contributed to a representational system that distinguished, ordered, and administered native populations.

Meanwhile the modern metropolis underwent a "dispersal of places"[25] as new sites of exchange and leisure sprang up. These sites also created refuges for those escaping patriarchal family structures such as urban gay and lesbian communities and other subcultures of marginal groups. The modern city itself had long been thought of as feminine because of its labyrinthine, centerless, unknowable qualities. It was replete with proximate mingling on the street, the sexual adventure of growing numbers of unchaperoned "public" women and the forbidden pleasures of the prostitute.[26] In her detailed cultural history of sexual danger in the city Judith Walkowitz notes, "By venturing into the city center, women entered a place traditionally imagined as the site of exchange and erotic activity, a place symbolically opposed to orderly domestic life."[27] Consumption was a feminized cultural loop, where the dream world of the department store interior created a paradoxically public site ingratiating and catering to women's desires. As Felski puts it, "Commerce's assiduous and exhaustive attentiveness to the fulfillment of every female whim gives women's interests a previously unimagined prominence in the public domain, while simultaneously obscuring the exploitive economic relations which underpin the modern cult of femininity."[28] The deliberate appeal of the spectacle was a means to imbricate women into new forms of modern identity through the "strategies of display"[29] of consumption. Consumption positioned women as public voyeurs constantly moving though a panoramic enchantment of visual pleasure. So too was travel newly available to women, often as requisite to migration and exile, but also very often as a leisure form.

Tourism and cosmopolitanism were key to the participation of women in the established circuits of internationalist networks, such as the missionary,

labour and anti-slavery movements. Fiona Paisley has documented the participation of women in internationalism, and the confluence of cosmopolitanism
with tourism, particularly in the pacific.[30] Through such tours modern women
encountered diversity and, through the resistance of indigenous women, were
forced to reappraise the ideal of modernization. Through cross-cultural exchange, however, many women traveling in the modern era sought to live out
an ideal of interracial harmony, that very often imposed the criterion of West-
ernization through the reform of local women. As the rapid changes and impacts of globalization were circulated through immigration and imperialism,
cooperation between scientific institutions, government administrations and
trade affiliations threatened the often newly asserted sovereignty of nation-
states and decolonized territories. The pleasures of travel were never innocent
from these constitutive agendas, nor from the transnational interdependence of
women, hierarchized in terms of resources and labor.

In Maureen Perkins's chapter on women and religion in this century she discusses the travels of Emmeline Pankhurst on lecture tours in the United States,
"often on themes to do with supporting the civilizing mission of the British
Empire." Like the women involved in internationalist networks Perkins notes
that Emmeline's sister Christabel moved between London, Paris, Canada, and
California, to speak publicly and act as a minister. The expanionist ethos of
Christianity was given moral legitimation as a project to civilize colonized
peoples. Whites such as Pankhust and Lindt embarked on colonial odysseys
that ironically aspired to fix the "roving native" through civilized cultivation,
or in photographic stills within historically moribund ethnographic sites. The
project took white women all over the world as missionaries, propagating, as
Perkins argues, "attitudes of benign superiority and a wish to rescue women
from the constraints of their 'traditional cultures.'"

The freedom of movement taken up by Christabel Pankhurst depended
paradoxically on the settlement of colonial-modernity. Migration, tourism,
commuting, are all forms of mobility that anticipate a "home-base," either at
both ends of the journey, or on arrival. This ideal of home depended on the
home-making of women settlers, and on the displacement of mostly indigenous women for whom the land had been part of their, or their parents' or
grandparents', homeland. These women were distinctly coraled from the freedom of movement that defines the modern era. Their initial displacement and
dispossession was only the first in a long march of itinerancy that could involve
removal, incarceration in ghettos or segregation and concentration on remote
reserves. Reserve leases were commonly revoked throughout the twentieth century and land handed over to white farmers—in Australia, particularly after

indigenous residents had shown it could be profitably farmed. Any "home" site designated by state authorities—who continually redrew the line of the frontier where such peoples were, yet again, in the way—was again and again pulled out from under their feet. If the frontiers of exploration of new territory had closed in 1911 when Roald Amundsen laid foot on the South Pole, the constant search for new lands to permanently occupy distinguished the particular expansion of the twentieth century. A permanent home, from which one might travel, tour or commute and then return, or to which one could migrate, defined the parameters of white identity. And again, it was white women assigned the work of building and maintaining the invisible economies of this realm. Indigenous women were accused of "primitive nomadism," and then denied the opportunity to settle and sustain their family economy. They had to respond to unimaginable shifts in "paradigms of Aboriginal landholding"[31] while very often they resisted the settlement of peoples who themselves sometimes harbored living, or generational, memories of the enclosure of common lands from British and Irish peasantry, or the degradation of ecologies through unsustainable agricultural practices, mega-projects such as mining, or displacement by war and civil strife. What is clear from the activism of the resulting indigenous diaspora throughout the twentieth century is that removal from homelands has rarely entirely severed custodianship, either for those removed, or for subsequent generations. For the displaced the loss of a territorial base did not disperse the identities that had been forged in homelands.[32]

The achievements of indigenous activists, and those of color, throughout the twentieth century overlapped with those sought by women, concerned as they were with political participation. At times differences between women, such as class-based, created tensions between rival reform organizations in the labor movement seeking protective legislation for women workers. As June Hannam details in her contribution on European women and power in the twentieth century, at the 1926 congress of the International Woman Suffrage Alliance in Paris, groups were formed to rival the Alliance over their different political strategies around women's workforce participation. Some opposed protective legislation while others sought legal equality in the workplace and by extension, all aspects of life. Suffrage was a central focus in the quest for equality with the antipodes creating the precedent, first in New Zealand in 1893 and for South Australian women in 1894, with federal franchise granted to Australian women in 1902. In Europe, women in Finland and Norway were included in the franchise just before the First World War, while Denmark and Iceland soon followed suit. Hannam documents a "spate of enfranchisement" after the war itself, including Britain, Germany, Czechoslovakia, the Netherlands and Sweden. France and Italy, however, waited until after the Second World War, while Switzerland was one of the last liberal democracies in Europe to enfranchise women in 1971. Fears that women's limited sphere of activity in the home would make them inherently conservative voters was initially borne out by their preference for moderate conservative parties; however, their choice was limited by the failure of parties to address the problems created in their daily lives by gender inequality, along with their needs for welfare reform policies, such as housing sanitation and maternity clinics. Perhaps for this reason women joined social democratic parties in large numbers during the interwar period, they also collectivized in women's organizations to counteract the difficulty of gaining preselection, and winning office as candidates. As Hannam argues, however, it wasn't until the Women's Liberation Movement commenced in the 1970s that women began to challenge the structures of power that marginalized them—cultural as well as economic and political—and to seek inclusion within those structures.

These claims were often set against those of indigenous activists, by commentators and legislators who variously decried the suffrage of either women or natives before one another as an insult to native manhood, or as a slight to white womanhood. In New Zealand the early suffrage of women was remarkable for its inclusion of Maori women. As Bronwyn Winter notes, Maori men had been elected under a special Maori electorate system in 1867 to New Zealand's parliament. Canada would remove their Indian disqualification clauses from its provinces from 1949 to allow indigenous suffrage, though Australia would lag behind by not extending its federal franchise to Aborigines until 1962.[33] Other gains were momentous. Apartheid collapsed on the release of Nelson Mandela in 1990, and land rights gains, such as the 1992 Australia Mabo decision, overturned the legal doctrine of *Terra Nullius*. In Canada the Inuit were granted autonomous political status over Nunavut in its Arctic territories.[34] These were dramatic wins, creditable to indigenous activists, amongst whom women were very prominent.

Also central to women's demands for political inclusion was education, as Deborah Simonton explains in her chapter. While middle-class women argued their education was a social good, working-class women had a vocational priority, and saw education as key to their demands for the right to work and soon after for equal pay. As modernity created new occupations filled by women, such as the assembly lines of large-scale manufacturers, perceptions of "work" that counted shifted to paid work while the unpaid work in the private realm was increasingly devalued and rendered invisible. Work ceased to be an interim activity for older girls, soon abandoned on marriage, and became an indispensable part of the family income, if not poorly integrated into the twin demands of housework and childcare. Compulsory primary education had been instituted in most European countries by 1900. By the twentieth century the education of working-class and rural girls was still hindered by the economic contribution demanded by their families, and class and ethnic differences played out through the attendance rates and leaving ages of girls in Europe, and race segregation in the United States, until reform for integrated education gained a foothold in the second half of the century. Curriculum however remained sharply differentiated for girls, who learnt homemaking skills, from boys, who dominated math and science, entrenching gendered vocational pathways. As Simonton shows feminists successfully challenged gender-bias in attendance, curriculum and access to tertiary education; however, women graduates then encountered discrimination in the workplace as to how work was defined, and how to combine their roles as caregivers and overcome the resistance of men's integration into caring and domestic work. The work lifecycle altered throughout the century, as women pursued education into their childbearing years. As more and more mothers worked, the demand for flexible hours could be conflated with "dead-end" positions entrenching a "vision of the woman worker" as "docile, malleable, unskilled and ultimately dispensable."

The impact of maternity on all aspects of Australian women's lifecycle in the twentieth century is explored in Catherine Kevin's chapter. Among non-indigenous women birthrates declined in the first half of the twentieth century, causing alarm among proponents of population growth in the newly federated nation-state of Australia. The fertility of British heritage women was impacted by the "elongation" of childhood as the education of children changed their status in the family from contributors to dependents. Women's reproductive life cycles were also limited by prolonged education, participation in the workforce and delayed marriage. Kevin notes, "the medicalization of childbirth, pregnancy, contraception, abortion, and infertility dramatically changed patterns of reproduction and the economic and political status of women during the course of the twentieth century." As Kevin demonstrates, IVF, ultrasound, the viability of extremely premature babies and neonatal technologies, have radically altered the meaning of women's fertility and their experience of the "uterine interior" and of maternal loss.

These advances in medical science are taken up in the chapter coauthored by Mary Rojek Kleinman and Alice Dan, and shown to have been carefully and consistently negotiated through the activism of women throughout the century. Health issues related to women have been of central concern to feminists around the globe, from "violence against women, reproductive health, sexuality and fertility." This chapter ranges over the key indicators of health pertaining to women, from increased life expectancy, immunization and the decline in infant mortality, improvements in nutrition, sanitation and education, through to contraception, STDs, and AIDS. They clearly show that "women's health status is related to their specific social, economic, and political status, and to the cultural and material context of their lives." The narrative of the gains in medical technologies equating with better health outcomes for women is also challenged by examining the complex scenarios of hormone replacement therapies, the medicalization of natural processes such as birth with its often unnecessary interventions. There have also been outright disasters such as the prescribing of thalidomide, all of which spurred women's activism around health, demanding greater autonomy and presence among health professionals and medical institutions.

The medicalization of women's sexuality also figures in Zora Simic's chapter on sexuality, focusing on the female orgasm and its remarkable course throughout the twentieth century from sexologists to feminists. From indicating dysfunction in the early part of the century, to becoming enshrined as a marker of well-being in recent decades, women's orgasms constitute a heuristic for women and sexual modernity in Simic's contribution. From the Freudian "invention" of the vaginal orgasm and his relegation of the clitoral orgasm to a secondary immature response, through to medical discourses of the "problem" of female sexual response and its need for intervention, to feminist debates about sexual liberation and essentialism, the chapter records how "sexual climax became increasingly synonymous with 'sexual truth.' In the overwhelming volume of literature devoted to female orgasm, heterosexist assumptions abounded, as did class-based, racialized, and "phallocentric definitions of female sexuality," also challenged by feminists and women demanding sexual liberation and autonomy. Yet despite feminist activism around women's sexual embodiment, inequality continues to pervade heterosexual relationships leaving sexual modernity an unresolved feminist project.

Such a proliferation of such explicit public dealings of women's sexuality was possible in the twentieth century because of the massive shift in the boundary between public/private realms, as Bronwyn Winter details in her chapter. Focusing on Australia and France Winter writes of "the great contradiction in the cultural framing of public and private in the modern age: the 'private' has become public—socially engineered, culturally represented, politically debated, commodified in the marketplace—as perhaps never before." Focusing on five related symbolic loci of women's public–private-ness: women and the nation; domesticity; fertility control; clothing; and place and space, Winter details the advances and backlashes against women's increasingly public presence and the peculiar dynamic that emerged in the twentieth century as state control of women's *public* display of their *private* roles became "national obsessions."

As each of the contributors shows the processes of modernization have been deeply ambiguous and unevenly distributed among women. The gains feminists have won, across political participation and citizenship, reproductive rights and sexual autonomy, legal protection and rights, education and work, cultural inclusion and expression, have been hard won, and accompanied by many reversals and backlashes at state, legal and cultural levels. The recurrence of chapter topics across each volume of this series captures the ambit of common experiences or exclusions amongst women that across eras played critical roles in defining the feminine.

The modern, as the period which laid down the conditions of our present lives, remains unresolved in terms of its offerings to women. As the finite resources of the natural world collide with entrenched habits of overconsumption, and we take the first steps toward a postcarbon economy, women are redefining their place within a new world order, from major brokers on the global political stage, to permaculturists pursuing a doctrine of simplicity and self-sufficiency in their own gardens. As the discrepancies of wealth widen both between countries and urban and remote communities, and within the megametropolisis themselves, women continue to be central to the maintenance of displaced cultural traditions, and the cohesion of their families, and for many it is an uphill battle. As women continue to organize around their demands they negotiate the ongoing tension between accommodating their diversity while politically strategizing as a unitary identity centered on their common concerns, for stability and peace, for security and justice, for the conditions of equal rights, access, and expression to make the transitions very manifestly and urgently before us.

CHAPTER ONE

The Life Cycle: Reproduction and Maternal Loss in a Modern Nation

CATHERINE KEVIN

The Australian nation was "born modern."[1] Emerging as a political and cultural entity in the late nineteenth century, it was recognized globally as a social laboratory. Its leading intellectuals were receptive to political and scientific theories that could be used in the service of securing a European—predominantly British—culture and population in the Southern Hemisphere. The dispossession of indigenous peoples, exclusionary migration policies, public health measures and pronatalist rhetoric were informed by evolutionary and eugenic theories and reflected this population goal. Reforms such as extending the vote to propertyless white men and to white women were the creative adaptation of European democratic ideals. Through these various innovations Australia earned its reputation for engagement in the modern experiment. By the end of the twentieth century, after fifty-two years of selective, though increasingly open, migration policies, Australia boasted a culturally and ethnically diverse population, a veritable "melting pot." And in response to political campaigns by indigenous and immigrant Australians, policy makers had further widened formal definitions of political and cultural belonging. In short, by the 1970s Australian policy makers had officially dropped their agenda for a white Australia—an agenda that profoundly disadvantaged indigenous mothers—and replaced it with multiculturalism.

While the population was changing its ethnic character and its minorities achieving increased status—at least formally and publicly—non-indigenous women's private experiences were transforming in particular ways with developments in the management of fertility and reproduction. These transformations reflected other, equally important, dimensions of white Australia's continuing desire to be modern. The medicalization of childbirth, pregnancy, contraception, abortion, and infertility radically altered patterns of reproduction and the economic and political status of women during the course of the twentieth century. Declining numbers of births and maternal and infant deaths, and the gradual rise in the age of first-time mothers reflected both changing educational and economic opportunities and desires, and new and effective medical management regimes. The history of Australian indigenous women's fertility and maternity is a starkly different one. Into the twenty-first century, the rates of reproductive and maternal losses through miscarriage, still birth, and infant death continue to be significantly higher for indigenous women.[2] The intertwining histories of land loss and the Stolen Generations are integral to an understanding of continuing poor access to and uptake of culturally appropriate medical services that would reduce rates of maternal and reproductive loss.[3] The scale and complexity of this history and its fraught relationship with the story of Australian modernity deserve far more detailed analysis than can be provided by this chapter.

Among non-indigenous women, demographic, educational, and economic shifts went hand-in-hand with a transformation in conceptualizations of the reproductive body. This was generated by a steady increase in detailed understandings of the body's journey from conception to birth. The arrival of ultrasonography on the obstetric scene in the 1970s, and the proliferation of fetal images in education literature aimed at pregnant women, was accompanied by the emerging discourse of responsible and informed pregnancy. As women were increasingly urged to monitor their behavior in the interests of healthy pregnancy they became more exposed to visual information that gave them the capacity to imagine their uterine interior. These factors generated an increased awareness of early pregnancy, and emotional and intellectual investment in its significance. Where miscarriage occurred and early steps in assisted conception were unsuccessful, this investment could produce or intensify experiences of reproductive loss by making them knowable and more meaningful.

The purpose of this chapter is threefold. The first section outlines demographic changes in the reproductive life cycles of non-indigenous women in Australia since the late nineteenth century, placing them in the context of major economic and political events. The second section elaborates developments in education and labor, and in medical and reproductive technologies that help to explain the broad-scale shifts described in section one and the changing conceptualizations of the body that inform the discussion in section three. The final section offers individual women's stories of reproduction and maternity. Zeroing in on accounts of the arrested development of infant life and pregnancy, and of infertility not chosen, this section describes the transformation of the range of possible experiences that maternal and reproductive losses have entailed for women, and the impact of these historical possibilities on the broader shape of women's reproductive life cycles.

AUSTRALIAN BIRTHRATES IN THE MODERN ERA

When we speak of nations we conjure up a concept of "the people." This concept is shaped by our sense of what it means for them, indeed for us, to belong to a community of country, to inhabit its land and to be integrated into its political systems. Doctors, lawmakers, and bureaucrats, the overseers and managers of modern nation-states like Australia, became increasingly enamored with the notion of population in the nineteenth and twentieth centuries. They directed and responded to demographers and statisticians who provided them with ways to imagine and "know" the subjects they governed. The state endeavored to shape these populations around concerns of security and prosperity, morality, and racial purity. This process was one of imagining the population both in the present and after existing aspirations had been achieved. It was also the enactment of governance via legal and public health measures, and the perpetuation of national myth. These imagined and governed populations were one and the same entity. They were nebulous, disobedient, and yet held the promise of the nation. A population's fertility was at the heart of this promise.

At the end of the nineteenth century, in a period of high anxiety about the future of the British race in Australia, women came under scrutiny due to the dramatically declining birthrate.[4] Between 1881 and 1911 the birthrate for all non-indigenous women dropped from seven to four. This decline, accompanied by a dramatic fall in European immigration rates, was considered enough of a threat to prompt the premier of New South Wales to establish a Royal Commission to look into the decline of the birthrate in 1903. The bluntness of the tools employed for this inquiry reflected demographers' lack of experience and expertise in bringing to light the reasons for population change. Rather than seeking explanations from women for the number of children they bore, the Inquiry asked doctors and clergymen.[5] The best known findings of the "men of substance" who made up the group of 1903 royal commissioners were that married women had begun to control their fertility on a wide scale from around 1880 and that the decline in the birthrate was caused by the "selfishness of women." Needless to say, more recent attention from historians of demography has complicated this picture. They have explained the Royal Commission's central concern as the combined effects of economic decline, most pronounced during the Depression of the 1890s, and the uptake of contraceptive techniques.[6] Looking through the lens of political and economic history, this fertility trend was sustained through two wars and the Great Depression until the post–Second World War period saw both an economic boom and a baby boom.[7] It was not until the mid-1970s that the birthrate began to decline dramatically again and its links to contraception, safe legal abortion, and changing attitudes to marriage were obvious. After a spike in 1972 of an average of three births per woman, the fertility rate fell to just under two in 1980. It has been less than two ever since.

As well as relative economic boom, the post–Second World War period marked a dramatic change in the ethnic and cultural make-up of the Australian population which impacted on overall birthrate trends in complex ways. In 1948 the Labor Government sought to solve economic problems and labor shortages through policies that actively encouraged British immigrants. These were soon expanded to include people displaced by war and living in refugee camps across Europe. The ideal of a white Australia informed the policies that determined who was invited and financially supported to immigrate and the style of reception they experienced until the late 1960s when raced-based elements of immigration policies began to be eroded. The fertility patterns of immigrant women from non-English-speaking countries have departed from those of Australian-born women in a number of specific cases;[8] however, in the period to 1991 there was a general trend among migrant women towards fertility patterns that were more similar to those of Australian-born women than those in their countries of origin. It is difficult to say to what degree this was due to the influence of Australian culture and economy, the particular priorities of people who choose to immigrate, or the disruptive effect of immigration on women's fertility.[9]

The history of demographic change offers a sense of the trends in choices women and men have made about sex, relationships, and the management of fertility, but it offers a mere sketch of the nature of women's experiences and the discursive resources they have had available for giving meaningful shape to their reproductive life cycles. More detailed histories of the relationships of birthrates to education and medicine can flesh out some connections between demographic change and women's subjectivities in the modern era.

CONTEXTS FOR DEMOGRAPHIC CHANGE

Education

Education has had a profound impact on the duration of women's reproductive years. The history of this impact in the Australian context enriches the picture of declining fertility in the late nineteenth and early twentieth centuries, so far attributed here to economic depression and increasing knowledge and uptake of contraception. While economic depression and contraceptive knowledge made the changes wrought by education more pronounced, education has had two major effects on women and families that are worth considering on their own terms. It has meant profound changes both to the linked economic and emotional relationships between children and their parents, and to women's aspirations and capacity for economic independence. Schooling has been an important change agent in the modern era, gradually removing children from the labor market and transforming their economic status for parents from asset to liability.[10] While in the late nineteenth century some working-class families made use of schooling in a way that accommodated children's paid work and therefore did not lead to an economic need for diminished family size, in middle-class families children became "beloved but costly burdens" and couples limited their fertility in order to cope with this cost. In the late 1880s and 1890s there was a subtle shift—more accentuated in the middle and upper classes than the working class but discernible to some extent across all classes—towards increasing periods of children's dependency. In working-class families, for example, girls who previously would have moved into domestic service were spending longer periods in the family home. While this was linked in part to their increased participation in education, Alison MacKinnon has argued that this reflected "the idea that girls belonged at home, that they acquired a new value, [and] points to the construction in that period of the notion of the male breadwinner family model in which the wife was viewed as a full-time homemaker."[11] In the modern era the family became a valued site for protecting the young, enabling their formal education and imbuing them with social values for a longer period of time. This elongation of childhood enhanced the role of the family and put further pressure on the resources it had available for raising each individual child.[12]

But of course assumptions cannot be made about the family being a harmonious unit in which members enjoyed equal and unchanging power relationships. This is especially relevant to a history of the impact of education and work on women's subjectivities and their capacities to determine their relationships to reproduction and maternity. Mass education frequently narrowed the emotional distance between husbands and wives and changed the distribution of power in their relationships. Dianna Gittens has drawn links between increased communication, greater equality within heterosexual relationships and fertility decline. She also points out that young women working in more isolated situations such as domestic service were less likely to bring knowledge of sex and contraception into a relationship than women working in factories or as clerks where there was greater opportunity for gossip and the exchange of information about love, sex, and fertility.[13]

Alison MacKinnon's history of university-educated women, whom she calls "those transgressors *par excellence*,"[14] found that among the women who graduated from Adelaide University between 1885 and 1922, almost half remained single, and therefore were much more likely to be childless. For those who did partner and/or become mothers, their average reproductive life cycles were shorter and less prolific than those of the majority—their less educated sisters—and on a par with their university-educated peers in Canada, the United States, Britain, and New Zealand.[15] Other studies have shown that in the period 1965–2000, a woman's level of education was still a predictor of her family size. The higher the degree taken, the smaller the family was likely to be. This highlights two things: first, the disincentives to marriage created by the serious pursuit of education; and second, the importance to women of making good their investment of time and resources in gaining qualifications by their participation in the labor market.[16] At the other end of the education spectrum, women who had left school before their seventeenth birthday and had not completed further study had much bigger families. Among women aged thirty in 1965, those who had left school before they turned seventeen on average had twice as many children as women their age with higher degrees. Not much had changed in the period from 1986 to 1996, when women aged 30–34 without post-school qualifications averaged just over double the birthrate of their contemporaries with post-school qualifications. Interestingly, in this later period, for women in the next age-bracket (between 35 and 39) those with degrees began to "catch up" with women without degrees, something I will come to later in this chapter.[17] Overall, increasing levels of school education, access to an expanding range of employment opportunities and higher education for women have been major contributors to the decline in fertility since the late nineteenth century.

Medicalization

Control of fertility—both its prevention and its materialization where desired—was made possible to an unprecedented degree in the twentieth century by medical interventions. Medicalized contraception and abortion had long lineages that lay outside of medicine and then at its margins. By the end of the twentieth century, the non-medical foremothers of the contraceptive pill (by then the most widely used birth control)[18] and medicalized abortion were a distant memory. Prevention of antenatal and postnatal maternal loss was also brought dramatically into the field of medicine in this period, and by the end of the century reproductive medicine had extended its reach to take in the diagnosis and cure of infertility. The intense medicalization of each of these domains pertaining to the reproductive life cycle has left a profound impression not only on Australian demography but on conceptualizations of pregnancy and women's relationships to fertility and maternity. In this section I examine changes to the medical management of reproduction that occurred during the twentieth century, and the impact of these changes on the meanings invested in reproduction and maternity at its different stages. These, in turn, have provided increasingly dominant discursive frameworks through which the experiences of reproductive and maternal loss have been understood.

The marginalization and near expulsion of lay midwives was necessary for the dominance of medical discourses of the reproductive body. During the long campaign to exclude lay midwives from scenes of childbirth, medical science achieved a number of milestones in the preservation of infant and maternal health which were crucial to its cause. The decline of the infant mortality rate in Australia can be traced from the 1880s and shown to have accelerated after 1900 when it stood at 10.3 percent of live births.[19] This was primarily an effect of the decline in mortality from infectious diseases due to improved sanitation and water supplies, the application of new scientific theories to the production of food, and the supervision of dairies. It is also possible that the decline in average family size decreased the chances of an infant coming into contact with other infectious children.[20] This improvement in child preservation coincided with the wider availability of medical care and improved feeding methods, which were largely the effect of a nationwide, state-supported infant welfare movement. The effects of these various changes on infant death-rates were a boon to the legitimization of medical practices.

Maternal mortality did not rate so highly as a medical and national concern. Between 1870 and 1939 a woman's access to medical attendance during pregnancy and birth was dependent on her willingness and ability to pay for it. This was despite the fact that pregnant women were vulnerable to a range of reproductive illnesses, and suffered and died from diseases such as tuberculosis in disproportionate numbers.[21] Medicine's growing ability to name and thus identify and understand bacteria between 1876 and 1940 enabled the profession to look critically at lay practitioners' techniques for delivering infants, and to claim superior expertise in infant and maternal health.[22] During the pre–Second World War period, without full knowledge of the aetiology of puerperal fever or of sulphonamides, doctors regulated their practices in the light of debates about antiseptic techniques and curettage. Meanwhile, they campaigned against "untrained" midwives whom they held largely responsible for high rates of maternal mortality.

Despite this new medical knowledge, puerperal infection remained a major cause of maternal deaths until sulphonamides became available in the late 1930s.[23] While infant welfare centres were being established throughout urban areas in the early 1900s, advocating regular feeding and weighing,[24] women were suffering from infections that intensified the risks of pregnancy and labor and would not be curbed before the start of the war. It was not until 1939 that maternity service, as medical care of the pregnant and parturient body was called, was available to most women and tied to the state. This reflected the government's continued interest in population growth and its recognition that healthy infants required healthy mothers. Penicillin and blood transfusions became treatment options in the war years[25] and by the 1950s more widespread, rigorous, and sophisticated antenatal care was an effective preventative of maternal death. Higher numbers of women participating in antenatal clinics from the mid-twentieth century were the effect of medical campaigns, particularly campaigns against eclampsia, and strategies for women's attendance.[26] They also indicate that medical discourses of pregnancy were making an increasing impact on women.

In 1948 Crown Street Women's Hospital in Sydney embarked on an ambitious and ultimately successful campaign to reduce the rate of eclampsia in pregnant women by increasing antenatal services and compelling women to attend.[27] Part of the incentive for the Crown Street campaign was the expense of trying to keep premature babies alive. Eclampsia endangered the fetus and many of those born alive to eclamptic mothers came too early and were too small. This was perilous, traumatic, and costly. While combating eclampsia reduced the possibility of prematurity, doctors were also developing ways of bringing the age of viability down by investing resources in neonatal care so that prematurity did not make neonatal death inevitable. In 1956 Professor Bruce Mayes gave a lecture, later published in the *Medical Journal of Australia*, outlining the success of efforts to prevent eclampsia. In it he referred to V-day, the point in pregnancy at which viability or capacity for a fetus to survive as an infant outside the womb is achieved. According to Mayes, V-day occurred at thirty-six weeks into a woman's pregnancy, four weeks before term. At this point, the fear of eclampsia became less pressing and a child could be delivered with a high chance of survival.[28] A number of Mayes's contemporaries used definitions of viability that were less conservative, some suggesting the possibility of infant survival as early as twenty-eight weeks.[29]

In 2001, almost half a century after Mayes spearheaded the eclampsia prevention campaign at Crown Street Women's Hospital, Sally Cornfield gave birth to twin boys only twenty-two weeks and five days into her pregnancy. Her first-born son, at just 650 grams, was rushed into the neonatal intensive care unit at the Royal Women's Hospital in Melbourne where his underdeveloped lungs were relieved by a ventilating machine. Cornfield's second son was born lighter and bruised from a struggle to pull him through her vaginal passage. He too was placed on the ventilator but by the next day his chances of ever surviving without it were deemed extremely poor and the machine was turned off.[30] In the 1920s, prematurity replaced diarrhea as the major killer of babies in Australia,[31] and babies weighing less than a kilogram did not survive.[32] In the 1930s, an American study indicated that a baby this small had about a one-in-twenty chance of survival.[33] By the end of the 1970s, she or he had a one-in-four chance of survival, and at the turn into of the twenty-first century, that figure was three-in-four.[34] Neonatal intensive care units, like the one that enabled the life of Cornfield's surviving son, have brought a concept of viability closer and closer to the moment of conception and the diagnosis of pregnancy.

Early neonatology relied heavily on close observation. Newborns could not communicate their symptoms to doctors and so required a rigorous and untiring clinical gaze to deduce the correct course of treatment.[35] While resuscitation, intravenous feeding, surgical, and transfusion methods were being designed for the infant, neonatal discourses also referred repeatedly to the management of pregnancy. In order to understand neonatal illness, it was necessary to understand the nature of antenatal conditions and their long-term effects. Dr. Kate Campbell, a pediatrician at Melbourne's Royal Women's Hospital, began working in the 1920s. Her career, which was most productive from 1948, is thought to have changed the face of neonatology in Victoria where she was a clinician and teacher. Campbell published on topics ranging from the care of newborns and the diagnosis of intra-cranial injuries to maternal diet and other aspects of pregnancy.[36] In the 1960s, the *Medical Journal of Australia*, which published frequently on the treatment of newborns, drew together the discourses of antenatal care and neonatology, emphasizing that supervision extended from neonates back to pregnant women. The journal expressed exasperation regarding the neonate's dependence on "the attitude, education, intelligence and initiative" of the pregnant woman, which would determine whether or not she presented herself for clinical observation.[37] Fetal mortality was the earliest mark of medical and/or maternal failure. Premature birth was the next. The goal of neonatology, a field that has experienced considerable success, was to reduce the morbid and terminal impact of prematurity. Since Kate Campbell's time, neonatal practices have become more refined to the point of enabling one of Cornfield's tiny babies to live. Neonatology meant that life for the struggling neonate in the absence of the mother's body no longer left the infant without means of survival. Instead, the possibility of this life came to depend on, in Australian hospitals at least, an ever-increasing range of medical aids, thus transforming the nature of precarious infant survival and maternal loss after premature birth. Contemporary viability, therefore, refers directly to the techniques of neonatology,[38] and access to this intervention can change the nature of the distinction between in-utero and ex-utero life.

The possibility of earlier and earlier pregnancy tests, the proliferation of pregnancy literature and fetal images, and the relatively recent emphasis on the responsibility of women to regard their pregnant bodies as risk-managed fetal environments have brought a new kind of awareness to pregnancy. To some extent this blurs the distinction between the role of pregnant woman and mother in relation to her offspring while elongating the period in which this is relevant to an understanding of the pregnant self. These conditions, in turn, have helped shape the meaning of miscarriage and stillbirth. As viability is reached at an ever-earlier point in pregnancy, we begin to imagine the possibility of the fetus's *ex-utero* existence. When terms like "fetal distress," "fetal well-being," and "fetal pain" enter the rhetoric of fetal medicine, along with more personal patient discourses of pregnancy, then the resemblance of the fetus to a neonatal patient, or in fact any patient with the capacity for pain, distress, and well-being, is increased. And when websites and advertisements use three-dimensional ultrasonography and images produced by the latest fetoscopic technology, our practice of looking at fetal images begins to feel as familiar as the practice of taking in a holiday snapshot; a relatively new concept of "baby's first picture" takes us into an imaginary uterine existence to explore the "beginning of life." The impact of these practices on investments in early pregnancy has been thoroughly exploited by the anti-choice movement but in more subtle ways it has impacted on dominant discourses of pregnancy. For those experiencing highly medicalized pregnancies the effects have often been more pronounced. Within this group, those whose conceptions have been managed by medical fertility specialists with technological interventions there is an even more powerful investment in early pregnancy.

By the end of the twentieth century, assisted reproductive technologies had increased the possibility of pregnancy for Australian women in their late thirties and early forties, for younger women facing infertility, and for those wishing to conceive in the absence of heterosexual sex. The first *in vitro* fertilization (IVF) procedure in Australia occurred in 1979 and the first Australian IVF baby (the world's fourth) was born in Melbourne in June 1980. Between 1981 and 1984, there were thirteen IVF babies born worldwide, twelve of them born in Australia, and in 1986 the first IVF baby conceived after the freezing and thawing of an embryo (now a routine efficiency in IVF clinics) was born in Australia. The development and availability of IVF procedures has been a significant factor in more highly educated women between the ages of 35 and 39 experiencing the fertility "catch up" that I describe above.[39] Although it is not possible to say how many of these women used technologies for assisted conception, in 2009 the mothers of just over three percent of babies born in Australia were assisted by reproductive technologies[40] and the majority of those using these technologies fell into the thirty-five and over age group.[41] The incorporation of assisted conception into the medical repertoire has intensified the medical gaze on women's reproductive bodies and opened up the possibility of a detailed medicalized self-awareness for women at the earliest point in the journey towards becoming a mother. In addition, IVF facilitates the creation of an embryo outside of the mother's body, bestowing on it a quality of separateness from its first moment.

Studies of the choices IVF patients make about the stored frozen embryos they do not wish to transfer for attempted pregnancy provide insights into the meaning they invest in pre-pregnancy conceptions. The choices provided are to dispose of the embryos; donate them to scientific research; or donate them to other patients unable to conceive using their own genetic material. Sheryl de Lacey's research found that donation to other patients was an option more often contemplated than pursued.[42] De Lacey highlights patients' difficulty articulating their ambivalence about donation due to the absence of relevant cultural scripts. She explores the rhetorical construction of embryos in the process of patients navigating through this difficulty. In patients' narratives, donation was described as much more than "the mere sharing of reproductive material and opportunity for pregnancy."[43] It was instead constructed as a form of relinquishment of full offspring. De Lacey describes sections of the narrative that referred to the memories of successful conceptions as a way of thinking through the significance of remaining embryos. These described the importance of early images of cells seen through a microscope prior to implantation, which were experienced as part of a continuum with ultrasound images. As one patient stated in reference to the microscope image, "We've got a photo taken the day they got implanted. So you look at it and think 'yeah well there's Kylie and Jason sitting there.'" And another explained, "They're real [the embryos], they're very real and not many people see their children at eight or ten cells."[44] The intersecting discourses of embryo as child and donation as relinquishment (and not dissimilar from adoption) had a deterrent effect on patients' preparedness to donate their embryos to other patients seeking fertility treatment. It also led to feelings of guilt and in some cases serious heartache for couples deciding on the fate of their excess embryos and choosing some form of disposal. The narratives de Lacey analyzed demonstrate the impact of the development of technologies of assisted reproduction on the meaning invested in the earliest stages of reproduction. In the context of these technologies, for which success rates continue to be low, the potential for a sense of meaningful loss is enhanced by the degree of early investment.

ACCOUNTS OF THE REPRODUCTIVE AND MATERNAL LOSSES OF INDIVIDUAL WOMEN

Birthrates and the histories of education reform and medicalization with which these statistics are strongly associated provide a partial picture of the maternal and reproductive experiences of women. This partiality can be described in numerous and fascinating ways, but the absences I wish to bring into focus here pertain to women's losses. These are the many children who did not survive their childhoods or even infancies; births that were not live births; pregnancies that did not make it to full term; and, in very recent years, failed assisted conceptions. These categories of maternal and reproductive losses are features of many women's reproductive life cycles and they have produced a wide variety of experiences, none of which are fixed to any single point in history. Their significance is contingent on dynamic discourses of maternity, life, death, loss, and grief, and can be attributed to both micro and macro changes. The following case studies add depth and nuance to histories of demography by closely examining reproductive events associated with loss, and therefore the plastic status of the infant and the unborn in changing historical contexts.

I begin my examination of case studies with accounts taken from two of Janet McCalman's studies. The first traces the trajectories leading to "friendless deaths" in the late nineteenth century but also, more pertinently, captures the extent of maternal loss experienced by the mothers of the cohort she examines. That cohort is the children born at the Melbourne Lying-In Hospital (now the Royal Women's Hospital) between 1857 and 1900.[45] In the second, McCalman uses oral testimony and archival records to explore the experiences of two generations of residents of working-class Richmond, in Melbourne, who lived through the First and Second World Wars.[46]

McCalman establishes the effects of impoverishment and instability in women's lives on the survival of their children in the mid- to late nineteenth century. For those born between 1857 and the mid-1880s to unmarried mothers, the rate of infant mortality hovered between 70 and 75 percent, and then declined steadily until it was about 55 percent for those born in 1900. McCalman attributes this change to the introduction of antiseptic midwifery in 1887 and the Infant Life Protection Act of 1893, which improved the standard of artificial feeding for babies in care. Babies born to mothers who were married to men with occupations either unskilled or unstated fared better than the children of single mothers. Those whose mothers were married to skilled or professional fathers did marginally better still. However, the overall infant mortality rate for the cohort was 50 percent (comprising 4,296 births). McCalman highlights the crucial role of birth weight as a risk factor for infant death—determined significantly by the age and marital status of the child's mother—and for the likelihood of the child surviving to forty: "It was a brutal biological and social selection determined by the level to which mothers were supported in pregnancy and early motherhood."[47] After infancy, these connections between biological and social factors for this cohort weakened, partly because so many of those worst afflicted by low birth weights had already perished. However, birth weight remained an indicator of longevity and the likelihood of descendents.

McCalman's work on the fate of this cohort is powerfully indicative of a grim reality for poor mothers, especially those who were unmarried. Other historians have provided insights into the conditions of marriage for many working-class women in the second half of the nineteenth century.[48] These give pause to any inclination to read McCalman's findings regarding the relative well-being of married women and their children as evidence of strong, mutually supportive marriages. This description may well have reflected some of the marriages enjoyed by mothers at the Lying-In Hospital but a more accurate reading of the data would interpret the contrasting outcomes for unmarried mothers as evidence of the dire material straits single women found themselves in. A paucity of work opportunities and the marginal social status of the unwed pregnant woman or mother translated into conditions so impoverished as to produce highly vulnerable pregnancies, infants, and children. Along with the exposure to disadvantage already inherent in their status as poor, single and confined, the potential for stillbirth and infant loss and the grief that might come with this were high. McCalman argues persuasively that the birth and death data for an individual, placed in the context of what we know about the impact of the circumstances of birth and the likely trajectories that produce particular kinds of deaths, "can be interpreted as inscription on the body of the quality of the individual's life-course; that is of the effects of insult accumulation on mind and body, of 'history.'"[49]

The oral histories informing *Struggletown*, McCalman's study of the first half of the twentieth century in working-class Richmond, offer a handful of more vivid images of the impact of maternal loss on the emotional life and well being of women. In the first decade of the twentieth century, Friedrich Smith's mother lost her own baby but continued to breastfeed a neighbor's child. She told him it was the hardest thing she had ever done, but in a community that saw a baby's first summer as the most dangerous period of a child's life and in which cow's milk as a substitute for breast milk presented all kinds of hygiene risks, this would have been understood as a profound contribution to the neighbor's child's survival.[50] Women like this showed impressive capacity to provide for others in the face of their own suffering. Phyllis Smith's mother had nine pregnancies, including "three deaths." The eldest daughter died from diphtheria; the other deaths are not described. The point Phyllis made in her interview was that in spite of these emotional and physical demands, her mother worked tirelessly each day, cooking and in other ways providing for her family, from dawn until just a short time before the following dawn, leaving only a few hours for sleep.[51] This degree of labor no doubt meant some distraction from her losses, but it probably indicates emotional neglect wrought by necessity as well. Phyllis Smith's testimony also offers insight into the ways in which families responded to loss, sometimes with terror that another child would perish, sometimes by spoiling a child after the death of her sibling or threats to her own life. When Phyllis was diagnosed with diphtheria, her mother fainted, fearing the worst.[52] Violet McLoughlin was spoilt by her father, which was understood as being due to the effect on him of her near-fatal episode of diphtheria.[53]

It was not only the very poor who suffered such reproductive and maternal losses. Professional women such as the lawyer Joan Rosanove, and even the most expert in maternal and baby care, such as the doctor and president of the Canberra Mothercraft society, Beatrice Holt, both began their reproductive life cycles with loss in the 1920s and 1930s, respectively. Rosanove's first child was stillborn[54] while Holt's died in infancy.[55] Both women went on to have other children but Holt's final pregnancy ended in the birth of a stillborn baby. The experiences of three generations of one middle-class family provide an illustration of the changing risks of loss to mothers and the enduring impact of maternal loss.[56] Mary became a mother five times between 1909 and 1916. A poor Irish child immigrant, she eventually trained as a nurse and met her future husband, a wealthy grazier, when he was in her care at a Sydney hospital. Three of their children survived into old age, one died from a probable burst appendix at the age of nineteen, and one was lost in her first month of life. Although infant death was common in this period, affecting more than one in ten babies, the sad memory of losing Florence has been handed down from Mary through four generations of her descendents. Mary's eldest daughter, Patricia, university-educated and married to a surgeon, gave birth to five girls between 1937 and 1952 but lost a son when he was stillborn in 1946. When Patricia's husband died she insisted that the death notice include that he was the loving father of a son as well as his five living daughters.[57] Patricia's eldest, Julie, had a reproductive and maternal life cycle that spanned twenty-two years, during which she experienced a number of losses and raised four children. Julie became pregnant for the first time at the age of twenty-one in 1958, long before she, her boyfriend, or her parents were prepared for such an event.[58] A university student from a Catholic family, she was desperate to keep her pregnancy a secret from her parents. Uncomfortable with the idea of abortion and believing a marriage would have compromised her boyfriend's future unacceptably, she left Sydney to become a live-in domestic in rural New South Wales while her belly grew. When she was thirty weeks pregnant she travelled to Melbourne to be cared for by Catholic nuns in a home for single expectant mothers. After an excruciating two day labor, during which she felt in turns ignored and chastised for being noisy, and a week of bottle feeding, her baby girl was placed in the care of adoptive parents. After a difficult marriage in which she had three sons, Julie married again. A new period of reproductive and maternal loss ensued. After a miscarriage she gave birth to a daughter in 1979. Fifteen months later, pregnant again and working full time, Julie's waters broke at 26 weeks. She went to the hospital and began to labor. When it became clear that the baby's shoulder was caught, a caesarean section was performed. As had been predicted

in the early stages of labor, the baby was stillborn. Julie had been given an epi-
dural for the procedure and valium in the immediate aftermath of the delivery,
a combination of drugs which left her barely conscious. She had wanted to see
her son, something she could only express when the sedative had worn off.

> When I asked to see the baby, the baby had already gone to the mortu-
> ary. John actually saw the baby and I was very angry that I never saw
> the baby. It was a little boy he called Jonathon. That wasn't good, that
> was bad.[59]

Julie felt blamed for this baby's fate.[60] She had delayed seeking help while she
assumed the leakage of amniotic fluid was urine. After explaining this, the
impression she had from her doctor was that he thought she should have acted
earlier, at the hint of anything suspicious, and that he regarded the event as a
"product of her folly."[61] A year earlier, Julie's sister Margie had had a similar
experience of stillbirth. The baby's body was disposed of before she could see
or touch her. When Margie returned to the hospital years later to inquire about
its fate, there were no clear answers.

Within two decades of the experience of these sisters, transformations had
taken place in the management of stillbirths in hospitals. Vanessa Gorman's
story of maternal loss was brought into the lounge rooms of ABC viewers all
over Australia in 2001 and then became a popular memoir in 2005.[62] It highlighted the depth of despair such an event can produce; the lengths to which
medical personnel can and will now go in their attempts to rescue a struggling
newborn; and new possibilities, made available by more flexible hospital policies and more individualistic discourses of grief, for mourning rituals centered
on the body of the dead infant.

Gorman's pregnancy occurred in the context of a relationship in which
she felt a strong desire to become a mother and her partner had made it clear
that he was not open to this. As a filmmaker, Gorman saw in this dilemma,
and in her open decision to try to become pregnant, a story worth recording.
She made a video diary that recorded her decision to conceive; her healthy
pregnancy; the long and arduous delivery of her little girl Layla and the drama
that immediately ensued of attempting to keep Layla alive. Most relevant here
is the mourning that was also recorded in detail. After meconium inhalation
Layla lived for only eight hours. Her body was brought home and placed in the
bed that had been prepared for her. Vanessa and her partner, their family and
friends, held the body of the baby and performed a series of highly personalized rituals to honor and bid farewell to her. Eventually there was a cremation

and Layla's ashes were scattered in the ocean near where the couple lived. Compare this to the whisking away of the body of Julie's son and the mysterious disposal of Margie's daughter just two decades earlier.

Susannah Thompson's history of practices around miscarriage, stillbirth and neonatal death at the King Edward Memorial Hospital (KEMH) in Perth offers an account of the transformation from an approach that did not address women's grief in the face of maternal loss to one that has created "a more supportive and protective environment for bereaved women."[63] By the early 1990s fetuses that previously would have been disposed of with hospital waste were cremated with ceremony in Australia's first fetal crematorium. The broader context for this and other changes to hospital policy at KEMH that responded to the needs of women experiencing reproductive and maternal losses were the emergence of grief theories and theories of maternal and infant bonding, both of which became increasingly acceptable to medical professionals in the 1970s, and the growing movement at the intersection of feminist and consumer rights agendas. The maternity reform movement that developed in the context of women's liberation and other feminisms sought to wrest discursive and material control from medicine, recognize the rights of women patients, and reinstate more woman-centered understandings of the female body. Inspired by women's accounts of feeling invisible, powerless and frightened during medically-managed obstetric and gynecological events, leaders within this movement, such as Janet Balaskas and Shiela Kitzinger, drew from renegade aspects of medicine, such as Grantly Dick-Read's natural childbirth movement and Fernand Lamaze's antenatal techniques, and feminist accounts of the outlawing of non-medical midwifery at the end of the nineteenth century, to develop a feminist discourse of the maternal body. By the 1980s, support groups were emerging that catered for women experiencing grief associated with miscarriage. The exact nature of the relationship between this trend and the wider feminist context in this period is unclear.[64] Whether they were the product of feminist maternity reform or were linked to an anti-choice agenda, as Leslie J. Reagan has argued regarding the United States,[65] they have provided an extension of the recognition and support for grieving women emerging among health care professionals, which is at least in part a product of an increased interest in women's perspectives on reproductive and maternal loss.

In addition to changes in some hospital settings, an effect of the broader cultural shifts Thompson describes is the increasing cultural space available for speaking about miscarriage.[66] This has mainly been made available by miscarriage support groups, in their publications and on their websites, but occasionally through newspapers as well. The accounts have much in common and their ready accessibility attests to a proliferation of writing about these experiences that is now available to those keen to seek it out. However, anecdotal evidence suggests that exposure to these accounts depends on the person exposed having experienced miscarriage directly, and this lack of broader engagement indicates both a continued reluctance to emphasize the risk of miscarriage in antenatal care; a tendency for women to keep a history of miscarriage a secret; and perhaps even a recoiling from accounts of miscarriage by those at some degree of remove from its events. These conditions reflect discomfort with experiences of death in contemporary culture despite the emergence of grief and bonding theories and the diversification of memorializing practices.

Overall women's writing and interviews express ambivalence about their experiences of maternal and reproductive loss. For some, such as Lisa, images of angels and heaven provide a comforting repertoire of signifiers. On the website of the Miscarriage Association she wrote: "our baby's spirit left its body when the heart stopped beating and is now in heaven with all the other angels, watching over us, waiting for its next chance to meet us."[67] However the language of failure, lost hope, and death is more ubiquitous than religious imagery. Another Lisa wrote, "I wasn't too sure what to say or to do as I have not had much experience of death in my lifetime so far and I wasn't even too sure how I felt."[68] Kate Evans described the death of a friend as being easier than this death, because it was tangible and could be shared: "we viewed the body, we buried him and we were able to say goodbye. We had the company of others who were as grief-stricken as I was."[69] In her other grief she was alone as she waded through the euphemisms presented by health care professionals and well-meaning friends. One woman raged against the idiom "I lost my baby," writing, "I did not lose my baby...My baby just died."[70] Other accounts focus explicitly on the search for meaning and express the inadequacy of discourses of death for the task of articulating the meaning of miscarriage. In her autobiographical piece Monica Dux wrote: "it can be hard to define what you're grieving. Yet this is what most of the women I spoke to longed for above all: to make their grief concrete, to frame it in a way that legitimised it."[71]

As I've already discussed, assisted reproductive technologies have provided the possibility for many women for whom the hope of becoming a mother would otherwise have been abandoned. However this sense of possibility is often accompanied by many disappointments and the narratives of assisted reproduction have the added dimensions of the degree of longing that often takes women to fertility clinics in the first place and the financial, physical, and emotional costs of undergoing the procedures. Medical technology has both increased our expectations of the possibility of pregnancy and proliferated reproductive losses. One interviewee explained:

> with IVF cos you know they've implanted a fertilised embryo you know, you're thinking ahead that you're pregnant and you might lose it. When you're going through a normal monthly cycle you don't actually think for ten days of the cycle, there's an embryo in there...I was absolutely devastated the first time when it didn't work. It's like, it's our big hope![72]

Another interviewee,[73] who also used IVF, captured the sense of failure, the sense of loss and also the complications of her miscarriage grief as a feminist whose previous conceptualizations of pregnancy and medical technologies had been shaped by pro-choice discourses and radical feminist perspectives on assisted reproductive technologies:

> And I got pregnant...But this is what happens to you. You get into this thing where you're talking about seven week old embryos which I used to talk about in terms of abortions, suddenly that was seven weeks closer to having a child than I'd ever been. I was like, completely jubilant. I was ridiculously ecstatic at that point. It was madness...But an IVF miscarriage is a terrible thing....I was never upfront about that miscarriage because most people, particularly my feminist friends would have gone "but oh, you're talking about a seven week old embryo...You have gone mad!" That's the response I would have got. So I didn't tell very many people at all.
>   ...we're talking about a massive failure couple here. You know, "that couple can't have a baby. They've done 20 million cycles on IVF. They've had miscarriages. She's ancient, he's a dud stud."...And we'd really come to accept failure.[74]

As this testimony makes clear, secrecy and shame can accompany pregnancy loss. These responses have been exacerbated when would-be mothers either have been subject to the punitive discourses that have characterized much public debate about older mothers and infertility, or the complication of reconciling pro-choice politics with their grief (or both). Among the miscarriage testimonies published in newspapers and online, accounts of women who have become pregnant with the help of reproductive technologies appear less common. Their private narratives are often more powerfully informed by detailed medicalized accounts of the numerous component parts of their conceptions and pregnancies. In the context of these conditions, the definition of "pregnancy" in "pregnancy loss" stretches to accommodate the dashed hopes that can occur anywhere along a continuum from egg collection to stillbirth. Thus the specific complexity of maternal desires and losses may account for the absence of IVF stories in some of the discursive spaces where miscarriage is publicly discussed.

CONCLUSION

Any account of the reproductive life cycle is always, inevitably partial in some respects. The work of historians of demography clearly indicates the defining features of populations and the fates of women whose physical pleasures and labors have produced and nurtured them. But only through an understanding of histories of education, health, and welfare can we begin to make these accounts more meaningful. And it is with detailed accounts pertaining to individual reproductive life cycles that historians can grasp the intersections between demographic shifts and the discursive frameworks that have given women the limits and possibilities of their sexual, reproductive and maternal bodies at any given point in time. Women's resistance to these frameworks and their attempts to forge new ways of understanding their experiences are particularly apparent in the articulations of loss. These demonstrate the difficulty entailed in attempting to engage in the production of new and resistant discourses. Through their descriptions of discursive dead-ends, future outlines for expansive and inclusive discourses pertaining to the sexual, reproductive, and maternal body are conceived.

Bodies and Sexuality: Twentieth-Century Orgasms; or, The Problem of Female Heterosexuality

ZORA SIMIC

An orgasm is an orgasm is an orgasm.

—Betty Dodson, 1974[1]

American sex activist Betty Dodson's characteristically pithy description of orgasm is especially impressive in its brevity given the cultural weight of all that she was rejecting at the time—the obsession of sex researchers with defining and cataloguing orgasm; the gendering of orgasm; the clitoral/vaginal distinction; the enduring "gold standard" of mutual, coital orgasm; the demotion of masturbation in the sexual repertoire; and the cultural status of orgasm itself. It was Dodson's vision that female orgasm did not have to be such hard work, or such a principle site for the perennial "battle of the sexes." Instead through developing sexual skills and intimate knowledge of their own bodies—particularly through masturbation, the "sexual base" of human sexuality—women could inhabit their sexuality more confidently than ever before—and have more orgasms. They would also have better sex with the significant others in their lives, be they man or woman, permanent or temporary partner.[2] In the twentieth-first century, Dodson has maintained her mission to liberate women "one orgasm at a time" through her masturbation workshops and writings,[3] and her no-nonsense approach to what mid-twentieth-century sexologists commonly labelled "female sexual response" did indeed demand a new cultural value for female orgasm. In this, she was hardly alone. In the late 1960s and early 1970s, women's liberationists in the United States, the United Kingdom, Europe, and elsewhere made the demystification of female sexuality one of their central projects. Yet by the 1980s, many Western feminists had shifted their focus away from the politics of sexual pleasure. Some even suggested that the efforts of Dodson and other "sex-positive" feminists had done more harm than good and that their "cult of the clitoris" merely replicated a male version of sexual liberation,[4] marginalized women who experienced their sexuality differently,[5] and privileged the feminist agenda of Western feminism's core constituency: white, middle-class women. In the millennium, feminists and others continue to debate what genuine female sexual liberation would look like—particularly for heterosexual women.[6] This debate is one of the legacies of sexual modernity, or the modernization of sex, which forms the wider context to this chapter.

Discourses of female orgasm are emblematic of the twentieth century obsession with sex. They illustrate how sexuality came to be recognised as a defining feature of modern individual identity—or even the "truth of our being"[7]—with the capacity to transform our lives for better or worse. Orgasm was allocated a major role to play in the attainment of "authentic" or "healthy" sexuality as sexual climax became increasingly synonymous with "sexual truth."[8] The historical backdrop to such popular, effusive, and largely heterosexist claims for the orgasm is a century of sexual revolutions, of which historians and feminists (amongst others) are still debating the after-effects.[9]

The twentieth century was one of major social upheaval and change, marked across the Western world by unprecedented numbers of women moving out of the home, into paid employment, and having fewer children. Two world wars brought anxiety about sex, population, and gender roles to the fore, but the obsession with female sexuality was hardly confined to these periods, and indeed peaked in the inter-war and post–Second World War periods. One way of understanding the twentieth-century fixation on female sexuality is as an ongoing attempt to comprehend larger processes of social change that continue to play out in the present. Another approach, not necessarily antithetical to the first, is to read attempts to define and regulate female sexuality as a permanent or transhistorical feature of patriarchal cultures. Female orgasm has been subject "to several millennia of theoretical interventions," the history of which offers a "veritable palimpsest of scientific attitudes toward gender and sexuality."[10]

In the twentieth century, sexuality became the domain of new experts, and a sign of the democratization of the West. Whereas in the past the authority to speak about sex and the body was largely confined to church, state, and the medical profession, modernity ushered in what sociologist Jeffrey Weeks has described as "a mass democracy speaking of sex" in which we "can all claim to be experts today, true to our own selves in our own fashion." Still, the enduring presence and influence of various sex experts with their diverse and sometimes spurious claims to knowledge also illustrates that sex remains for many of us a source of contemporary anxiety and confusion. This is hardly surprising: sex is an incredibly subjective and often keenly felt experience, while at the same time "a peculiarly sensitive conductor of cultural influences, and hence of, social, cultural and political divisions."[11] The proliferation of information on sex may also appear to offer strong evidence of a less sexually-repressed era, but the volume and content of this knowledge also testifies to what Michel Foucault has identified as the disciplinary basis of modern sexuality: sex was no longer merely to be judged, but also to be administered.[12] At the same time, while Charles Darwin's theory of evolution, outlined in *Origin of the Species* (1859), profoundly challenged Christianity's grip on explaining the human condition and its history—and thus Christianity's influence on Western sexuality—it hardly eradicated it. Evolutionary thinking, and the Christian distinction between "good" and "bad" sex, each powerfully informed discourses of sex and gender in the twentieth century.

More specifically, this is a chapter about "female orgasm," a contested term that was heavily debated throughout the twentieth century, most often within the context of what feminist poet Adrienne Rich would influentially describe as "compulsory heterosexuality."[13] As the nineteenth century turned into the twentieth, women who regularly experienced and enjoyed clitoral orgasm—whether alone or in company—could be diagnosed as "abnormal" and prescribed various remedies, including in some cases removal of the clitoris. Over a century later, healthy female sexuality and general well-being is often indexed by regular orgasms, while a lack thereof can constitute "female sexual dysfunction," an official diagnosis that has spurred a range of pharmaceutical and therapeutic responses. In the wake of mid-century sex research, the clitoris was also rehabilitated after its extended spell as secondary to the vagina or merely a "secret," though knowledge about this built-for-pleasure body part (or "little penis," to use a crude Freudianism) can still be vague or problematic.[14] This chapter traces how the female orgasm acquired its contemporary status as the optimum expression of embodied female sexuality. I will do so by traversing the three foremost discourses on the female orgasm that positioned it as the exemplar of female sexuality, and that continue to inform how we comprehend female pleasure, female experience, and female politics and the relationship between them in the present. These discourses are: Sigmund Freud's theorizing on female sexuality, in particular his distinction between clitoral and vaginal orgasms; the ongoing obsession of sex research with female orgasm within an enduring paradigm of female sexuality as a "problem" in need of clinical intervention (or at the least explanation); and finally, second-wave féminist debates about the place of orgasm in feminist sexual politics. To begin I will re-state the quintessentially twentieth-century question—what *is* female orgasm?—as an entry point into a closer examination of Freud, sexology, and feminism.

WHAT IS FEMALE ORGASM?

There is great variation in both the intensity and the duration of female orgasmic experience, while the male tends to follow standard patterns of ejaculatory action with less individual variation.

—William H. Masters and Virginia E. Johnson,
Human Sexual Response, 1966[15]

Female orgasms usually involve the clitoris. In short, this was the great revelation of twentieth-century sex research, particularly in the wake of Alfred Kinsey's 1953 study into female sexuality. Yet, the clitoris also confounds heterosexuality. What is the role of the penis if the clitoris is the primary organ of female sexual pleasure? Freud's answer to this dilemma was to theorise the clitoral orgasm as "immature" and the vaginal as "mature." Popular sex educators such as Dutch gynaecologist Dr. Theodore Van de Velde recognized the significance of the clitoris, but quarantined it to foreplay in service to the holy grail of twentieth-century heterosexuality: simultaneous, mutual orgasm; a highly coveted though elusive sensation, frequently described in hyperbolic terms in manuals and novels alike (Van de Velde, a man of medicine, still described it as "Sexual Communion"[16]). But while mutual orgasm may be rare, or even a myth, and difficult to clinically measure, the "scientific" rediscovery of the clitoris in the 1950s and 1960s was not necessarily experienced as a catalyst for heterosexual intimacy. In her 1962 novel *The Golden Notebook*, Doris Lessing offered this insight into what was at stake, post-Kinsey:

> A vaginal orgasm is emotion and nothing else....The vaginal orgasm is
> a dissolving in a vague, dark generalised sensation like being swirled in a
> warm whirlpool. There are several different sorts of clitoral orgasms, and
> they are more powerful (that is a male word) than the vaginal orgasm.
> There can be a thousand thrills, sensations etc., but there is only one real
> female orgasm and that is when a man, from the whole of his need and
> desire, takes a woman and wants all her response. But when she told him
> she had never experienced what she insisted on calling a "real orgasm"
> to anything like the same depth before him, he involuntarily frowned and
> remarked: "Do you know that there are eminent physiologists who say
> women have no physical basis for vaginal orgasm?"
>   "Then, they don't know much do they?"[17]

Female orgasm here moves between the cracks of culture and biology, exposing
a major faultline in heterosexual relationships.

To subscribe to a particular definition of female orgasm runs the risk of
reproducing discourses of female sexuality as "problem" or hierarchies of orgasm. Female orgasm itself resists a stringent definition, despite ongoing clinical attempts to do so. Ejaculation of semen provides male orgasm with both an
objective marker that orgasm occurred, and a reproductive function. Female
orgasm had not been as easy to explain or quantify, though at various points
throughout history, female orgasm has been conceptualized using reproductive, physiological, and/or psychological criteria. The American Psychiatric
Association currently defines human orgasm as "a peaking of sexual pleasure,
with release of sexual tension and rhythmic contraction of the perineal muscles
and reproductive organs...In the female, there are contractions (not always
subjectively experienced as such) of the outer third of the vagina. In both genders, the anal sphincter rhythmically contracts."[18] This definition privileges the
physical experience of orgasm, and aims for a unisex application that is nonetheless undermined by female subjectivity; it also contradicts research that suggests a greater variability among the physical responses of women.[19] Masters
and Johnson's 1966 research into human sexual response certainly affirmed
this variance, but in doing so their benchmark remained the "standard" of
male orgasm.

The female orgasms referred to throughout this chapter are both real and
imagined: real in that orgasms are part of many women's embodied experience,
and imagined insofar as what an orgasm "is" has been constructed and recon-
structed across the twentieth century. Competing and shifting notions of what
constitutes an orgasm have also informed women's own understanding of their

bodies and sexuality. One oft-cited example of this is the case of psychoanalyst and friend of Freud, Marie Bonaparte, who in her quest for vaginal orgasm, conducted research into female sexual response. In the 1920s, after measuring the proximity of the clitoris to the vagina in 243 women, the majority of whom exhibited the capacity to orgasm from intercourse, Bonaparte concluded that her best course of action was to have her own clitoris relocated to the optimum position. After two surgeries, she declared the experiment a personal failure, though she remained committed to somehow reconciling her own sexuality, and female sexuality in general, to psychoanalytic thought.[20] Bonaparte's experience is singular and rather sensational, and her legacy is a patchy one (sexual pioneer or Freudian dupe?),[21] but her example does emphatically illustrate how influential discourses about orgasm have played out on women's bodies. In her defense, it should also be pointed out that Bonaparte's own sexual history and investigations into female sexuality meant that she could never entirely concur with Freud's theorising which made the clitoris (and thereby clitoral orgasm) subordinate to the vagina. Nor did Bonaparte "fake" it. In this respect, she aspired to the "authentic" orgasm, rather than its binary opposite the "fake" orgasm.

As Marie Bonaparte's quest demonstrates, the theory and practise of orgasm have not always worked in tandem. And while designated experts certainly adjusted their theories in the light of "new" discoveries, old frameworks were often hard to shake. Take, for instance, sexologist husband-and-wife team Josephine and Irving Singer who, in response to Kinsey and Masters and Johnson, and the more specific "discovery" that some women claim to experience orgasms without any contractions in their vulva, proposed in 1972 three new types of orgasm they claimed would resolve the "value-laden connotations" of the terms "clitoral" and "vaginal" orgasm: the "vulval orgasm" (not dependent on "coitus" and thus, to infer from their tone, quite ordinary and easy to achieve); the "uterine orgasm" (not defined by contractions of the "orgasmic platform" but instead subjectively and emotionally experienced as "deep" and dependent on "repeated penis-cervix contact" that "occurs in coitus alone"); and finally the "blended orgasm" which combines aspects of the first two in that the "orgasmic platform" does contract as with a vulval orgasm, yet is experienced as a "deeper" sensation as with the coital orgasm.[22] In other words, the blended orgasm is a vaginal orgasm, involving some clitoral stimulation. In fact, the Singers' theory of orgasm can also be described as a "blend" of influential twentieth-century theories of female sexuality—in particular, of Freud's vaginal orgasm, of the purportedly evidence-based and "neutral" taxonomies of the American sex researchers of the mid-century, and of the pervasive heterosexism that marked them all. Their incorporation of subjective accounts of orgasm—not always easy to measure using the laboratory approach favored by Masters and Johnson—also alerts us to one of the more positive legacies of Freud: the recognition that orgasm is both a psychological and physical experience, mediated by bodies and by culture.

This history of female orgasms is partial, based as it is primarily on "expert" discourses of orgasm, and feminist critiques of these. Historicizing female orgasm is a task constrained by what Nancy Tuana has described as "the politics of ignorance," exemplified by the historic fate of the clitoris which has been constantly rediscovered and redefined since its initial "discovery" by Renaldus Columbus in 1559. (Centuries later, in 1980 to be precise, British feminist Beatrix Campbell would quip: "Presumably its discovery was as much a surprise to its owners as the discovery of America was to its indigenous occupants."[23]) Ignorance, argues Tuana, is not merely a simple lack of knowledge, but an active production that is related to power. What we do and do not know about women's orgasms inevitably emerges from, and intersects with, the dominant knowledge of what constitutes "normal" female sexuality and the "normal" female body at any given time. The ancient belief that female orgasm was necessary for reproduction privileged knowledge of women as sexually robust and multi-orgasmic. Yet once the connection between women's orgasms and conception was refuted in the nineteenth century, female sexuality was refigured as passive and/or passionless, a discourse that prevailed well into the twentieth century.[24]

Of course, not all women at the dawn of sexual modernity were assumed to be passionless or sexually repressed. If the desirable state of Victorian femininity was "passionless," then "fallen women" were their mirror opposite: voracious, insatiable, and "morally corrupt."[25] Whether as victim or agent of sex, working-class women and racial "others" were frequently depicted—often in crude Darwinian terms—as inherently and even wantonly sexual. Victoria-era porn was full of accounts of maids, servants, and prostitutes as "wayward, insatiable women who experienced overwhelming orgasms at the hands of inexhaustible men,"[26] while the colonial encounter itself was eroticized via images of invitingly assembled "exotic" women. The sexuality of these women was of a different order of problem or panacea to that of middle-class wives and mothers: on the one hand, their presumed sexual availability threatened class and racial boundaries, and on the other, they provided an outlet for the "natural" sexual urges of men, and an escape from bourgeois domesticity. Both the "respectable" and "deviant" (or "pure" and "impure") models of female sexuality were subject to regulatory control, ranging from moral censure

or guidance to government intervention, and each was articulated in relation to a normative idea of male sexuality as naturally promiscuous and in
constant need of sexual release (in other words, the sexual double standard).
These often racialized and class-based models of female sexuality lingered
well into the twentieth century, manifesting themselves in pornographic and
mainstream representations of sexually desirable and/or available women,
and underpinning debates about contraception and population. For instance,
Marie Stopes—author of the best-selling *Married Love* (1918) and the founder
of the British Society for Constructive Birth Control and Racial Progress—
made the case in 1920 that birth control would be particularly helpful in curb-
ing the breeding habits of the "diseased, racially negligent, the thriftless, the
careless, the feeble-minded, the very lowest and worst members of the community [who] produce innumerable tens of thousands of stunted, warped, inferior infants." With fewer undesirables draining "the resources of those above
them," she continued, "[t]he better classes, freed from the costs of institutions,
prisons and so on, principally filled by the inferior racial stock, would be able
to afford to enlarge their own families."[27] It was for these better classes that
Stopes encouraged better orgasms.

The origins of Bonaparte's somewhat extreme experiments resided in her
own sexually unsatisfying marriage. Female sexual response became a specific
sort of problem in the twentieth century as female sexual pleasure became a
desirable component of marriage and then, heterosexual encounters in general.
In service to this ideal, and in response to patients who reported sexual unhappiness, sex researchers increasingly turned their attention to "normal sexuality" or heterosexual problems. The nineteenth-century market that purported
to cure a range of sexual problems became a more respectable enterprise in
the twentieth century; it also became far more visible as the mass media and
popular culture disseminated new information and ideals about sex. The shift
to sexual modernity epitomized by expectations of love, sexual pleasure, and
individual satisfaction, has been variously dated to the 1890s emergence of the
New Woman, the growth of sex radicalism in the early decades of the twentieth century, the alleged "first" sexual revolution of the 1920s, the sex research
of Alfred Kinsey in the 1950s, and the introduction of the contraceptive pill
and the sexual revolution in the 1960s.[28] Whatever the origins of sexual modernity, by the release of the Masters and Johnson report into human sexual
response in 1966—in which they reinstated the clitoris as the primary site of
female sexual response and pleasure—it was obvious that the female orgasm
was well-established as one of its most contested features.

To return to Bonaparte one last time, her painful pursuit of a "real" vaginal
orgasm alerts us to a parallel or counter-history of fake orgasms, typically read

as anti-feminist insofar as faking it is presumed to collude with male heterosexual imperatives. Annamarie Jagose has suggested that fake orgasms are a distinctly twentieth-century phenomenon or invention that elucidates the "open secret" of the "sexual incompatibility of the heterosexual couple" and "the normalising discipline of sexuality."[29] The topic of fake orgasms also reminds us of the huge (and contested) influence pornography would come to have in representing female orgasm in the highly visual twentieth century. Writing in 1989, before the rise of Internet pornography, Cindy Patton reflected on the sexual scripts embedded in heterosexual porn; a genre that typically presupposes a male viewer. Her wider observations of how male and female orgasms (and sexualities) are differently represented are still relevant:

> Male sexual fulfilment, in Western culture, is synonymous with orgasm. The discourse of male orgasm is generally limited to how to achieve one. There is no question that men have orgasms: the proof is ejaculation.... No come shot, no narrative closure.
>
> [But] there is cultural uncertainty about what constitutes female sexual pleasure. Female sexual pleasure is not synonymous with orgasm, and images of female sexual pleasure have been used to indicate male sexual pleasure, as in mainstream movies, and product satisfaction, as in glossy advertisements. Even though the nature of female orgasm has come under debate in the last two decades—the clitoral orgasm, G-spot, anal sex—female sexual pleasure is still depicted through facial expressions: the transcendent glazed-over eyes, lips glistening and slightly parted, head thrown back.[30]

And while the Internet has certainly expanded the range of porn on offer—with "real porn" depicting "real sex" being especially popular—the twenty-first century has already been described as exhibiting an unprecedented mainstreaming of pornographic behaviours and aesthetics, which some feminists argue has been particularly damaging for heterosexual pleasure.[31]

Throughout modernity, debates about, and investigations into, the content, frequency, and purpose of female orgasms have been conducted within what has been called an androcentric model of sexuality. Within this heterosexist model, sex is defined as an activity that involves preparation ("foreplay"), penetration, and leading to male orgasm. And while it may be preferable for the female participant to also reach orgasm, her inability to do so does not undermine the status of coital sex as "real sex."[32] Within this paradigm, female heterosexuality was arguably defined as a problem from the outset. Feminist critiques attest that the androcentric model hardly went unchallenged, yet female heterosexuality—when indexed to orgasmic capacity within coital sex *or* as paradigmatic of female oppression—remains problematic. A specifically *feminist* heterosexuality or feminist politics of heterosexuality has been identified as one of the unfinished projects of women's liberation.

FREUD AND FEMALE SEXUALITY

> The elimination of clitoridal sexuality is a necessary precondition for the development of femininity.
>
> —Sigmund Freud, 1925[33]

The path to sexual modernity was marked by a reversal of what had been commonplace thought about female sexuality for thousands of years: women were more pleasure-seeking than men, female orgasm was necessary for reproduction, the clitoris was "the seat of woman's delight," the clitoris was the female version of the penis (or a part of the vagina), and female physiology was in effect the male body turned inside out, with some variations in heat distribution. Then, as Thomas Lacquer has influentially demonstrated, in the late eighteenth century, medical science advanced a radical interpretation of the female body in relation to the male, inaugurating the two-sex model and a sexual difference that was (among other markers) indicated by the presence of orgasm in one sex (male) and absence in the other (the increasingly passionless female). It was this "purported independence of generation from pleasure that created the space in which women's sexual nature could be redefined, debated, denied, or qualified."[34] It was in this space that the father of psychoanalysis Sigmund Freud—using the authoritative language of science to posit a "narrative of culture in anatomical disguise"[35]—theorized female orgasm. In tandem with his theory of penis envy as constituting the "repressed wish" of female sexuality, Freud made a distinction between the clitoral orgasm (typically synonymous with masturbation, the "executive agent of infantile sexuality") and the vaginal orgasm (as the culmination of mature, "normal femininity").[36] He thus problematized female sexuality in very specific terms (she is effectively castrated and defined by what she does not have) and further consolidated its clinical and general reputation as mysterious or, in Freud's words, a "dark continent."[37]

Freud looms large over any discussion of female orgasm in the twentieth century, and indeed of modern sexuality in general. As Freud's interlocutors have emphasized, and many of his detractors conceded, he did substantially expand and refine notions of sexuality; for example, in his insistence on inherent bisexuality and by privileging pleasure over reproduction, and personal history and social context over mere genital function. Freud was also as interested in normative sexuality, epitomized in the unit of the bourgeois family, as his predecessors in sexology had been in sexual "perversions," and indeed in his focus on childhood sexuality, found origins for all sexual behaviors.[38] Perhaps even more significantly, Freud suggested that perversions were common property, rather than exclusive to sick or immoral minorities.[39] And while Foucault famously rejected the distinction between Victorian sexual repression and modern, liberated sexuality purportedly represented by Freud,[40] other historians have emphasized his profoundly original conception of sexual desire (beginning with the "polymorphous perversity" of childhood sexuality),[41] his insistence on sexual fulfilment as a fundamental component of status and well-being (an affirmation Freud shared in common with his sexologist contemporaries),[42] and the subversive effect of psychoanalysis, the signature of which, as Paul Rutherford has pointed out, was "an obsession with sex, more particularly with the power of the sex drive and the intensity of sexual desire, as the key to understanding the psyche and behaviour of men and women."[43] The novelty of this proposition (and his emphasis on the unconscious) meant that Freud's work was simultaneously hailed as unlocking the key to modern civilization and as fraudulent nonsense.[44] His influence on modern sexuality was particularly marked in the "optimistic" culture of the United States, where therapists popularized among their bourgeois clientele the idea that it was possible to adjust one's sexuality to meet society's demands.[45] Later, it would be American feminists that would launch some of the most scathing critiques of his ideas.[46]

The "caricatured portrait" of Freud was of "some sort of sex-crazed Viennese professor intent on violating every taboo."[47] However, despite Freud's radicalism, he was also a man of his times: nowhere was this more apparent than in his theorizing on female sexuality, premised as it was on penis envy, female passivity, and reproductive imperatives, all of which demanded a demotion for the clitoris as a locus of female sexual pleasure. If his theory of femininity allowed for the then-radical proposition that women are socialized into their feminine roles, Freud also left little doubt that the optimum outcome of this process was a vaginally orgasmic, reproductive heterosexual female. "We are entitled to keep our view," wrote Freud, "that in the phallic phase of girls the clitoris is the leading erotogenic zone. But it is not, of course, going to remain so."[48] The move from clitoral to vaginal orgasm posited a "mature" model of female sexuality, defined by passivity, in which the female desire for a penis was surpassed by the desire for a child. And while the 1905 publication of his *Three Essays on the Theory of Sexuality* caused a sensation, arousing what his daughter Anna Freud later described as "outbursts of indig-nation...[over] what was then a shocking and prohibited attack on human dignity,"[49] the downgrading of clitoral pleasure to auxiliary for vaginal sex, or in Freud's words to "pine shavings [that] can be kindled in order to set a log of harder wood on fire,"[50] was not particularly contentious. As Angus McLaren puts it, "Freud was attacked for saying many things, but never in his lifetime for the notion of this unlikely migration of a woman's pleasure centre from her clitoris to her vagina." "Freud's unlikely scenario," suggests McLaren, of-fered some solution to contemporary anxieties about declining birthrates and increasing female independence.[51]

Given Freud's medical training, Laqueur contends that he "must have known that there was absolutely no anatomical or physiological evidence" for the transfer of clitoral to vaginal stimulation. Thus, Freud would have been aware that "he was inventing the vaginal orgasm and...at the same time giving a radical new meaning to the clitoris."[52] What Freud did then, via the vaginal-clitoral distinction, was to attempt to align female sexuality with the reproduc-tive imperatives of Western civilization. That the vaginal-clitoral distinction ran counter to biological evidence was perhaps precisely the point of his theoriz-ing on female sexuality. Unpacking Freud's arguments, Laqueur interprets the move from clitoral to vaginal pleasure as "hysterical" rather than biological in that it "works against the organic structures of the body. Like the missing-limb phenomenon, it involves feeling what is not there." Thus, becoming a sexual mature woman means "living an oxymoron [and] becoming a life-long 'normal hysteric.'" Freud's contribution to twentieth-century thought then was to pose so richly the problem of sexual difference,[53] rather than to solve it. As for his "evidence," Anna Freud has argued that the basis of psychoanalysis was clinical case histories, and as such, Freud's theories of female sexuality can be explained as descriptions or critiques of patriarchy rather than prescrip-tions for it.[54] In a similar vein, Jacqueline Rose has argued that psychoanalysis was born not in the Viennese parlor, but during Freud's time working under Jean-Martin Charcot in the 1880s at the Salpetrière Clinic in Paris, a hospital for women comprised of the "dregs" of society, alleged "incurable" hysterics, whom he was determined to understand in general and psychic terms, rather than as examples of individual pathology.[55]

Freud both acknowledged female sexual desire and pathologized female sexuality in new and/or updated ways. As Rachel P. Maines has traced, while Freud's theorizing of female sexuality maintained a prevailing emphasis on penetrative, heterosexual sex as the "real thing," he also moved away from earlier diagnoses of female "hysteria" that had frequently diagnosed sexual deprivation as a cause—with some form of sexual gratification—preferably not through masturbation, and not often directly called "orgasm"—as a cure. Instead, Freud elevated hysteria to a "psychopathology," rooted in childhood experiences and commonly manifested in adulthood as a propensity to masturbation or "frigidity" in coital sex. With vaginal orgasm as the measure of mature female sexuality, the two-thirds to three-quarters of women who did not commonly experience orgasm this way were ascribed a pathological condition.[56] Female sexuality was thus not only mysterious, but also most often cast as a problem requiring diagnosis and treatment, which in psychoanalytic terms was most commonly the "talking cure," with Marie Bonaparte's failed surgical attempts to relocate her clitoris representing an extreme example of the pursuit of vaginal orgasm. Psychoanalysis then can be understood to have assigned women a problem, while also giving them a way to talk about it.

Freud's theorising on female sexuality and female orgasm were not accepted wholesale within psychoanalysis: Melanie Klein, Ernst Jones, and Karen Horney (who declared his theory of femininity "androcentric" and would eventually break away from Freud) each rejected or refined his vision of the female orgasm,[57] while William Reich—psychoanalyst, sex radical, author of The Function of Orgasm (1927) and acknowledged inspiration for the 1960s sexual revolution—took Freud's theories in what has been described as a more "optimistic" (though no less androcentric) direction, investing orgasm (still heterosexual, still vaginal, and ideally mutual) with the capacity to cure neurosis, rather than produce it.[58] Freud's ideas, in the hands of "inter-war misogynists" such as Antony Ludovic, Robert Teutsch and K.A. Wieth-Knudsen, also inspired what would become well-worn twentieth-century stereotypes of sexual identity, including the boy with the overbearing mother who becomes homosexual; the girl driven away by a cold, distant father to lesbianism; and the feminist as a man-hating frigid with lesbian tendencies.[59] And though initially Freud's theory of the vaginal orgasm remained largely absent from marriage advice manuals, and were not particularly common outside Freudian circles, it had taken firm hold by the 1940s.[60] Perhaps the most influential Freudian of this period was psychoanalyst Helene Deutsch, author of The Psychology of Women (1944), who—while rejecting the notion of penis envy—also endorsed Freud's transfer theory of female sexual development by using vaginal orgasm as a mark of a healthy woman, or the "feminine woman" who "adapt themselves to their partners and understand them [and] are easily excited and rarely frigid." In making this case, Deutsch was perhaps most loyal to the basic tenets of Freud in her conflation of the vaginal orgasm, heterosexuality and women's mental health,[61] and most representative of the kind of increasingly popular thinking that would convince a married woman who could not orgasm vaginally that something must be wrong with her rather than with the sort of sex that she was having. Deutsch's work in particular was made accessible through the work of Marynia Farnham and Ferdinand Lundberg, authors of the American best seller *Modern Woman: The Lost Sex* (1947), whose promotion of vaginal sexuality contained a virulent strain of anti-feminism that consigned women who were not married and/or mothers to frigidity and gender disorder. "Normal" women were vaginally orgasmic, and also passive: sex, they declared, "is not as easy as rolling a log for her. It's easier. It is easy as being the log itself."[62]

Whatever the origins or intent of Freud's theory of female sexuality, his valorization (or "invention") of the vaginal orgasm emerged from and clearly influenced the "new heterosexuality" that was one of the markers of the alleged shift from Victorian to modern sexuality. According to Jonathan Katz, heterosexuality began the century "defensively" as the "publicly sanctioned private practice of the respectable middle-class, and the publicly put-down pleasure-affirming practice" of everyone else. Yet by the end of the 1920s, aided by Freud and others, heterosexuality had "triumphed as dominant, sanctified culture."[63] Heterosexual female pleasure in particular became one of the most important signs of sexual modernity, and the "New New Woman" or flapper the most obvious (and contentious) example of this new ethos.[64] Onto the flapper, and young women in general, were projected a host of post–First World War anxieties about what it meant to be "modern" and in particular the perils of new sexual freedoms, including declining birthrates, sex and pregnancy outside of marriage, promiscuity, contraception, venereal disease, sex across class and racial boundaries, and homosexual desire. In the inter-war period, representations of the flapper, and younger female sexuality, also often contained mixed messages, including that premarital sex was acceptable as long as it had no public consequences, and that sexual experience was both desirable and dangerous.[65]

The New Woman generated anxiety because it was feared that having tasted some form of unprecedented freedom (whether it be political, financial, or the freedom to manage fertility) she would no longer settle for traditional gender roles and the inequality of a heterosexual relationship.[66] Modern marriage began to be promoted—via "sex experts" and through popular culture—as a romantic, mutually pleasurable union based on sexual compatibility, of which the simultaneous orgasm—achievable through sex education—was the ultimate expression. This "eroticization of marriage" was due partly to the efforts of sex reformers such as Stopes in Britain and Margaret Sanger in the United States, both of whom won over their target middle-class audience by "cloaking the discussion of sex in a terminology that was both romantic and religious." The percentage of women getting married also rose to include approximately 95 percent of women,[67] a figure which would not significantly change in most Western countries until at least the 1960s. As Anna Clark and others have pointed out, much of the early sex advice in the twentieth century was developed "on the job": by "renegade doctors" such as Dr. Theodore van de Velde and the German socialist Max Hodden who treated sexually frustrated patients, and by female scientists such as Stopes, who as a young ignorant wife, experienced the frustrations of sexual ignorance and incompatibility first-hand. Foreplay, both loosely and specifically defined, was prescribed, typically with the clitoris having a role to play[68] (indeed Van de Velde described it as "an organ of voluptuous sensation exclusively"[69]).

The ongoing popularity of instruction manuals from the likes of Stopes and Van de Velde obviously indicates that heterosexual couples were eager for more sexual knowledge (*Married Love* went through seven printings, and sold over a million copies;[70] Van de Velde's *Ideal Marriage: Its Physiology and Technique* was first published in Holland in 1926, and was reprinted forty-three times in English alone;[71] and *Marriage Manual: A Practical Guidebook to Sex and Marriage* by husband-and-wife doctor team Abraham and Hannah Stone, first released in 1937, had already been reprinted twenty-nine times and translated into numerous languages by the time the revised 1952 edition was published[72]). Some of what was presented was refreshingly matter-of-fact, and decidedly risqué for the period. Stopes lamented that the sexual pleasure of women was often cut short by the premature ejaculation of their partners. Van de Velde advocated "the genital kiss, by gentle and soothing caresses with lips and tongue" as the ideal lubricant,[73] and included information about genital odors, erogenous zones, and menstruation. For Van de Velde, the failure of women to achieve orgasm was "deplorably frequent" and in most cases could be blamed on "the inadequate technique of the husband, or to his absolutely unfair and fraudulent behaviour in coitus."[74] British doctor Helena Wright, author of a series of sex advice manuals published throughout the 1930s and 1940s, counseled her patients and readers that the clitoris was essential for sexual satisfaction, and offered women instructions on how to find it: "Arrange a good light and take a mirror.... The instant the clitoris is touched, a peculiar and characteristic sensation is experienced."[75]

Yet, read together, the sex manuals from the first half of the twentieth century, however well-intentioned or instructive, maintained heterosexual coitus "as the central act of sexual significance," and mutual orgasm as its fullest expression, and in doing so explicitly or implicitly assigned women the blame for any sexual failures in this arena.[76] Some of these authorities were less committed to the pursuit of simultaneous orgasm—Wright, for example, after decades of speaking with her patients, began to challenge the "efficacy of the penis-vagina combination for producing an orgasm"[77]—yet in taking marital sex as their basis, each writer circled back to a central problem: the lack of correspondence between the reproductive act and female orgasm.[78] Freud's theory of transference from clitoral to vaginal sexual pleasure had offered one route out of that impasse, but the experiences of sexually frustrated couples exposed the after-effects and limits of his thinking.

Natalie Angier has argued that Freud's proposed vaginal-clitoral orgasm distinction "was an anomaly, a blot on history's understanding of female sexuality," in which the clitoris had been long understood as central to female sexual satisfaction.[79] This recognition did not suddenly disappear with Freud, only to reappear with second-wave feminism: renegade and professional voices positively affirmed the clitoral orgasm prior to its resurgence in the 1960s. Marriage manuals that typically assigned the clitoris a supporting rather than starring role were not necessarily direct proof of Freud's influence, as evidence of a shared goal to somehow reconcile heterosexual intercourse and male climax—the prerequisites for reproduction—with female sexual pleasure. Even after the Freudian hierarchy of female orgasm was challenged by sex researchers and feminists alike, the vaginal-clitoral distinction never entirely disappeared, at least within discourses of heterosexuality. For instance, the 1980s discovery of the "G-Spot," the erogenous zone within the vagina that purportedly produces female climax and ejaculation in some women, has been interpreted by some commentators as not so much a coda to the vaginal-clitoral orgasm distinction as a resurgence of it.[80] Research has also shown that Freud's clitoral-vaginal opposition continues to provide some women with a vocabulary for talking about their sexual experiences, even if they cannot link this distinction explicitly to Freud.[81]

SEXOLOGY AND THE FEMALE ORGASM

For all of his distinctiveness, Freud was also part of the emergence of modern sexology, or the science of sex, that had its roots in Germany in the clinical work of Richard von Krafft-Ebbing (psychiatrist), Iwan Bloch (dermatologist), and Magnus Hirschfeld (physician). Hardly a uniform group—Hirschfeld was an early campaigner for gay rights who challenged the prevailing professional opinion that homosexuality was "abnormal"; British doctor Havelock Ellis advocated female sexual pleasure, and masturbation[82]—early sexologists nevertheless reflected and reinforced the social hierarchies and social and political

concerns at the turn of the twentieth century. Among them were the enduring sexual double standard of "normal" women as sexually passive and mo-
nogamous and men as naturally sexual and inclined to promiscuity, and the
widespread obsession with public health (or, as it was sometimes called, racial
or social hygiene).[83] Yet while they broadly espoused the Darwinian line that
heterosexual gratification was essential for human evolution and "thus" natural, some early sexologists also provided contrary evidence that undermined
the axiomatic link between sex and reproduction. Krafft-Ebing, for instance,
while declaring women less sexual than men, also asserted that they needed
to have orgasms in order to prevent hysteria or neurasthenia. Swedish sexologist Anton Nystrom warned that sexual abstinence could cause what he called
"female diseases."[84] Some physicians and psychiatrists, under the influence of
various sexological theories, treated their "hysterical" female patients with or-
gasm-inducing massaging of the genitals, using either their hands or electronic
vibrators. Others prescribed clitoridectomy.[85] Meanwhile, sexology also inter-
sected with the rise of eugenics. As forced sterilization laws were introduced
across Europe throughout the 1920s and 1930s, it was those women deemed
socially deviant or inferior—a marker of which was an allegedly uninhibited or
excessive female sexuality—who bore the brunt of this legislation.[86]

Still apart from Freud and Ellis, so-called "normal" heterosexuality was
of secondary concern to early modern sexologists. After the two world wars,
sexology shifted its centre to the United States where entomologist Alfred Kinsey, prompted by the sexual ignorance of the students he taught at Indiana
University, began his major studies into human sexuality. The results of the first
study were published as *Sexual Behaviour in the Human Male* in 1948, followed by the companion volume on female sexual behavior in 1953 (the same
year *Playboy* was first published; the magazine's founder Hugh Hefner would
share with Kinsey the title of Father of the Sexual Revolution). In the massive publicity that greeted both volumes, orgasmic words such as "explosive"
and "mind-blowing" littered the more sensationalist accounts of his research
findings. Almost 46 percent of the male population had engaged in both heterosexual and homosexual activities (compared to approximately 28 percent
of females). Roughly 50 percent of married men, and 26 percent of married
women, had had extramarital sex. Fifty-four percent of marital sex included
"oral stimulation of the female genitalia"; 92 percent of men masturbated, as
did 62 percent of women, and 40 percent of females experienced their first
orgasm through masturbation. Premarital sex occurred in approximately 50 percent of the female sample. From an overall sample of 18,000 cases covering a
large social spectrum, results were mostly sourced from "in-depth, face-to-face

interviews," conducted by "highly trained interviewers," with 5,300 white males and 5,490 white females, most of them college-educated. Subjects were asked up to 521 questions about their sexual histories, as Kinsey sought out what he described as "quantifiable" and "objective" evidence of sexual behavior—of which frequency of sex and orgasm were the most obvious indicators.[87] Sexual acts, rather than sexual identification, were his concern. In adopting this methodology Kinsey sought to avoid what he criticized as the flimsy evidential basis and moral tone of earlier studies, and by doing so he argued that he would access the "facts" or "truth" of sex, or to put it another way what people were actually doing in the bedroom, rather than what they should be doing.[88] For his efforts, Kinsey was variously hailed as a menace to society, a threat to the Western family, a heroic figure who battled against moral conservatism at the high point of the Cold War, a flawed scientist, and the first proper scientific sex researcher.[89] Kinsey died in 1956, two years after losing funding from the Rockefeller Foundation.

Kinsey defined orgasm in broad unisex terms as the "explosive discharge of neuromascular tensions at the peak of sexual response," to be achieved by six potential routes: masturbation, nocturnal emission, heterosexual petting, heterosexual intercourse, homosexual relations, and intercourse with animals.[90] Using this criteria, Kinsey broke down the distinction between heterosexuality and homosexuality, replacing it with the Kinsey Scale, a seven-point classification system that ranged from exclusively heterosexual to exclusively homosexual, with the majority of cases falling somewhere between. After initially categorizing female orgasm as "clitoro-vulvar," Kinsey abandoned the vaginal orgasm altogether in the 1953 volume, declaring that women could only achieve orgasm via the clitoris, and that masturbation was beneficial to coitus.[91] It was this finding that particularly endeared his research to early women's liberationists, yet other feminist critics have pointed out that Kinsey also peddled earlier essentialist ideas about "higher sexual capacity" in men, privileged the institution of marriage—even after the results of his study revealed that wives typically had far fewer orgasms than their husbands—and ignored the cultural and social context of sex altogether.[92] Fertility control and sexual disease were outsourced to gynaecology and urology, leaving orgasm as the premier subject for sexology, and curing "sexual dysfunction" rather than cataloguing deviance as its motivation.[93]

Sexology's new status as a science dedicated to the study of human orgasm was further consolidated with the laboratory studies of William Masters, a gynaecologist, and Virginia Johnson, a behavioral scientist whose first book *Human Sexual Response*, released in 1966 at the height of the sexual revolution (and thus far less controversial—though no less sensational or influential—than Kinsey's Cold War-era investigations[94]), was based on empirical data of over 10,000 orgasms from 382 female and 312 male subjects, most of them white, educated, and middle-to-upper class.[95] This material was augmented by reports, or subjective accounts, "given in the laboratory in the immediacy of the postorgasmic period"[96] of the experience and sensation of orgasm. Masters and Johnson observed, measured, and sometimes filmed their subjects reaching orgasm, which in the case of females was focussed exclusively on the clitoris ("a unique organ in the total of human anatomy"[97]), with the authors following Kinsey in rejecting vaginal orgasm. Women were filmed reaching climax (or "contractions of the orgasmic platform"[98]) in response to vibrators, fingertips, pornography, and intercourse with an artificial coition machine. As with Kinsey, while the results pointed to major differences in male and female orgasms (including length, variety, and the influence of psychological factors—all higher in the female), the authors chose to stress the similarities, selectively using their material to espouse "ideology rather than science."[99] Their ideological commitment was to marriage, an institution under threat as divorce rates soared: if both couples had orgasms, a successful marriage was assured. And while Masters and Johnson moved on from Kinsey in asserting female sexual response "*infinitely* surpasses that of a man," they shared his larger neglect of the social subordination of women to men. Instead, women were now burdened with the task of eliminating bad sex from the marriage by making it better. To this end, Masters and Johnson provided sexual instruction and recommended sex therapy—rather than "any lengthy discussion of women's personal histories or experience of sex and relationships."[100]

Masters and Johnson created sex therapy for what in retrospect seems a ready-made market. By the late sixties, the contraceptive pill and the intrauterine device (IUD) were widely available, and although fertility rates were dropping, and the American magazines *Playboy* and *Cosmopolitan* extolled the pleasures of the single lifestyle for bachelors and single girls respectively, the percentage of women getting married and having children had actually increased: a general pattern of small family size that gradually extended to all social groups throughout the Western world. Sexologists, and other sex and reproduction experts, had "successfully implanted the notion that a woman who did not reproduce was incomplete."[101] More marriages—and changing laws—also meant more divorce. There was increasing tolerance of extramarital affairs, at least if popular culture was any indication.[102] The "new orthodoxy" that women needed more than a penis to have an orgasm opened up a whole new market in sexual self-help, including Alex Comfort's *The Joy of Sex* (1972) which celebrated a "sexual menu" of pleasures including anal sex and sado-masochism. Masturbation and oral sex became signs of liberated heterosexuality,[103] yet the sexological conflation of sexual and psychological well-being with orgasmic capacity produced a new set of problems: women reported pressure to have multiple orgasms, men worried their partners were faking it,[104] and the discrediting of vaginal and mutual orgasm—while experienced by many women as genuine sexual liberation since their inability to have one was no longer their fault—also meant the loss of one way to talk about heterosexual pleasure and intimacy (or pain, miscommunication, and inequality) that did not necessarily focus on orgasm. For this reason—and many others, not all of them relating to heterosexuality—the sexual revolution of the 1960s has been widely assessed as incomplete or a failure. Sex was commercialized, not liberated.[105]

By the 1970s, when Shere Hite was conducting her own sex research into American women as an explicitly feminist project that was critical of earlier studies into female sexuality and of the sexual revolution, feminism was clearly influencing sexology at least insofar as female sexuality was extended unprecedented investigative attention. Yet her best-seller *The Hite Report on Female Sexuality* (1976), clearly modelled on Kinsey while at the same time critical of him, also bore the marks of the sexological obsession with orgasm, leading her to interpret her finding that only 30 percent of women reached orgasm during penetrative sex as an indication that most women did not like coital sex at all—a conclusion, says Lynne Segal, that simplified the "complexity of feelings that Hite herself uncovered."[106]

The "new" sexology of Kinsey, Masters and Johnson, and to a lesser extent Hite, through their focus on orgasm as the key indicator of sexual health, ultimately maintained and reinvigorated the old paradigm of the sexually dysfunctional female who is in need of medical intervention or guidance, whether it be psychological, physiological, or both. This framework for comprehending female sexuality endures: in 2010, it was reported that almost a third of women express little or no interest in sex, or to put it in medical terms, these women suffer from hypoactive sexual desire disorder or HSDD. One sex researcher has reported that exposing women to pornography in her laboratory in order to illicit genital response has been effective in curing or alleviating this condition.[107] In the lab, the social and cultural construction of heterosexuality—experienced differently by men and women—is muted by evidence that women can have an orgasm if experts intervene.

FEMINIST HETEROSEXUALITY

In the late 1960s, Sigmund Freud ("Father of the Vaginal Orgasm") was an obvious starting point and target for women's liberationists eager to advance a less phallocentric model of female sexuality emanating from, to use the argument of American feminist Anne Koedt, author of "The Myth of the Vaginal

Orgasm" (1970), the biological facts of female anatomy rather than spurious assumptions about female inferiority. To make her case, Koedt turned to Kinsey and to Masters and Johnson for anatomical evidence of the centrality of the clitoris to female sexual pleasure. Women and men, she went on to argue, had different investments in maintaining the myth, an inevitable result of the inequality of the sexes. Lacking knowledge about their own anatomy, women could confuse a clitoral orgasm with a vaginal one. Some women were also motivated by a "desire to fit her experience to the male-centered idea of sexual normalcy." Faking orgasm became a way to "get the job" of functional female heterosexual, and the primacy of male sexual pleasure—and male social dominance—was maintained. Men perpetuated the myth because they preferred penetration of the vagina for their own orgasms; because their penis is the "epitome of masculinity"; to control women and because they are threatened by lesbianism and bisexuality. In place of this sexual status quo, Koedt insisted women "redefine our sexuality. We must discard 'normal' concepts of sex and create new guidelines that take into account mutual sexual enjoyment....New techniques must be used or devised which transform this particular aspect of our current sexual exploitation."[108]

Koedt delivered her indictment of the vaginal orgasm at the first national Women's Liberation Conference in the United States in 1968. At the same conference, she also ran a workshop where women shared "wonderful, detailed stories" about their sex lives and fantasies well into the night.[109] By the time an expanded version of her essay was published a year later, it was already a feminist classic, having circulated with impressive speed around the English-speaking feminist world. And Koedt was hardly alone in identifying sex as key to women's liberation: as historian Jane Gerhard has traced, from 1968 to the mid-1970s the meaning of female sexual pleasure in patriarchal societies was *the* topic for many Western feminists as different from one another as Australian libertarian Germaine Greer (who broke ranks and celebrated a new version of the vaginal orgasm in *The Female Eunuch*), orgasm sceptics such as Dana Densmore of Boston's Cell 16 (who rallied against a new form of post-sexual revolution oppression, labelling it "orgasm frenzy," and instead sought a sexual politics focussed on intimacy) and The Lavender Menace/Radicalesbians (authors of "Woman-identified Woman," who espoused the primary importance of emotional—rather than merely physical—relationships with women as a personal and political choice). Too diverse in their critiques and visions to be reduced to what would by the 1980s become vulgarized as the pro-sex and anti-sex camps, these early women's liberationists collectively offered a radical re-working of contemporary theories of female sexuality that rejected the divide between heterosexuality and lesbianism by variously celebrating clitoral sexuality, revolutionizing the meaning of lesbianism and championing intimacy over orgasmic sex. They also creatively and selectively reworked the aspects of Freudianism and modern sexology that best suited their purposes—so they embraced the instability of female heterosexuality that Freud had plotted as a problem as a powerful source of self-identification, and quoted from sexologists who championed the clitoris without reproducing their focus on marital sex.[110]

The injunction to "think clitoris"[111] has been recognized as one of the most significant feminist interventions of the 1970s. Without the clitoris, wrote feminist literary critic Paula Bennett in 1993, "theorists have no physical site in which to locate an autonomous sense of female sexual agency." As an organ entirely devoted to female sexual pleasure, the clitoris exists outside of the reproductive economy and the exchange of women.[112] Not surprisingly, given the special status assigned to the clitoris, female masturbation was promoted in feminist terms by the likes of Betty Dodson and the Boston Women's Health Book Collective (authors of the classic feminist "self-help" medical guide *Our Bodies, Ourselves*, first published in 1974). In this task, and aided by women's magazines that assumed a readership of sexually active women, feminists were enormously successful: by the end of the century, female masturbation had become rather respectable, especially in comparison to male masturbation which maintained a furtive, rather than therapeutic, association.[113]

Still, the limits of the utopian ideal of autonomous female sexuality were soon revealed. The promotion of clitoral orgasm as the route to female liberation, sexual and otherwise, gave way to larger questions and doubts. Did a focus on clitoral orgasm liberate female sexuality, or add another layer of anxiety and oppression? And what did female sexual liberation mean under patriarchy, and was it even possible? Some feminists decided not, and pledged allegiance to political lesbianism, regardless of sexual persuasion. Identifying sex as the fundamental site of male dominance over women, the Leeds Revolutionary Feminist Group, for example, concluded that to sleep with men was to collaborate with the enemy. Lesbian separatism, always a minority position with Western feminism, was nevertheless influential enough in the late 1970s to divide the women's movement in the United States, the United Kingdom, France, and elsewhere.[114] This splintering was symptomatic of wider divisions within 1970s feminism: by the end of the decade, it was impossible to speak of a coherent women's movement, divided as it was not only by the issue of sex and sexuality, but also by issues of race, ethnicity, class, and other political influences.

At roughly the same time the G-spot was discovered, or rather rediscovered, in the early 1980s,[115] British feminist Beatrix Campbell lamented a fading feminist sexual politics, epitomized in her view by a woeful neglect of heterosexuality as part of the feminist political project. For Campbell, the feminist sex wars had reached an impasse in which feminist sexual politics was. conflated with lesbian politics, an analogue that took the sex out of lesbianism and left heterosexual feminists to struggle for sexual freedom "more or less on their own."[116] Writing in 1983 from another angle, but also in pursuit of a wider definition of feminist sexual politics, Lynne Segal acknowledged that sex research had taught women to orgasm, but did not offer much in the way of theorizing intimacy: understanding the clitoris was not enough.[117] Campbell proposed that feminism reorient itself by returning to its focus on the transformation of heterosexuality, "and the possibility of a politically supported sexual practice which engages both men and women, and which is neither categorically heterosexual or lesbian."[118]

Campbell and Segal made their interventions in the context of ongoing debates within Western feminism over what constitutes sexual oppression or liberation for women—reductively categorized as the Feminist Sex Wars with "pro-sex" feminists promoting female sexual pleasure on the one side, and "anti-sex" feminists campaigning against the sexual oppression of women epitomised by pornography and prostitution on the other. Each deliberately presented their critiques from the periphery of the Sex Wars, and both Campbell and Segal foreshadowed in their own way the preoccupations of third-wave feminism and queer politics, which emerged in the late 1980s and early 1990s in the aftermath of women's and gay liberation. These political projects attended to what they saw as the unfinished business of the 1970s: for sexual politics, this included (for the third-wavers) the unrealised potential for feminist heterosexuality and (for queer activists and theorists) the necessary deconstruction or rejection of fixed or "normative" gendered and sexual identities. As part of this work, male heterosexuality and "hegemonic masculinity"[119]—relatively unexamined compared to female sexuality and femininity in twentieth-century psychoanalytic thought and sex research—began to be interrogated within a general critique of heterosexuality (or "heteronormativity") as privileged, fragile, pleasurable, and/or oppressive: in short, "queer" and open to transformation.

CONCLUSION

The twentieth century saw the emergence of what influential sociologist Anthony Giddens has described as "plastic sexuality"; that is, "decentred sexuality, freed from reproduction."[120] The three discourses covered in this chapter—psychoanalysis, sex research, and second-wave feminism—all sought in their own ways to elucidate female sexuality within this larger context. Each invested female orgasm with special explanatory power. For Freud and his followers, a theory of femininity that plotted a transference of female orgasm from the clitoris to the vagina acknowledged female sexual pleasure on the one hand, and maintained women's primary identity as mothers (and "castrated") on the other. Mid-century sex researchers, concerned primarily with the accumulation of facts drawn from the body and its sensations, produced ground-breaking and sensational evidence that female orgasms were clitoral, multiple, and easier to achieve through masturbation and "foreplay" than via coital sex. Yet though they rejected Freud's distinction between clitoral and vaginal orgasm, Alfred Kinsey and Masters and Johnson each shared Freud's conclusion that heterosexual marriage was normative and ideal. Some early women's liberationists criticized the heterosexist bases of sex research, while optimistically drawing on its findings about female orgasm to argue that the clitoris was the key to female sexual liberation. Their celebration of an autonomous female sexuality, freed from centuries of misinformation and miscomprehension about female orgasm, enjoyed wider influence, filtering through to popular culture, yet within women's liberation, a feminist sexual politics inclusive of heterosexual women has been persuasively critiqued as one of the casualties of the Sex Wars. Towards the end of the twentieth century, third-wave feminists, often aided by queer, postcolonial, and/or postmodern theory, began to revisit the possibility of "feminist heterosexuality and its politically incorrect pleasures," cognizant that the "question of a proper feminist sexuality is an issue that mostly women in the orbit of the First World have the luxury to pursue."[121]

Each of these discourses produced new knowledge about female orgasm (some of it onerous) and provided new ways to talk about sexual difference and heterosexuality. Their legacy is mixed: female sexual pleasure is both celebrated and expected, yet orgasm's capacity to define female sexuality as healthy or dysfunctional has been both maintained and enlarged. And while orgasm is now officially defined in unisex terms, and the burden of sexual dysfunction is shared, sex research focussed on heterosexuality suggests that the "orgasmic imperative" has produced a "gift" economy in which male and female orgasm continue to have a different status: his is non-negotiable and mutually attained; hers is a "gift" that her male lover delivers.[122] This is merely one of the ways that sexual inequality and sexual difference continue to play out in heterosexual relationships, making a feminist sexual politics as urgent as ever.

CHAPTER THREE

Religion and Popular Beliefs

MAUREEN PERKINS

The twentieth century was thought of, for a time, as an increasingly secular century. Claims that "God Is Dead" signaled the belief that Western society was becoming increasingly indifferent towards religion.[1] Cultural historian Callum Brown writes, "It was taken for granted for half a century that religion was sliding from cultural and political life in a calm, secularising reverie."[2] But the significance of religion took a surprising about-turn with the terrorist attacks of the early twenty-first century. These appeared to break the secular reverie, vindicating Samuel Huntington's 1993 "Clash of Civilisations" thesis, which had suggested that culture and religion would be the main fault lines of global conflict after the end of the Cold War.[3] After 9/11, the interplay of religion and modernity was portrayed as more complicated than a simple story of decline, and the re-evaluation of the role of gender became a key part of new discussions about that complexity. It was already widely recognized that women's religious involvement has often been greater than men's in many different societies and religions, especially within a Christian context, and discussion about the changing role of religion increasingly recognized that changes "occurred differently for women and men."[4] Religious modernity and secularization are more complex processes when considered in the light of gender.

What, though, is religion? Although a commonsense assumption may be that religion means a belief in a supernatural being and adherence to rituals

associated with that belief, in fact no uncontested definition exists. The very
term is closely connected with the colonial era of the nineteenth and early
twentieth centuries, when European powers undertook the task of categorizing and defining the cultures with which they came into contact. Part of that
classification project involved deciding whether the "superstitions" of primitive peoples counted as religion. One effect of this process was to encourage
colonized communities to make their beliefs and rituals fit more closely to a
colonial template. Sikhism, for example, which had previously emphasized the
ineffable and unsayable name of the transcendent, took on the terms *God* and
Lord to translate into English what had previously been closer to a sense of
the "uncreated."[5] The status of Buddhism as a religion was—and continues to
be—problematic for the purposes of Western classification because belief in a
supernatural being is not essential to its practice. Moreover, the term *religion*
has implied different things at different historical periods.[6] Peter van der Veer
argues that in India "religion" is a modern category, applied to Hinduism as
part of the colonizing process, but also applicable to Christianity: "The difference, however—and this remains crucial—is that Christianity...is portrayed
as the rational religion of Western modernity, whereas Hinduism is mystified
as Oriental wisdom or irrationality."[7]

Despite historical changes in the meanings of the term *religion*, most writers
aim for at least a working definition.[8] Such practicality is evident in the field
of international and constitutional law, where the right to freedom of religion
is commonly stated but rarely defined. T. Jeremy Gunn, a leading expert on
human rights and religion, refers to the "understandable, but misguided, quest
for a legal definition of 'religion,'" and says that whereas academics have the
luxury of debating the term, judges and lawyers (for example, asylum-case ad-
judicators) must make some decisions about what it means in individual cases.[9]
In fact, the search for a definition, he feels, may lead up a dangerous blind alley,
in which misunderstandings about the concept may result in a "failure to take
sufficient cognizance of the nature of religious discrimination and persecution":

> Rather than focus on defining "religion," it would be much more valu-
> able for adjudicators of claims involving religious discrimination and
> persecution to heed the words of Professor Amor, the UN Special Rap-
> porteur on Freedom of Religion and Belief: "The victims of intolerance
> and discrimination on grounds of religion or belief are quite diverse: they
> may be believers or non-believers, communities of religion or belief or
> they may belong to society at large. Particularly affected, however, are
> vulnerable groups, such as women and minorities."[10]

A broad definition, allowing for great diversity, is well captured by Alison Jasper, when she suggests that "although difficult to define," religion might be taken to refer to "beliefs and practices through which people express their understanding of divine powers or of the spiritual dimension of human existence, and structure an appropriate response." She goes on to carefully point out that this is not limited to "belief in a single transcendent and masculine divine being...within and beyond terrestrial existence."[11]

Including the term *popular belief* alongside religion, as this chapter does, eases the pressure to achieve a watertight definition of either. For example, some people will consider Wicca, discussed later in this chapter, a religion, part of an organized structure with its own orthodoxies and power struggles. However, for others, it may be more a personalized, individual, and amorphous belief, and "popular" in the sense of being slightly marginal and antiauthoritarian. Drawing a distinction between *popular* and *elite* must allow for the interchange that can take place between the two. The term *popular* implies "of the populace," and for that very reason, it signals a "from below" process rather than "top down," but influences can travel in either direction and may not always be easy to distinguish. Christian churches that use meditation, influenced by the popularity of Westernized forms of Hindu practice, are probably a clear example of a response to demands "from below"; whereas the use of the veil among Western Muslim women is much more difficult to describe as either popular or elite, since it is often enthusiastically embraced as a sign of identity and agency, not necessarily as a mark of obedience to religious authority.[12]

In an attempt to capture something of the complex role of religion and popular belief in women's lives during a century of very great change, this chapter will consider three themes: first, the enormous influence of feminism; second, the influence of transnational syncretism, such as the incorporation of Eastern religions; and third, the growth of paganism and forms of worship linked to environmental concerns. It will also make use of the *subjective turn*, which has emphasized personal experience as the criterion for judging truth, and has increased the responsibility of individuals to participate in a process of *self-making*, which has stressed the role of individual development and understanding, often in contrast to an interpretation of religion as obedience to some external authority. Strongly influenced by feminism's claim that the personal is political, as well as postmodernism's emphasis on the role of narrative in constructing knowledge, the subjective turn has encouraged the use of memoir and autobiography as a means of accessing the historical experience. This survey of these themes will inevitably use more English-language material, and therefore be partially, though not exclusively, skewed toward Christian experiences.

FEMINISM

Feminism among the ranks of religious women in the twentieth century was a spur to reframing doctrine and practice. Perhaps one of the most wide-reaching achievements of the broader feminist movement was discussion about the whole field of linguistic usage in which masculine terminology was shown as masking gender inequality. Christian feminists applied these arguments to translations of the Bible and in Christian liturgy, with demands for nonsexist and feminine terminology and images for the Divine. Recognition of women as equal in many spheres was also demanded, not least in church governance and leadership. Campaigns for the ordination of women became a focus for change, and they were often seen by opponents as symbolic of a process that might threaten the very authority of Christian doctrine, "the last straw in a whole bale" as one government minister in England put it.[13] Nevertheless, in 1974, eleven women were ordained to the priesthood in Philadelphia, Pennsylvania, and four more in 1975 in Washington, D.C. The Church of England authorized the ordination of women in 1992 and began ordaining them in 1994.

Questions of sexual freedom and morality, including contraception, abortion, divorce, and homosexuality, were battlegrounds from the late 1960s on, often bringing feminists into conflict with ecclesiastical authorities. These struggles were not exclusively undertaken by women, since for many men the tension between personal freedoms and religious teaching have also been an inspiration towards a campaign for gender and sexual equality. In fact, the identity issues of the later twentieth century have meant that religious feminism and feminist theology now generally welcome the overlap of many social justice issues across gender, religious affiliation, and race.[14]

Feminism has, of course, been much broader than simply a British or American phenomenon, and feminist demands have been heard in churches other than Christian. The growing participation of women in public life in the twentieth century has made critiques of religious/social constraints in the Arab world, for example, more common and more accessible to a world audience. Frequently, such critiques have taken the form of memoir, in keeping with the subjective turn. As Amira Hassan Nowaira writes, "Many educated women found the directness of autobiography the best form in which to express their grievances."[15] Huda Sha'rawi (1879–1947), one of the pioneers of the feminist movement in Egypt, wrote *Harem Years: The Memoirs of an Egyptian Feminist 1879–1924* (not published until 1981), challenging the tradition that "women should always observe silence, especially concerning their private lives."[16] Perhaps the most famous and influential feminist writer on Islam has been the

Egyptian Nawal al-Sa'dawi (*Memoirs from the Women's Prison*, 1983), but use of memoir has also marked the more recent and controversial criticisms of Islam from Ayaan Hirsi Ali, the former Somali writer resident in Holland (*Infidel*, English trans., 2007), and from Irshad Manji, the Canadian author of *The Trouble with Islam* (2004) and founder of Project Ijtihad, a charitable organization promoting a tradition of critical thinking, debate, and dissent in Islam.[17]

Irshad Manji's call for the best of secular modernity's rationalism to be applied to Islamic belief and practice is a reminder that feminism opposes religious patriarchy and authoritarianism, not religion itself. The decline of institutionalized religion, once forecast as part of the rise of secular government in the modern world, has clearly not been inevitable. Secularization does not necessitate the abandonment of religion, but rather provides a greater emphasis on the responsibility and freedom of the individual to make choices about religious commitment not necessarily based on tradition, that is, increasing religious choice rather than decreasing it.[18]

A demonstration of the way in which the values of a secular society can promote religious commitment as opposed to undermining it can be found in the lives of some first-wave feminists, a group often portrayed as in conflict with the conservatism of the Christian church.[19] The life of Emmeline Pankhurst (1858–1928) offers an example. Pankhurst's work in advancing the cause of female suffrage was renowned even during her lifetime. The president of the Women's Freedom League said at the time of her death: "Not only all women in Britain, but all women in the world, owe a deep debt of gratitude and honour to Mrs Pankhurst. Without her genius and courage they could not have attained for many, many years the position they hold to-day."[20] Even at the end of the twentieth century, several surveys among newspaper readers voted her the most outstanding woman of the century. Her highly visible campaigns probably make the term *suffragette* more widely known than the less militant campaign of the suffragists.

Pankhurst's bold stand on civil disobedience was paralleled in her youth by a rejection of religion: she was an avowed atheist and married to an agnostic. Yet by the time of her funeral at St. John's Church, Smith Square, and her burial in Brompton Cemetery, she had become a devout Christian.[21] This highly regarded woman of the twentieth century provides an example, through her decision to change her spiritual allegiance, of the more fluid relationship of modern women to religious belief and practice. Pankhurst's stand as a declared atheist was an unusual and unpopular position at the time, requiring considerable personal courage.[22] Her later disapproval of Communism in Russia led her to react against what she saw as Communist attacks on Christian civilization and made her more open toward Christianity, so that in her later years, she "mellowed" toward religion.[23] Her daughter Christabel went through a more dramatic conversion to evangelical Christianity and devoted her life to publishing and speaking about the imminent return of Christ.[24] In marked contrast, Emmeline's younger daughter Sylvia was noted for her atheism and free thought, an aspect of her commitment to Socialism.

Changes in society itself presented a number of opportunities for women to make personal choices that were historically unprecedented. Emmeline Pankhurst benefited from the huge developments in steamship travel of the previous fifty years to travel and lecture in the United States, often on themes having to do with supporting the civilizing mission of the British Empire. This became for her intimately connected with the role of Christianity as an essential part of that civilizing force. Similarly, Christabel moved between London, Paris, Canada, and California, enjoying a career as a public speaker and minister, and living a modern life familiar with rapid change. As one biographer, Timothy Larsen, points out, she made a point of tailoring her message to acknowledge the growth of scientific knowledge that was such an exciting part of the intellectual ferment of the early century, but she tailored her intellectual curiosity to the service of her own religious argument. For example, on the question of whether the Second Coming presented logistical problems, she wrote:

> [O]ne clergyman…actually argues that "if Christ were to appear tonight in the clouds over England, the people in Australia would not see him, because Australia is beneath our feet." Extraordinary idea in these days, with television already a fact and only needing to be perfected to make the people of London visible in Australia! Sound and sight girdling the earth is a modern possibility which helps us to understand that Christ, as Lord of all the marvellous powers of the universe, can, when He returns, make Himself visible by world-circling rays which will act direct upon the human eye.[25]

As Larsen, who quotes the previous passage in his study of Christabel and her religious belief, comments, "Pankhurst was determined to claim modernity for Christ and his word."

Deep divisions on the subject of religion were a factor in the severing of relations between Emmeline and Christabel Pankhurst, on the one hand, and Sylvia and her sister Adela Pankhurst, on the other. However, despite the Pankhursts' own estimation of the importance of religion, its role in first-wave feminism has not been widely studied. As Larsen says, "Many feminists have not known what to do with Christabel Pankhurst's religious turn," despite her being "arguably the most significant Anglican female preacher after Maude Royden in the first half of the twentieth century."[26] He argues that it has been widely accepted that fundamentalism and feminism are incompatible, but challenges this view and argues that, especially in the first third of the twentieth century, there were women who saw feminism and fundamentalism as being "in coalition."

War increased the potential for division, both among suffragists and among Christian women. Whereas Emmeline and Christabel Pankhurst campaigned strongly against the threat of Germany at the time of the 1914–18 war, Maude Royden (1876–1956), a suffragist who was elected to the executive committee of the National Union of Women's Suffrage Societies (NUWSS) in 1909, broke with the NUWSS over its support for the war effort and espoused Christian pacifism. In 1917, she became assistant preacher at the City Temple in London, the first woman to occupy the position, and in 1929, she began the official campaign for the ordination of women, founding the Society for the Ministry of Women. Royden traveled widely in the 1930s and 1940s promoting this cause. However, war again was a catalyst for personal change, when in 1939 she renounced pacifism, believing Nazism to be a greater evil than war. She lived long enough to see the question of the ordination of women seriously engage the Church of England, although the first successes were not within the English Communion. In 1944, Florence Li Tim-Oi, in Hong Kong, became the first woman ordained to the Anglican priesthood.

Another dramatic turnabout was that of Maud Gonne (1866–1953), an outspoken campaigner for the end of the British colonial occupation of Ireland, who in 1904 converted from a seemingly inactive form of Protestantism that reflected her birth and upbringing in Surrey to Roman Catholicism. This move was shocking to many who knew her, even prompting William Butler Yeats to dream with foreboding that it was about to happen. It was not that the critics were ideologically opposed to Catholicism, but rather that Maud Gonne's long history of involvement with occultism suggested that her views on religion and sexuality were not consistent with doctrines of salvation, confession, and obedience. Gonne was an Englishwoman who had taken up the cause of Irish independence but had also chosen to live a life of exceptional freedom and nonconformism. Yet this unconventional woman was not welcomed into the ranks of contemporary feminists. Many of the early suffragists considered respectability an important component of their armory and disagreed not only with the suffragettes who espoused violent action but also with those women, like Gonne, who were achieving notoriety by breaking moral boundaries.

The figure of the woman as guardian of family morality was an extremely powerful one, in Britain at least, from the early nineteenth century to the middle of the twentieth century. The "angel in the house," whose quiet religiosity was seen as essential to the efficient functioning of society, was an important part of the "feminisation of piety" that had worldwide consequences.[27] Christian values were closely connected to gender roles, and both were spread by colonial culture and by missionary endeavor, with women an important part of the "civilising mission." By 1900, Callum Brown writes, "Women were an accepted part of the professional mission scene, and female missionaries became role models in the popular magazines."[28]

Brown, a leading figure in the history of religion in Britain, sees women's role and influence in the Christian church as reaching their zenith in the nineteenth and early twentieth centuries, but then disappearing dramatically in the mid-twentieth century. Until this time, he suggests, Christian piety was located in femininity, as part of a gendered discourse. Indeed, the rapid decline of Christian influence in Britain as a whole, he suggests, can be related to the depietization of femininity, "when women cancelled their mass subscription to the discursive domain of Christianity."[29] The "death" of Christian Britain, which Brown argues has taken place, was, then, closely connected with the changing role and self-image of women: "The reconstruction of female identity within work, sexual relations and new recreational opportunities from the late 1960s, put not just feminism but female identity in collision with the Christian construction of femininity."[30] It has surely been the work of Christian feminists to critique and reshape the Christian construction of femininity. Some, at least, have looked outside the older boundaries of what constituted spirituality, to non-Western forms of belief and older pagan terminologies.

GLOBAL INTERCONNECTEDNESS

The late twentieth century was a time of huge population movements. In Europe, for example, the "foreign resident" populations grew by a factor of four between 1950 and 1990.[31] Many of these new residents came from countries that had once been colonized by European powers in the earlier twentieth century, and the changes they brought to Europe were huge, not least in the religious landscape. In discussions about how different religions could coexist in a previously Christian-dominated society, the status and freedoms of women became iconic issues. A sense that European culture offered a unique role model of respect for and protection of women had been an important part of imperial ideology, and much recent research has explored Western attitudes to Other women. These were often attitudes of benign superiority and a wish to rescue women from the constraints of their traditional cultures.[32] Women's rights movements in Europe, such as the campaign for the franchise, were secular in nature, and secularism was considered to be essential to gender equality. Hence the new Indian constitution of 1947 declared India to be a secular state at the same time as enshrining the principle of gender equality. Both principles were simply two aspects of what were considered to be important legacies of empire, laying the foundations for future progress and development. National identity was promoted above religious identity, and the limitation of religious influence on political decisions was considered an essential qualification for joining the modern world. Yet for some in the postcolonial world, secularism was suspiciously connected to imperialism. The rise of late twentieth-century religious and ethnic nationalism has been explained as a reaction against the previous authoritarian imposition of the western European model of state secularism and nationalism.[33] As with the backlash against imperially created national boundaries, many religious movements of the second half of the century reconceptualized gender issues to address and contest the discourses of European and American feminisms. The question "How can a Muslim woman be French?" typifies the tensions between secular national identity and transnational religious affiliation that complicate the multiple roles of many modern women.[34]

Connections between nationalism and religion are an important factor in the twentieth century. Maud Gonne's embrace of Catholicism was closely connected with her love of Ireland, and her sense that to be truly Irish was to be Catholic. Many other women, too, decided that changing religion was one aspect of a conversion to a whole culture. Some European and American women found fulfillment in Hindu life in India but went on to campaign for Indian independence. Madeleine Slade (1892–1982) became a follower of Gandhi, changing her name to Mira Behn, or Sister Mira. She lectured in Britain and the United States with a view to presenting an accurate—and favorable—interpretation of Gandhi and his goals. The historian Kumari Jayawardena writes that there may have been other Western women devoted to Indian religious-cum-political gurus in subsequent years, but with the end of colonialism, "such conversions became drained of any nationalist or political content and acquired significance only within a purely religious context."[35]

The protracted end of the British Empire during the course of the century and its replacement by globalization led to increasingly hybrid forms of culture and religious identity. Under the rubric of the alternative movement of the 1960s, eclecticism was common, with groups taking teachings from a wide variety of religious sources. For some, a core thread of common philosophical approach could link practices and beliefs that had no apparent historical connection. Some religious leaders taught the existence of a Western mystery tradition that had progressed from the mystical teachings of Persian masters, through European romanticism, to modern movements of monism and magic. Like paganism later in the century (see the following section), an ancient lineage conferred authority. One of the esoteric leaders whose ideas were adopted by the New Age was Madame Helena Blavatsky (1831–91), founder of the Theosophical movement, and one of the leading figures of the Western mystery tradition. Her mantle passed to Annie Besant (1847–1933), who in 1907 became the second president of the International Theosophical Society. Madame Blavatsky's insights, she said, came from masters living in the high mountains of Tibet, and Annie Besant made her home, and the effective center of international Theosophy, in India, drawing increasingly on Hindu traditions and beliefs.

Hybrid mixtures of religious belief have been labeled "pick-and-mix," and there has been an attempt in the sociology of religion to differentiate between the "spirituality" of such belief as contrasted from traditional "religious" affiliation.[36] This differentiation may be to miss the point of how women's religious affiliation is being transformed. Spirituality is well known as having a high correlation with gender: "Besides the young and the well educated...women of course also stand out with high levels of affinity with spirituality."[37] Dick Houtman and Stef Aupers link this relationship with gender to a "sacralization of self," that is, a search for meaning and identity that results from the pressures of women's changing gender roles. Such sacralization of self and the belief that personal growth may be achieved (indeed, ought to be achieved) through a combination of all that is best in many paths seems, in fact, to be increasingly underpinning even secular accounts of the nature of the self, so that the growth of multireligious practices blurs the boundary of where secularization begins and ends: "Even management courses may today stimulate one to embark on a spiritual journey to the deeper layers of the self."[38]

PAGANISM AND GROWING ENVIRONMENTAL CONCERNS

In 1979, James Lovelock published *Gaia: A New Look at Life on Earth*, a book that rapidly achieved a high public profile. In it he argued that the earth itself was a living organism, "a self-organizing and self-regulating system," and "alive" in its own right. This portrayal fitted well with growing environmental concerns and also with late twentieth-century feminism, since Gaia was the name of an ancient mother goddess associated with the earth. Although not generally accepted by the scholarly scientific community, and recently much modified by Lovelock himself, the Gaia hypothesis was one manifestation of growth in the second half of the century of beliefs that claimed to revive pre-Christian goddess-centered traditions, and that linked these beliefs to a need to care for the earth, represented as feminine in essence. These beliefs sometimes took the form of a neo-paganism, and the last decades of the century saw a sharp rise in paganism in Britain and the United States.

Pagan beliefs and growing environmentalism were linked, and both in turn had associations with feminism and gender. In 1998, John P. Newport wrote, "Many contingents march under the banner of Gaia. Among these are groups that are prepared to embrace Gaia as the rebirth of paganism in our time; others take her as a basis for nature mysticism; others see her as an ally in the development of ecofeminism."[39] The earth as a mother goddess, concerns about environmental degradation, and feminist resistance to patriarchal exploitation came together in the last decades of the twentieth century to form an array of groups, not all concerned with spiritual development, but many of them prepared to explore European history in search of premodern, preindustrial modes of social and economic organization.

One of the leading historians of modern paganism, Ronald Hutton, cites a rise in the "idealization of rural England" as directly attributable to increasing urbanization. In 1810, about 80 percent of English people lived in the countryside; by 1910, about 80 percent lived in towns.[40] A longing for rural life and for the community that had supposedly centered around country rituals was expressed in many major works of literature. Among those who were of a spiritual turn of mind, this representation of the countryside could lead to an interest in pre-Christian beliefs. The groundwork for this interest was being laid throughout the century. The women who contributed to it came from varying ideological positions. Jessie Weston, for example, was a nonprofessional folklore enthusiast, whose work on the Arthurian legend and the symbolic meaning of the search for the Holy Grail was popular in the 1920s and 1930s. Margaret Murray, on the other hand, was an established academic and Egyptologist, whose work on the history of witchcraft, such as *The God of the Witches* (1933), was hugely influential. Others, again, were practicing witches, part of a growing number of practitioners of modern pagan witchcraft.

Among the most important factors contributing to the rise of modern forms of witchcraft was the claim that their practices and beliefs linked back to ancient traditions, which had been thinly overlaid by an exploitative and repressive Christian church. Margaret Murray was foremost in advancing this thesis. It has recently been challenged, perhaps most notably by Ronald Hutton, who argues that ancient paganism and modern paganism are best understood within the context of their own times, not as a seamless progression of continuing belief. In particular, he links the development of Wicca, probably the best-known form of modern paganism, to the influences and decisions of several twentieth-century figures, notably Gerald Gardner.[41] Gardner himself and his followers understood their work to be the survival and revival of an ancient body of wisdom. No doubt the 1951 repeal of the Witchcraft Act and the reform of the Vagrancy Act, which since the mid-nineteenth century had made fortune-telling a crime on the grounds that it was fraudulent, made it easier for Wicca to gain visibility.

Discussion in the British Parliament about repealing the Witchcraft and Vagrancy Acts centered on a responsibility to protect the public, but reference was also made in the debate to religious toleration. This was in part because the pressure to change the law came largely from the spiritualist movement. In a century when two world wars produced loss of human life on a massive scale, the services of clairvoyants and mediums were used by all classes of society. So in June 1951, the "concept of witchcraft" disappeared from the statute books.[42] The last person to have been successfully prosecuted was Helen Duncan, in 1944.

Increasing paganism and witchcraft did not necessarily mean that these were forms of religion, though they can certainly be thought of as forms of popular belief, and Andrew Dobson identifies a virtually deified Nature as the religion of environmentalism: "Spirituality ghosts Green politics; Green politics is a filling of the spiritual vacuum at the center of late-industrial society, and the land itself is the cathedral at which we are urged to worship."[43] Hutton writes that the image of the witch advanced by the radical feminists Mary Daly and Andrea Dworkin in the United States had "no necessary religious dimension at all," and that it "depended upon the concept that witchcraft was something inherent in all women."[44] However, in the work of "the most famous witch in the world" in the 1980s, there was a clear religious substratum. Miriam Simos, known as Starhawk, published a book called *The Spiral Dance* in 1979. This built on the concept of witchcraft as the "Old Religion" of Europe but reworked it using it as a form of psychological therapy to become a craft to transform its practitioners,[45] in "an Earth-based, feminist spirituality" as her website has described it.[46]

THE SUBJECTIVE TURN

If the nineteenth century was one where "the angel in the house" might be said to be the dominant ideal of the Western religious woman, then the twentieth century was one where changing work patterns, political emancipation, and increased access to education allowed women to become more independent and public in their religious lives. Carol Hanisch's 1969 essay, "The Personal Is Political," hit a resonant chord with feminists in the midst of the consciousness-raising movement, but its title encapsulates broader twentieth-century developments in religion. In her 2006 introduction to the reprinted essay, she writes, "A theory is just a bunch of words—sometimes interesting to think about, but just words, nevertheless—until it is tested in real life." It is this testing in real life that has been the touchstone of modern religious life, and one which many access through a globalized circulation of the writings of other women who are trialing diverse spiritual paths. What has been called "the biographical turn," the increasing interest at the end of the twentieth century in biographical and autobiographical writing, has been part of a widespread increase in the role of narrative in how we conceptualize our lives, including how to use the experiences of others as a guide to our own understanding, broadening the stories available to us for making sense of our lives.[47]

This emphasis on the personal is explored in depth by Paul Heelas and Linda Woodhead who call it "the subjective turn": "'The turn' is shorthand for a major cultural shift...towards life lived by reference to one's own subjective experiences (relational as much as individualistic)."[48] They see this massive turn of modern culture as the key to understanding why there has been an increase in spirituality (manifested in spiritualities such as New Age movements) while at the same time institutional religion (manifested in expectations of conformity to an external authority) has declined. This also helps to explain what has seemed to be a contradiction between women's increasing visibility as participants in religious movements like Wicca as contrasted with academic debates about secularization. Heelas and Woodhead offer a useful distinction between "spirituality," which is "often used to express commitment to a deep truth that is to be found within what belongs in this world," and "religion," which "is used to express commitment to a higher truth that is 'out there,' lying beyond what this world has to offer, and exclusively related to specific externals (scriptures, dogmas, rituals, and so on)."[49]

There are many reasons for this increased emphasis on the subjective or the personal, and one factor must surely be the work of Sigmund Freud. While it would be inaccurate to describe Freud (1856–1939) as the father of the biographical turn, he did emphasize the creative work of "the interpretive mind," and in drawing the soul in to the field of scientific study, he has had an enormous influence on the stories that both women and men construct about their religious experience. It may seem unusual to link Freud, an avowed atheist,

with the concept of the soul, but the sociologist Bruno Bettelheim has argued
that Freud's use of *seele* (soul) was carefully chosen in order to convey an in-
nermost being separate from the rational mind. The English translations, according to Bettelheim, have left the concept out entirely or mistranslated it as
"mind," indicating the rising scientific status at the turn of the twentieth century of rational secularism. Ian Hacking is among those who have claimed that
Freud advanced the secularization of the soul, treating it as a subject that could
be studied by science, and thus diminishing its transcendent status.[50] Freud's
use of case histories and "psychoanalytic narratology" can be interpreted as
examples of the autobiographical process, which relies for its coherence on the
construction of a story, or framework;[51] and his sense of conflict within the self
was an important influence on the belief that identities are plural and often
competing. Freud's first research was conducted into the illnesses of women
institutionalized in the mental hospital of the Salpetrière in Paris, but in a famous extract in a letter to Marie Bonaparte, he described his work as research
into the soul: "The great question that has never been answered, and which I
have not yet been able to answer, despite my thirty years of research into the
feminine soul, is 'What does a woman want?'"[52]

Freud saw religion as the adult attempt to ward off a sense of helplessness,
a substitute for the infant's need of a loving father's protection, and he implied
that women were particularly prone to this impulse. Judith van Herik has described a "gender a-symmetry" revealed in Freud's work on religion, that is,
women were portrayed as more prone to succumb to an irrational desire for
a god figure. She argues that in Freud's theory as a whole, renunciation and
fulfillment are central interpretive categories. Renunciation is viewed as the
source of intellectual and moral achievements such as scientific attitude, ethical
behavior, and principled thought. Conversely, for Freud, fulfillment of wishes
actually obstructs such achievements, and, while he linked masculinity with
renunciation, femininity was linked with wish fulfillment and was therefore
more distant from the therapeutic ideal of rational autonomy.[53]

Several leading second-wave feminists addressed what they saw as the negative impact of Freud on society's concepts of *woman*. The portrayal of God as
father, suggested by Freud but already embedded in patriarchal society, was
one of the key elements to be attacked by feminist philosophers, such as Mary
Daly, whose influential book *Beyond God the Father* (1973) analyzed and
challenged the misogynistic nature of the Christian church. However, Freudian
concepts have permeated society in ways that stretch far beyond academic and
professional discussion. Many writers reconstructing their own and others' religious experiences testify to the huge impact that Freud's portrayal of the mind

had on the twentieth century: belief in the formative role of childhood; the fragmented, tortured self; and the tendency to look for unconscious motivation as the force behind spiritual quest. This is not to say that recognizing Freud's huge influence necessitates the portrayal of religion as a neurosis, but simply that concepts such as *the unconscious*, *repression*, and *sublimation* have all entered the modern world's understanding of identity and are frequently used when describing the role played by religion.

In the later twentieth century, Freud's theories were reworked to form the basis of influential psychoanalytic theories of feminine identity, which have in turn influenced feminist thought on religion. Foremost among those who developed Freudian ideas in this way was Jacques Lacan (1901–81), who influenced Julia Kristeva (1941–) and Luce Irigaray (1932–). Irigaray, in particular, has written about religion, arguing in "Divine Women" (1993) that it is necessary for women to rethink the notion of God.[54] Her "sensible transcendental" locates divinity and carnality together, so that the divine "comes to represent the accomplishment of the flesh":

> This is a project of becoming that is simultaneously conceptual and corporeal. In *An Ethics of Sexual Difference,* Irigaray asks: "Why do we assume that God must always remain an inaccessible transcendence rather than a realisation—here and now—through the body?" (148). The sensible transcendental is a phrase that emphasises the primacy of the body, and its relation to the elements through the senses, in considering questions of transcendence and incarnation. It encompasses both physical sensation and the recognition of a beyond.[55]

An attempt to draw the body into discussions about the spiritual is in keeping with the late modern desire for holistic approaches, reconciling mind and body. This desire can be seen in Starhawk's earth-based spirituality or in more complex form in Irigiray's recent work on Christ as encompassing both male and female bodies.[56]

CONCLUSION

In postindustrial society, Penny Long Marler identifies "a dramatic shift from the home as the site of piety and the woman as its moral hero or guardian to the piety and industry of the woman herself. The woman's role moves from homemaking to self-making, a shift which legitimates her changed position in the labour market."[57] Rather than emphasizing increased freedom for women

in the religious/spiritual sphere or focusing on freedom *from* religion in a secu-
larized society, this interpretation suggests that the structures of the economy
continue to bind women, but with constraints which have the superficial appearance of liberty and choice. Linda Woodhead also seems cautious about the
liberating potential of modernity's "project of the self":

> The late modern condition can be characterized by the extensive and in-
> tensive way in which the self becomes disembedded from established tra-
> ditions, roles, regimes and rituals. Even if this is a social process, brought
> about by a nexus of factors including the modes of production and con-
> sumption characteristic of late capitalism, it is integral to it that it is *read*
> as a matter of individual choice and responsibility...Representations of
> the self as free, responsible, self-propelled, self-made and independent
> become dominant...
>
> Thus late modernity spawns dominant modes of selfhood which stress
> individual worth, entitlement, self-propulsion and independence. This is
> not because the anomic individual is set free in a world of normless pos-
> sibility, but because—on the contrary—guidelines, targets, demands and
> "opportunities" spread their tendrils as never before...this new regime
> compels self-organization and the constant exercise of choice and self-
> assertion.[58]

An influential example of the role of postindustrial, late modern self-
fashioning might be Karen Armstrong, the English writer whose account of
joining a religious order as a teenager and then leaving seven years later has
formed the core of two autobiographical accounts as well as the background to
a prolific output about religion. Her work has been an outstanding example of
the personal as political, using *political* in the sense in which Hanisch meant it,
as concerned with power relationships. It is Armstrong's own personal struggles, setbacks, and successes that thread through all her explorations of various
religions, and that lead her to the conclusion that religion is not about doctrine
or belief, but about living with compassion. She exemplifies not only the turn
to experience as the litmus test of authority, but also the twentieth-century need
to respond to diversity in religious experience, as migration and globalization
have brought many religions into the same space. In seeking to understand
both Islam and Buddhism better, and to relay her search to a reading public,
she has written two major biographies of religious leaders, *Muhammad: A
Biography of the Prophet* and *Buddha*, as well as writing the biography of a
city, Jerusalem, stressing its importance to three major world religions.[59] She

is also a visible example of the defeminization of piety. What could be a more compelling example of this important change in twentieth-century discourse than a woman who chooses to leave a religious order and sets out on a search that will be devoid of a husband and of children—those necessary accoutrements of the angel in the house—and rewrites femininity as intellectual courage and stamina. Her holistic approach to her own self-making is testimony to the truth that it is not only history that every generation must rewrite but also the meaning of the "spiritual."[60]

The so-called subjective turn and the increasing emphasis on self-making may be a response to what Woodhead and others have called the "stalled gender revolution." Woodhead and Sointu borrow the term to argue that the shift to a postindustrial context has meant that women have had to negotiate a new mode of selfhood, while men have merely had to intensify existing modes of masculinity. The impact for women of new modes of employment in the public sphere has been "qualified or contradicted by continuing ties to traditional roles of domestic care." Women—particularly middle-class women—in contemporary Western societies are forced to negotiate two different modes of selfhood: the feminized, immanent "self for others"; and the masculinized, transcendent "self for itself."[61] The self-making that this tension seems to have brought to the fore in Western societies is often expressed in terms of the desire for holistic well-being where "talk of wholeness slides naturally into talk of a 'soul' and the spiritual depths of selfhood."[62] Described in this way, the subjective turn (self-work) can be seen as melding with "global inter-connectedness," transnational syncretism, and even forms of pagan holism, emphasizing an ideal of unity between humanity and environment, between the spiritual and the physical. The goals of wholeness and expressive self-hood foreground experience more than authority and may be a factor in tensions within religious affiliation nationally and internationally. In short, at the start of the twenty-first century, women have not abandoned belief but are searching for ways in which it can be made relevant to their gendered experiences.

CHAPTER FOUR

Medicine and Disease: Women, Health, and Medicine in the Twentieth Century

MARY ROJEK KLEINMAN AND ALICE J. DAN

During the twentieth century, major changes in health and medicine took place, including public health measures such as clean water and sanitation, drugs to counter infectious diseases, and remarkable advances in the medical sciences with new imaging techniques, medical devices, and pharmaceutical treatments. Despite these advances, and while acknowledging their importance to effective medical treatments, experts recently identified "increased health education for women and increased empowerment of women across multiple spheres as the major advances positively impacting the health of women."[1] Thus, scientific advances are not enough. A supportive social, cultural, economic, and political environment is essential to women's health.

This chapter places women's health activism and the women's health movements of the twentieth century in the context of women's struggles for recognition, equality, and self-determination. We will begin with a review of changes in major health indicators, including life expectancy, and changes in causes of mortality and morbidity during the century to provide a context and a basis for our discussion. Next, we will consider some of the key health issues on which women's activism has focused in the modern age in order to gain an understanding of the forces that influence women's health and their health care. These include violence against women, reproductive health, sexuality and fertility, and health issues related to the work that women do. At the same time, we integrate the emergence of scientific medicine as the dominant approach within the twentieth century as another key influence on women's health.

The application of scientific knowledge to medical theories, training, and practice provided physicians with increased authority, government support, and public faith in medicine's ability to improve health. Technological and pharmaceutical innovations further strengthened the medical profession's authority and expanded the range of life issues for which their consultation was sought or deemed appropriate. The development of laboratory testing, imaging technologies, and genetic medicine enabled physicians to see inside the body, inside cells, and even inside smaller cellular components, giving them seemingly objective information only interpretable by other scientifically trained physicians. Their control of access to drugs and devices for fertility control, and of pharmaceuticals for lifestyle problems, increased their authority and influence over women's lives.

Women's health movements occurring worldwide throughout the century have influenced many governments and the United Nations World Health Organization (WHO) in their approaches to women's health. The WHO recognized the importance of adopting a holistic perspective toward health, taking women's social and economic status into account, and including not just physical but mental and spiritual aspects of their lives. Health then is an interdisciplinary responsibility, not limited to medical practitioners or the health care industry; women, families, businesses, and communities all have a role in promoting health. In a holistic health model, women are considered in the context of their unique situations across their life spans, and they are seen as full citizens, students, and workers, as well as friends, daughters, wives, partners, mothers, and grandmothers. The key value of self-determination is reflected in the emphasis on women's control of their own bodies, from their own points of view, which often vary across cultures and across time. Recognizing the importance of all contributions to the health of women and their families, women's health activists, in individual efforts and in movements, have sought to improve many areas of women's lives, including health education and women's safety in and outside of their homes, and to equalize health care relationships by working across many areas to challenge biomedical models, demystify health information, and empower women.

THE GENDER PARADOX, LIFE EXPECTANCY, AND MORTALITY AND MORBIDITY

There is a gender paradox in health: overall, although women experience more illness compared with men, they have a longer life expectancy.[2] The way this manifests varies by country and varies within any single country across different socioeconomic and ethnic groups. Researchers are uncertain about the exact cause of the gender paradox, but biological, social, and behavioral theories have been offered as explanations.[3] What is clear is that women's health status depends on their specific social, economic, and political status, and on the cultural and material context of their lives.

Worldwide, overall life expectancy at birth increased dramatically during the twentieth century from 31 years in 1900[4] to 46.5 years in midcentury and 65.2 years in 2002.[5] Life expectancy refers to the *average* expectation for the length of life in a population.[6] It can be influenced by many things, but there were primary contributing factors to increasing life expectancy at different points in time. In wealthier countries, in the early twentieth century, it was due to decreases in infant and maternal mortality rates (especially among younger women).[7] In the mid-twentieth century, it was due to the new availability and use of antibiotics and immunizations. In the latter part of the century, it was the result of declines in mortality rates among older persons due to the development and use of new medications, increased standards of living, and improved access to health care. At the beginning of the century, women were considered the weaker sex, but by the end of the century, they were viewed as the sturdier sex.[8] In less developed countries at the end of the century, increases in life expectancy were due primarily to decreases in infant and maternal mortality, owing to the use of skilled birth attendants who reduced the rates of preventable deaths.

Scientific medicine applied to public health helped to improve women's health, especially in wealthier countries. Early in the twentieth century in the United States, improved sanitation and clean water greatly reduced death rates from infectious diseases, leading to increased life expectancy. Diseases such as tuberculosis were controlled by quarantine measures and, later, with newly developed drugs.[9] In contrast, the inadequate implementation of public health measures in poor countries at the end of the century led to infectious diseases being major causes of illness and death.

In general, the wealthier a country, the longer the life expectancy, but there are cases of poor countries having relatively high life expectancy rates. For example, Jamaicans have a life expectancy that is near U.S. levels due to their public health practices, maternal child health programs, and educational system.[10] Women also have a relatively high degree of social equality in Jamaica, protective legislation regarding women's physical safety was passed late in the century.

While life expectancy is a general measure of health in a population, mortality and morbidity statistics reflect more proximate causes of death (mortality) or illness (morbidity) from diseases and conditions. Early in the twentieth century in developed countries, the primary cause of mortality in the general population was infectious diseases such as smallpox, pneumonia, and influenza.[11] Young children were especially vulnerable to dying from diarrhea, diphtheria, measles, and other intestinal pathogens.[12] Hookworm was a major source of morbidity for both women and children, but serious illnesses from it decreased after a public health education and eradication campaign was implemented. Both public health measures and improvements in the standard of living contributed to increasing life expectancy. Public health measures included sanitation, sewage systems, and access to clean water.[13] As incomes rose, nutrition improved. In contrast, medical advances played a minor role in reducing deaths, and hospitals were major sources of infection where people often died.[14] For women in childbirth, the primary cause of mortality was poor obstetric practices.[15]

In developed countries in the latter part of the century, degenerative and chronic diseases became the primary cause of mortality, morbidity, and disability. Cardiovascular disease has been the primary cause of death in women, followed by cancer.[16] Stroke has been especially debilitating for women, who experience higher rates compared with men. Contrary to popular belief, lung cancer is the primary cause of cancer deaths in women and not breast cancer. As women's rates of smoking increased during the twentieth century, lung cancer deaths increased even more because women are more susceptible to lung cancer from smoking compared with men.[17]

In poor countries during the twentieth century, maternal mortality was a leading cause of death. By the end of the twentieth century, women died of pregnancy-related causes at a rate of about one per minute, with more than half a million deaths annually.[18] Millions more experienced permanent injuries. Of all maternal deaths, 99 percent occurred in poor countries so that maternal deaths show the largest gap between rich and poor countries of all health indicators.[19] The primary causes of maternal death are hemorrhage, sepsis (infection), unsafe abortion, obstructed labor, and hypertensive disease during pregnancy. Almost two-thirds of maternal deaths occur during labor, delivery, or immediately thereafter. For every woman who dies of childbirth-related causes, another twenty are severely injured or disabled. The majority of these injuries are preventable. Infectious diseases are also a major cause of mortality and morbidity, including HIV, tuberculosis, and malaria. In many ways, the health issues currently facing women in poor countries are similar to those of women in wealthier countries about a century earlier. Poor sanitation and sewage treatment, lack of clean water, poor nutrition, inadequate reproductive health care, poverty, violence, lack of education, and women's low social, economic, and political status all affect their health.

By the end of the twentieth century, there was an increased focus within scientific medicine on the treatment of chronic illnesses in the elderly such as cardiovascular diseases and cancer. Almost all of this medical knowledge was based on the study of men and was then often inappropriately applied to women.[20] When women exhibited symptoms or experienced illnesses in ways that differed from men, their illnesses often went unrecognized. Even when women had the same symptoms, discriminatory beliefs and biased knowledge held by those in the medical profession resulted in physicians ignoring women's problems. For minority women, their discriminatory experiences were compounded because of their race and sex. These remain major problems in the twenty-first century.

VIOLENCE AGAINST WOMEN

Violence is one of the most common causes of injury and death to women throughout the world. It takes different forms and includes honor killings, acid attacks, dowry murders, sex trafficking, incest, forced early marriage, female genital cutting, rape (including rape as an act of war), assault, and intimidation.[21] After 1970 in the United States, public focus was finally directed at the issue of domestic violence (DV), also known as intimate partner violence. Throughout most of the century, DV had been viewed as a private matter, and official incidence statistics were not maintained. Although DV is under-reported, the U.S. Justice Department conservatively estimated that one out of six women has been the victim of rape or attempted rape, and about one out of four has been physically assaulted.[22] Incidence rates vary by social group within the United States, with younger women, pregnant women, and African American and Native American women being more likely to be victimized. Incidence rates vary throughout the world, with the highest levels estimated at 60 percent in some parts of Africa.[23] Women of all social and economic classes are abused, but those of lower status are more vulnerable because they have limited ability to remove themselves from dangerous environments.

Throughout the world, women have organized and rallied on behalf of abused women and girls. They formed organizations to support and protect women, and to lobby governments for assistance. By bringing attention to this problem, violence against women was transformed from a private matter into a public health problem, and also into a human rights problem. While the American Medical Association finally identified DV as a public health problem in 1992, estimates are that U.S. physicians do not recognize the signs of DV in about 98 percent of cases; and health care workers throughout the world have also been known to be perpetrators of violence.[24] At the 1995 4th World Conference on Women in Beijing, Hillary Clinton[25] argued persuasively that violence against women was more than just a women's health problem, that it was a gendered problem that was a violation of human rights.[26] Governments around the world agreed. Throughout the century, it was women's activism on the issue of DV that moved the world forward to reinterpret and address this problem.

REPRODUCTIVE HEALTH ISSUES

Although late twentieth-century women's health movements have brought attention to the many issues beyond reproduction that affect every part of women's bodies, their health and their lives, reproductive health remains a central concern to many. Early in the century, the still-limited social roles available to women directed activists' focus toward maternal and child health. At that time, the United States had the highest infant and maternal mortality rates in the Western world.[27] Various reformers, medical professionals, and lay-women advocated for safer childbirth. Childbirth was dangerous for women, and most people knew someone who had suffered pain, been injured or disabled, or died while giving birth. Desiring to have safer childbirths, women with access to physicians and hospitals began to place their trust in physicians and scientific progress.[28] Physicians claimed that they were better birth attendants than midwives because they had received medical training. In the first decades of the twentieth century, this training often consisted of a several-week course in which no patients were actually seen, while some lucky physicians received training from experienced female midwives.[29] Many women sought out a physician-attended childbirth, even though in many areas, maternal mortality rates were higher for women attended by physicians than by midwives.[30] This held true even in rural areas where female midwives attended at both normal and complicated deliveries. The higher maternal mortality rate among physicians was due primarily to their poor hygienic practices—especially their negligence in washing their hands, which led to fatal infections.[31] By the Second World War, approximately half of U.S. women had a physician-attended childbirth, and two decades later, almost all U.S. children were born in hospitals.

At the beginning of the century, many U.S. government officials, lay activists, and health care workers were troubled by the high infant and maternal mortality rates, particularly among the middle and upper classes. They were concerned that future generations would not be adequately populated with the children of the privileged classes, and that instead, the country would be dominated by immigrants.[32] Because it was viewed as women's job to produce and care for the next generation, reform efforts were directed at mothers. Educational programs were developed to teach women how to better care for their children. Reformers also established clinics for infants and for prenatal care, and they provided poor women with clean milk for their children.[33]

In 1912, this early activism led to the creation of a new federal office, the Children's Health Bureau, with Julia Lathrop as its first head.[34] Lathrop decided to study the issue of infant and children's health systematically via the collection of health statistics. Upon discovering that women's and infants' health were linked, she directed government efforts toward both maternal and child health. Lathrop designed programs responding to the needs about which women had written her. She later drafted a bill, passed by Congress in 1921, initiating the federal government's role in the provision of health services for women and children via state grants.[35] These state programs funded educators who taught mothers about nutrition and hygiene; prenatal and child health conferences were coordinated for health workers such as public health nurses, midwives, and social workers; and visiting nurses were sent to care for pregnant women and new mothers. The extensive use of various health care workers concerned physicians about state infringement on their role in health care. Many physicians coordinated with political conservatives to successfully oppose the act's renewal, and it expired in 1929. Nonetheless, a precedent had been set for government involvement in maternal child health. In 1935, Title V of the Social Security Act reestablished government's role in health care, with a special provision funding maternal and child health programs. These programs had four foci: aid to dependent children; maternal and child welfare programs; welfare services for needy children such as orphans and neglected, homeless, or delinquent children; and vocational rehabilitation for the disabled.[36] This measure provided a legitimate basis for future maternal child health programs in the United States.

During the Second World War, an Emergency Maternal and Infant Care Program (EMIC) was established for women with children whose spouses were serving in the military.[37] In attempting to fulfill its primary goal of improving military men's morale, the program provided payment for women and children's health services. Consequently, many more women gave birth in hospitals where, by this time, physicians had implemented hygienic obstetric practices, dramatically decreasing the maternal mortality rate. In 1965, Medicaid legislation provided poor women and their children with expanded access to a broader range of health services. In 1972, the Women, Infants and Children program (WIC) was established, assisting poor pregnant or postpartum women and their infants or young children in obtaining food and other necessary health services.[38] Women beyond the postpartum period were not eligible for nutritional support under WIC.

As the federal government became more involved in maternal child health, physicians' role in women's health care also increased. Once insurance and federal funds became readily available to reimburse physician-attended births in hospitals, it was expected that prudent women would choose these types of deliveries. By the end of the century, physicians dominated childbirth, but some feminists began advocating returning control of childbirth to women.[39] They objected to what they perceived to be the overmedicalization of childbirth.

THE MEDICALIZATION OF CHILDBIRTH

The medicalization of childbirth refers to treating the childbirth process as a medical event requiring intervention rather than as a natural life event. The extent to which any one woman's childbirth experience is medicalized depends on a number of social factors, including access to high-technology health care, health insurance, income level, institutional factors, country, and so forth. The central actor in a fully medicalized childbirth is the physician who delivers the infant using all the technology at his or her disposal to evaluate how childbirth is proceeding and when intervention is needed. In contrast, the central actor in a childbirth defined as a natural event is the woman. Modern Western societies have been criticized for overly medicalizing childbirth, while in poor countries, the limited availability of trained birth attendants and other medical resources results in high rates of infant and maternal death and disability.

When childbirth is medicalized, medical monitoring and advice begin before a woman conceives. Recommendations are made regarding nutrition, vitamins, and the ideal health status that will provide a welcoming fetal environment. After conception, women's bodies and the developing fetus are monitored for changes and potential dangers. During childbirth, the woman and the fetus are subjected to intense monitoring, including the intravaginal placement of fetal probes to assess fetal distress. After childbirth, medical advice and education may be given to women about breast-feeding or infant care.

A medicalized childbirth can lead to unnecessary and harmful surgical interventions for women. If distress is noted or if labor doesn't proceed according to a predefined normal time frame, then a Caesarean section may be performed. This is a major surgery from which it takes several weeks to heal. Inappropriately applied medical definitions of normalcy[40] and overly cautious interpretations of information from monitoring devices contribute to excessive Caesarean rates. When an infant is delivered vaginally, U.S. women often have a surgical incision known as an episiotomy made in their vaginal opening to ease the process. Although research has shown that this procedure does not provide the medically claimed health benefits and is unnecessary in almost all vaginal births,[41] more than one million episiotomies are performed in the United States annually. It can harm women, leading to sexual problems and incontinence, and can cause permanent damage.

While international studies monitor poor countries' maternal mortality and morbidity rates, studies of problems associated with Caesarean sections, episiotomies, and other aspects of medicalized childbirth in wealthier countries are limited, making it difficult to assess the true degree of injury from medicalization.

SEXUALITY AND FERTILITY: RIGHTS AND CHOICES

In many societies, women's ability to become mothers is socially valued. However, bearing, nursing, and raising children can be burdensome and may have negative health consequences. Therefore, the effects and effectiveness of fertility control methods have always been important to women everywhere.

Women's ability to control fertility is related to their social status. Fertility control may be viewed as a private matter, but in patriarchal societies, women's fertility and sexuality is generally under the auspices of male family members and other powerful men. This makes women vulnerable and dependent on the men in their lives, and it puts them at risk of sexual violence and sexually transmitted diseases. It also makes social and political issues out of some of the most pressing reproductive health issues for women, such as birth control, abortion, sterilization, assisted reproductive technologies, and sexually transmitted diseases. Each of these has been a point of advocacy and contention in legal, medical, political, and religious domains.

At the beginning of the twentieth century, women had limited ability to control their fertility. Many physicians opposed women's access to contraceptives.

U.S. laws made access to information about contraceptive devices or abortion illegal, and many state governments passed similar restrictive legislation.[42] These were known as "obscenity laws" because of the concern that contraceptives would promote lewd and immoral behaviors, and that women would not perform their womanly duties. It was thought that women's morals had to be protected because a moral society depended on mothers' good morals.[43] These laws hindered women's ability to limit their family size, learn about their bodies, and obtain health information. Restrictions on access to birth control and abortion continued throughout the twentieth century.

In the late nineteenth and early twentieth centuries, a group of feminists asserted the sacredness of motherhood and recommended that women control their fertility by abstaining from sexual intercourse. This would allow them to space out their children and provide children with the best mothering possible.[44] As women accepted these ideas, especially among the upper and middle classes, fertility rates began to decrease. At the same time, immigrant women were having larger families, prompting eugenic concerns among social conservatives.[45]

Margaret Sanger, a nurse in New York City, observed that mothers who had many children and were living in slums suffered from poor health.[46] She believed that in order for women to be healthy, they needed to control the timing, spacing, and number of their children.[47] Sanger became a birth control advocate, and in 1916, she opened the first clinic providing birth control, for which she was arrested.[48] In 1921, Sanger and other women founded the American Birth Control League (ABCL) and began opening clinics across the country. The ABCL later became known as Planned Parenthood of America. Sanger believed that physicians should provide contraceptive information to their patients. Her efforts and those of other activists led to changes in laws, making physicians exempt from restrictions on distributing birth control.[49] This benefited the growing medical specialty of obstetrics and gynecology by providing women with another reason to seek medical care. However, broader contraceptive restrictions enacted by individual states remained in effect, and it was not until 1965 that the U.S. Supreme Court ruled that married persons had a right to access to birth control in the landmark case *Griswold v. Connecticut*, while the 1972 ruling in *Eisenstadt v. Baird* gave unmarried persons that right.

Fertility control changed after synthetic hormones were developed. Birth control pills became available in the 1960s, making private fertility control possible for many women.[50] The Pill also made possible the separation of intercourse for pleasure from procreation, enabling women to have some control over their sexual expression. However, the Pill and other hormonal contraceptives such as Depo-Provera, Norplant, and the morning-after pill were only available through physicians. While hormonal contraception increased women's self-determination, their access to these modalities often depended on males: male physicians prescribed contraceptive methods, male pharmacists sometimes refused to dispense them, male insurers limited reimbursement for them, male policy makers and government leaders directed their availability, and male religious leaders dictated the morality of their use.

Throughout the twentieth century, women's access to information about their bodies was limited because this knowledge was viewed as being under the predominantly male medical profession's jurisdiction. In response to the control of information and services, and because of the many negative and dangerous experiences women had as a result of medical care, a women's health movement arose in the 1960s and 1970s.[51] Groups of women joined together in the United States to share health information and educate each other. In Los Angeles, women were arrested for practicing medicine without a license because they were encouraging women to understand their own anatomy.[52] A group of women in Boston, later known as the Boston Women's Health Book Collective, published an educational booklet for women in 1970, which was expanded into a book, *Our Bodies, Ourselves*.[53] It has been updated many times and has been published in more than twenty languages throughout the world. It continues to be produced by and for women within their own countries, integrating women's health concerns within their respective cultural contexts. The Boston Women's Health Book Collective has helped women worldwide to take control of their own health.[54]

Women's health activists were also concerned about pregnancy termination. Prior to 1973, abortion was illegal in the United States, and many women either died or experienced debilitating injuries from unhygienic and dangerous abortion providers and practices. In Chicago in the 1960s, a group of women known as "Jane" learned to perform abortions for those who needed them.[55] In 1973, the U.S. Supreme Court ruled that women had the right to abortion until the fetus was viable, and under certain circumstances thereafter, on grounds of an individual right to privacy. While abortion is currently legal in the United States, there are many restrictions on access. For example, in some states, women must travel hundreds of miles to reach an abortion provider, and late-term abortions are very difficult to obtain, even when the mother's life is at risk. About half of all pregnancies are unplanned in the United States,[56] and many women do not want or cannot afford to have a child. Late in the twentieth century, mifepristone was developed as a pharmaceutical abortifacient for use in the early stages of pregnancy. It increased women's options, but access has been controversial and limited. In poorer countries, women have fewer options. If abortions are not readily available, abortifacients may be sought from traditional healers. The debate about women's right to control their bodies continues.

Of all family-planning methods used worldwide, the most common is sterilization among both men and women.[57] In the United States, sterilization rates are highest among women who are members of stigmatized or poor groups such as black women, Puerto Rican women, welfare recipients, and minors who receive health care in government clinics.[58] Even when women voluntarily choose sterilization, it raises questions about the true voluntary nature of these choices given that in the United States and in other countries, sterilizations have been integral to eugenic practices. Early in the century, women who were viewed as inferior in some way, such as intelligence, disability, race, or ethnicity, were sterilized after childbirth to prevent future conceptions. Physicians often refused to deliver infants unless a woman agreed to sterilization after delivery. Eugenic practices often occurred without women's knowledge or consent, and they continued throughout the century.[59]

In contrast, reproductive health technologies have made it possible for women to have children and families when they would otherwise be unable to do so, either because of one partner's infertility or the absence of a male sexual partner. These costly technologies are rarely reimbursed by insurance. For many wealthier childless women who wish to be mothers, the availability of these technologies can become an imperative for their use. In their efforts to conceive, women may begin fertility procedures that are often lengthy, difficult, painful, and emotionally wrenching. While wealthier and higher status women can access technologies enabling them to increase their family size, poor and stigmatized women often experience social pressures to limit their family size.[60]

For women who lack power in their relationships, sexual activity may be hazardous to their health. They may not be free to refuse a partner's sexual demands, use birth control, or use methods to prevent sexually transmitted diseases. In both poor and wealthy countries, women may be beaten for making such requests. This has had especially tragic consequences in Africa, where the majority of those infected with HIV are women, and among those aged fifteen to twenty-four with HIV, three-fourths are women.[61] AIDS has the potential to kill an entire generation of young women in Africa and decimate many communities. While AIDS in Africa is a complex issue, women's low social status and male assertions of authority contribute to the problem, rendering women incapable of protecting themselves.

MENSTRUATION AND MENOPAUSE

From the time of menstrual huts and blood taboos until the present, menstruation and menopause—these most personal of women's experiences—have had political, economic, and social implications. Like pregnancy, these normal life events are subject to being defined as pathological. Over the course of the twentieth century, women have been told that menstrual cramps were due to their inadequacy in the female role—if they would just be satisfied with their role in the family, if they would only have a child, then their cramps would dissipate.[62] Once it was discovered that menstrual cramps resulted from an oversupply of certain uterine prostaglandins and were generally quite treatable with medications like ibuprofen,[63] one no longer heard much about this theory.

Premenstrual syndrome (PMS) is associated with physical and emotional changes and has been used to women's disadvantage.[64] It has long been blamed on hormonal fluctuations, despite a lack of evidence of a causal link. Researcher and psychoanalyst Therese Benedek referred to these as changes of "climate" in the body.[65] For most women, most of the time, these changes are interesting but not significant. Symptoms increase with high caffeine intake and also under stressful conditions.[66] More recently, the American Psychiatric Association defined premenstrual distress as an emotional disorder, naming it premenstrual dysphoric disorder. The association is currently considering whether to move this diagnosis from an experimental (needing more research) to a permanent place in its *Diagnostic and Statistical Manual of Psychiatric Disorders*, a standard tool for mental health providers. While this classification could provide insurance coverage for treatment with psychiatric medications, women worry that the diagnosis will be overused, leading to overmedication when stress relief might be all that is needed.[67]

A serious, sometimes fatal illness, toxic shock syndrome, was reported in the United States in the early 1980s shortly after the introduction of a new form of "superabsorbent" tampon for use during menstruation. Women activists learned that there was no regulation of tampon content or advertising, and they began demanding the necessary information so that women could make informed choices about the lowest tampon absorbency needed for their purposes. In the United States, tampon packages must now contain absorbency information and warnings about the potential for toxic shock.[68]

A menstrual technique used to remove menstrual blood with a simple apparatus known as menstrual extraction was pioneered by the Feminist Women's Health Centers. Groups of women gathered to assist each other in performing the extraction. If done regularly, the technique could obviate the need for abortion.[69]

For many years, the view that menopause is a "hormone deficiency disease" rather than a normal life process was used to justify the use of postmenopausal hormonal treatments for otherwise normal women. Some feminists referred to this as the largest undocumented experiment ever done, and gradually the activist community joined with the research community to demand an actual randomized controlled trial of these hormonal therapies.[70] In 1991, with the support of the U.S. National Institutes of Health (NIH), a large nationwide study began enrolling menopausal and postmenopausal women at more than twenty clinical sites around the country. This research, called the Women's Health Initiative, eventually enrolled more than 60,000 women and examined the effects of postmenopausal hormonal therapy, low-fat diet, and calcium supplements on cancer, bone density, and heart disease. The initial dramatic results were published after ten years, showing that the standard postmenopausal therapy of estrogen with or without a progestin did not prevent heart disease. Instead, it caused higher risks of stroke and cancer. While it protected bone, the overall risks outweighed the benefits so greatly that the study was halted early.[71] Other results have shown that estrogen does not protect cognitive functioning and, in general, should not be recommended for women, except briefly for those women experiencing distressing menopausal symptoms during the climacteric transition.[72]

In the latest installment of controversial medical proposals for menstruation, new cycle-stopping hormonal contraceptives have appeared on the market. They are being sold as completely safe and convenient, since women will no longer have to menstruate at all. Thus far, studies following groups of women for up to five years do not appear to demonstrate harmful effects, and many medical professionals believe they are safe. Time will tell whether it is indeed safe to stop hormonal cycles in normal women, especially among younger women.[73]

HEALTH HAZARDS AT WORK

The economic transformations experienced by wealthy countries during the twentieth century have commonly been referred to as shifts from industrial to service and then to global economies. Poorer countries' economies have industrialized more recently, while agrarian economies continue to exist throughout the world. Women work in each of these sectors and systems in ways that their societies permit, while bearing primary responsibility for doing the work of caring for the home and their families.[74] All of this work has consequences for women's health.

At the beginning of the twentieth century when wealthier countries industrialized, the majority of laborers in many factories and industries were women.[75]

They were exposed to occupational hazards such as industrial chemicals and solvents. Women exposed to phosphorus or radium developed a disease that caused their jaws to slowly disintegrate.[76] As men went to war during the First World War, many women working in munitions factories became sick and died of TNT exposure. Poor air quality in factories and extreme dust caused respiratory problems and lung cancers.

One of the first individuals to examine the effect of poor work conditions on health was Dr. Alice Hamilton, the "matriarch of industrial medicine."[77] Influenced by the diseases she observed among immigrant workers living near Hull House in Chicago, she studied the cause of what she believed were occupational illnesses. She identified lead toxins as hazardous to workers and to children's health. Her research into reproductive health hazards became the basis for social activism, resulting in the passage of protective occupational legislation. Unfortunately, employers later used these laws to justify keeping women from higher-paying industrial jobs. Hamilton lobbied for safer work environments and compensation for women's occupational injuries.

As industrial economies became service economies, the numbers of women working in offices increased, especially in low-wage jobs. These service jobs are often thought of as low risk, but they allow for little control over work and have been linked to health hazards.[78] Common problems include increased stress, cardiovascular disease, depression, and higher rates of mortality compared with those who have greater control over their work.

In the last decades of the century, the world economy was transformed into a global economy, meaning that the production of goods and services has been disaggregated throughout the world, resulting in additional trade, investment, and communication linkages between countries. For example, corporate ownership could be located in one part of the world, resources could come from another part, manufacturing and assembly could occur elsewhere, and supporting financial and business services could be performed in yet other locations. Globalization meant that many industries shifted their production from higher-cost wealthier industrialized countries to lower-cost poorer countries. Many firms hired female workers for jobs where they could pay women less and women would not object to exploitation.[79] In most cases, the health protections established in wealthier countries did not apply in poorer countries. Female workers in Mexican, Philippine, and Asian factories have been exposed to health hazards comparable to those during early Western industrialization. The benefits of cheap global female labor have accrued primarily to home governments, large corporations, and consumers in wealthier countries who benefit from lower-cost goods and services. The cost associated with job creation in poor countries is often disability and death from exposure to toxic industrial hazards. The magnitude of the effect on women's health in general and on women's reproductive health is unknown.

Women grow more of the world's food than men, but they toil on land that is usually owned by men.[80] These men may be the executives who own large agribusinesses, local men who own community plots, or male spouses who own the family's subsistence plot. Farmwork is especially hazardous to women's health in poor countries.[81] Women working for large corporate interests are often exposed to dangerous pesticides, which may affect their fertility, and risk their future children's health. Even though women in developing countries produce most of the food and are responsible for processing and cooking it, they generally have less access to food than male household members.[82] Men are often fed first; women and female children receive any remaining food. When there is not enough, this can lead to malnutrition, anemia, exhaustion, dizziness, other illnesses, and even death. Even housework, for which women are primarily responsible, may be hazardous because it continually exposes women to many chemicals. Very little research has been done on the potential chemical toxicity or the long-term health effects of such exposure, but it may contribute to a portion of the excess morbidity experienced by women compared with men.

Wealthier women in the West may obtain domestic labor from lower status women in their own communities, or from migrant female workers from poorer countries who have traveled to be domestic workers, often at a great personal risk to their own physical, sexual, and emotional well-being.[83] Income from these domestic jobs enables foreign women to provide financial support for their families in their home countries. These remittances are a large source of funds for many economies and are often relied on by governments. Such work arrangements link the lives of women across the globe; at the same time, they link the governments of the respective nations in complex geopolitical relationships. In this and many other ways, the global economy has intertwined women's lives, while shifting a portion of the illness burden associated with housework and child care onto poorer women.

Overall, women have lower income levels and less wealth than men, and they are more likely to live in poverty, which affects their health negatively. Studies have consistently shown that the greatest factor affecting mortality and morbidity is socioeconomic status. Women are generally compensated at lower wage rates than men, regardless of the type of work that they do. Women who are farmers are more likely to be laborers rather than land owners. Women are less likely to own property. While women work two-thirds of all the hours worked in the world, they earn 10 percent of the world's income, and they only own 1 percent of the world's wealth.[84] Worldwide, women are less likely to be educated than men, and two-thirds of all illiterate people in the world are women.[85] There is a positive correlation between education and health, so that when women are denied an education, it also results in greater mortality and morbidity.

Cultural expectations associated with women's gender roles also affect women's health. Within their homes, women's lower status means that they have less decision-making power, and in most countries, they have fewer rights. In a world where women are expected to be the primary caretakers of children and elders, this responsibility limits their ability to earn an income.[86] Women are far more likely to work part time or in the informal sector, which pays low wages and provides few benefits, but which allows women the time to care for family members. In the United States, women's greater likelihood of irregular or low-wage employment due to caretaking responsibilities affects their eligibility for Social Security and pension benefits. Consequently, women are more likely to live in poverty in old age compared with men, and poverty is related to ill health. This cultural expectation is reflected in government measures of productivity. Unpaid domestic labor such as housework, child care, and elder care is generally not considered in official government labor statistics because it is performed in the direct service of the household.

Workers throughout the world have lobbied for their rights and for safe work environments, and women have fought for equal wages and for family-friendly policies. While some progress has been made and protective legislation has been enacted in many countries, there is still a long way to go. Health equity will not be achieved until women and men have equal responsibility for the home, social policies account for the necessity of child and elder care, and proper compensation is provided for the work that is done in caring for others.

SCIENTIFIC MEDICINE: A DOMINANT AND GENDERED APPROACH

Scientific medicine emerged as a new approach toward medicine and health care and became dominant in Western societies during the twentieth century. Scientific medicine is a tool, an approach to practicing medicine, and a meaning system. Within this framework, physicians and scientists have the authority to define what a disease is, how disease states are determined, which factors lead to illness, how patients should be treated, and how to regain health. Government support of scientific medicine contributed to its growth, as did the public's expectations that science would solve many problems. Many areas of our lives have been reinterpreted within a medical framework, including grieving, sexuality, physical activity, gender identity, and so forth, and for women, that has occurred in gendered ways.[87] Although the medical/scientific framework is dominant, it is characterized by gender bias. Activists have challenged medical professional authority, especially as it relates to women's health given that almost all medical knowledge is based on research conducted solely on men.

Early in the twentieth century, the greatest successes from the application of scientific medicine were those directed at public health practices. By midcentury, vaccines became more readily available, and pharmaceuticals grew in importance. The midcentury development of mood-altering medications such as tranquilizers, sedatives, and antidepressants provided an opportunity for physicians to treat their female patients' depression, anxiety, and unhappiness. Psychotropic medications, often referred to as "mother's little helper," became widely available in the 1960s, but their use was often geared toward encouraging women to fulfill their traditional social roles.[88] Valium became a huge commercial success and was the first billion-dollar drug in history, paving the way for the increasing use of similar psychiatric medications. This facilitated the expansion of the medical profession's authority into lifestyle issues and the medicalization of women's normal life events such as menstruation and motherhood.[89] Some feminists have claimed that the goal of these medications was to adjust women to their subordinate social status rather than actually relieve them of suffering, thus maintaining the status quo.[90] The medical profession has also been criticized for establishing a double standard in psychological health for women and men, reinforcing traditional gender roles for women.[91] Physicians encouraged men to be productive workers, while encouraging women to care for their appearance and care for others. By the end of the century, an active antipsychiatric movement had emerged, with roots in feminist critiques.[92]

Some scientific medical advancements had had a negative impact on women's health. In the 1940s, menopause was viewed as a deficiency disease, and menopausal women were prescribed diethylstilbestrol (DES), a carcinogen. Beginning in 1949, DES was approved to prevent miscarriage in pregnant women (for which it did not work) and as postcoital contraceptive method (a morning after pill). DES caused cancer in some women, and it caused cervical cancer in some of their daughters. Many of these DES daughters have become DES health activists.[93] In another case, between 1957 and the early 1960s, tens of thousands of pregnant women throughout the world were prescribed thalidomide to prevent morning sickness, but this drug caused severe birth defects. Birth control pills are widely used, but they have been linked to stroke, hypertension, and cardiovascular disease in women—more so with the higher-dosage preparations used in the 1960s and 1970s.[94] Similar health hazards apply to medical devices. The intrauterine device (IUD) is a contraceptive device that caused women's deaths in the 1970s. One such model, the Dalkon Shield was banned in the United States, but the device continued to be sold to women worldwide.[95] More recent models of the IUD appear to be safe. In the 1980s, a commonly used antiacne drug, Accutane, was linked to birth defects.[96] There are countless other examples of drugs and devices that were developed, approved by the U.S. Food and Drug Administration following accepted scientific procedures, and later shown to produce harm and even death. Many of these technologies were developed to help women fulfill their expected social roles. These drugs and devices were accepted and sometimes desired or requested by women. Women sought physicians' help in managing the most intimate aspects of their lives, but scientific medicine's ability to help was limited.

It was only late in the twentieth century after challenges from women's health activists and female physicians that the medical profession began to acknowledge this gender bias. Dr. Lila Wallis, an early advocate of teaching physicians about women's health problems, spearheaded the development of an Advanced Curriculum in Women's Health in 1983 in collaboration with the American Medical Women's Association.[97] In 1990, Dr. Ruth Kirchstein established the Office of Research on Women's Health at the NIH to focus on research and training related to women's health issues. In 1991, Dr. Bernadine Healy became the first female head of the NIH. She initiated the systematic research program on older women's health issues known as the Women's Health Initiative.[98] Each of these female physicians contributed to changing U.S. policies about women's health. As early research findings about women's health emerged, they invalidated long-held medical beliefs, but this has not yet translated to changes in medical practice. The medical profession has been resistant to changing medical training and medical practice to integrate and apply this emerging knowledge. Some researchers continue to ignore the directive to include women in research studies or to analyze their data by sex, thus reproducing the gender bias in scientific medicine. Ironically, by the end of the century, scientific knowledge about women's health was in its infancy, but the medicalization of women's lives was widespread and well established.

ENDURING CHANGE AND FUTURE DIRECTIONS

Women have a rich history of women's health activism, individually and collectively, in the United States and throughout the world. It has had enduring consequences. Women established new areas of medicine such as occupational health. Women's support of physicians, and especially of physician-attended childbirths, fostered the development of obstetrics and gynecology as a medical specialty. Women lobbied for their right to medical information, and they demanded to be partners with their physicians, contributing to the informed consent movement. Women's consistent efforts to obtain information about birth control and other drugs resulted in the legalization of contraception, the accessibility of birth control information in the United States, and later, the availability of drug information for all patients. Women's demands for access to information about their bodies and about health and illness contributed to the explosion of health information available to the public by the end of the century from lay sources, professional sources, peers, and the Internet. Domestic violence and rape are now considered to be crimes, and rape during wars can be designated a war crime. Women's lobbying for additional research into women's health resulted in the federal support for the Women's Health Initiative research program. This is slowly beginning to change medical practice because while physicians remain the ultimate authority, they now work more collaboratively with patients.

Women everywhere experience common problems in the primary domains of their lives. They bear children, need to control their fertility, care for others, suffer from violence, and do work that can damage their health. The commonality is that women's unique social position and activities expose them to similar health hazards, make them vulnerable in their relationships, and affect their ability to respond to their own health needs.[99] In order to be healthy, women must have the right and ability to control their bodies and protect their bodily integrity. When understood in this way, we see that women's health depends primarily on their social, cultural, political, and economic situations.

The medical profession needs to adopt a more holistic approach to health and illness, incorporating a broader range of factors in health models, as is done by the WHO. Women's perspectives and lived experiences must become central in our approach to health and illness. Health care practices must be culturally sensitive to women's needs and allow women to be equal partners with their health care providers. Only by recognizing the complexity of women's health and the many individual and social factors affecting it, and by acknowledging that women are differently situated and need solutions relevant to their specific cultures, can we begin to truly address women's health issues and make women healthier.

CHAPTER FIVE

Public and Private: Politicizing the Personal— Questioning the Public/ Private Divide

BRONWYN WINTER

In 1997 renowned French feminist historian Michelle Perrot published *Femmes publiques*, the title being a deliberate play on words.[1] In French, *femme publique* means "woman of loose morals," usually prostitute (cf. "ladies of the night"), but Perrot uses it in another way, to denote the occupation by women of the public sphere and their representation within it. In the opening paragraphs of her introduction, she notes the enduring cultural and political demarcation between a *femme publique* and a *homme public*:

> In public space, that of the City, men and women are located at the two extremes on the scale of values...Invested with an official function, public men play a role that is important and recognized...Depraved, debauched, lewd, venal, public women—who are just as often called "girls"—are "creatures", women who commonly belong to all.[2]

The "City" to which Perrot refers is as it was understood in antiquity, or, in other words, the community of citizens, and by extension, the public urban space associated with citizens. Women who have ventured into this City have always been viewed with distrust. Women "belong" in the private realm, it is their nature: Rousseau, that celebrated visionary of Enlightenment equality among men, told us so, in Book V of *Emile, ou de l'éducation* (1762), which is dedicated to the inculcation, into the mind of Sophie, Emile's wife-to-be, of her "natural" and very publicly private role of wife and mother.[3] (The unfinished Book VI deals with Sophie's adulterous and whorish behavior following her marriage.)

But that was the eighteenth century. By the twentieth century, that epoch of breathtakingly rapid change and postenlightened modernity (which by its end was also presumed to be postfeminist, postcolonial, postmodern, and a number of other "posts"), surely things had changed, or would change. Well, yes, and yet no. Let us take two snapshots of the eve of the last century and the beginning of this, a sort of graphic bookending of the modern age of women. The first, dated 1893, is a New Zealand antisuffrage cartoon of which Rousseau would surely have approved. The second is a 2009 photograph of Johanna Sigurdardottir of Iceland, the first openly gay prime minister in a world where female national leaders of any sexual persuasion remain relatively rare. In setting these two photographs side by side, one might exclaim, "My, how things have changed" (subtext: for the better). Yet, one might, on further reflection, simultaneously lament, *plus ça change, plus c'est la même chose* (the more things change, the more they stay the same), for reasons I will explain presently.

This chapter, then, will look at some of the ways in which the public/private divide was challenged or reinforced, its boundaries shifted or blurred, in the twentieth century, through the combined impact of feminist challenges and the socioeconomic conditions that enabled or disabled them, and co-optations of such challenges, or backlashes against them, by a range of actors including the state, the media, and culture industries. I will focus on five related symbolic loci of women's public/private-ness: women and the nation, domesticity, fertility control, clothing, and place and space. In looking at these areas, I will also be focusing on the great contradiction in the cultural framing of public and private in the modern age: the private has become public—socially engineered, culturally represented, politically debated, commodified in the marketplace—as perhaps never before.

NATIONALIZING WOMEN

In 1893 an extraordinary event happened in New Zealand. For the first time anywhere in the world, women acceded to full human status as it is constitutionally recognized in modern nation-states: they got the vote.[4] They became fully fledged citizens, with rights, responsibilities, and a formal voice equal to men's. Even if the battle for full-functional equality in the public sphere is far from won anywhere in the Western world, that moment in time marked the beginning of a profound transformation in the representation of women (in all senses of the word) in modern societies. It was all the more extraordinary in that Maori (indigenous) women were included; in fact, the first Maori men had been elected to New Zealand's parliament under a special Maori electorate system in 1867 (the Maori seats survive to this day). For Australian indigenous people, the history was more checkered: they had the vote in all states except Queensland and Western Australia before federation but were barred from voting in national elections after federation in 1901 due to a restrictive interpretation of the constitution. They were not formally enfranchised at the national level until 1962 and not included in the census until 1967. White women, on the contrary, had voted nationally since federation in South and Western Australia, and since 1902 in other states.[5] Indigenous Australians did, however, get the vote almost a quarter of a century before women in the Swiss canton of Appenzell Innerhoden became the last Western women to obtain the vote, in 1990.

Women's full enfranchisement in the West is thus a much more recent occurrence than one might assume, and not necessarily ahead of the non-West. For example, Azerbaijan gave women the vote in 1918, Uruguay in 1932, and Indonesia in 1945. In fact, at the time of this writing, only a handful of nations maintain formal prohibitions or restrictions: Saudi Arabia and the Vatican (complete prohibitions), Lebanon (which places basic education requirements on women but not men), Bhutan (where the one-vote-per-household law effectively means that few women vote), and finally, Brunei and the United Arab Emirates (where no one has the vote, although the United Arab Emirates is moving toward establishing suffrage).

Of course, the New Zealand government, like any other government that has granted women the vote, did not do so out of some sudden act of enlightened magnanimity, nor did it do so, as we can see from Figure 5.1, without facing considerable opposition. The history of the Western world (and indeed, other parts of the world) reminds us time and again that any legal, political, and socioeconomic gains that women (even the most privileged) have obtained have been the result of a fight.[6] The battle has, moreover, often been protracted, and women who have waged it have suffered backlash that has ranged from public humiliation to death. The latter was indeed the price paid by Olympe de Gouges in 1791 for daring to claim women's right to citizenship, and equality in marriage and before the law, in revolutionary France. Happily, late nineteenth-century and early twentieth-century suffragists did not suffer as final a fate, and it is thanks to them that women have a public voice today. Indeed, if one were to name the most profoundly transformative social movement and political philosophy of the many seen by the twentieth century, one must surely be compelled to name feminism. It is, after all, thanks to feminism that half of humanity came to be recognized, legally, politically, and philosophically, as, indeed, human. Moreover, it is because of this accession to legally encoded citizen's status that feminists have been able to accomplish another revolutionary act—that of publicly positing and theorizing the "private" as a site of male domination and thus a political terrain, as reflected in the second-wave feminist slogan "The personal is political."

Over the eighteenth and nineteenth centuries, the state had largely taken over from the church the role of supporting men in controlling women's behavior in the private sphere, at least in the West. In doing so, it used modern liberal constructions of separate public and private life, accompanied by modern "scientific" ideas about women's "nature."[7] As women massively entered the public sphere from the latter half of the nineteenth century, in education,

FIGURE 5.1: "What, Dinner Not Ready Yet?" Cartoon in the *New Zealand Mail*, September 29, 1893. Courtesy of the Alexander Turnbull Library, Wellington, New Zealand.

work, cultural production, and politics, they challenged that divide. The impact of those challenges was to be profound and, notwithstanding backlashes and regressions, enduring.

This is the "My, how things have changed" story. The *plus ça change* story is that just as feminists challenged patriarchal configurations of the public and private (or fraternal configurations, to use Pateman's reading of the Enlightenment's "sexual contract"[8]), existing institutions—themselves undergoing rapid technological and cultural transformation—were preparing their responses. For the men of the political class, the emancipation or otherwise of women was quickly harnessed to a national project: women's public and private roles and behavior were increasingly seen as measures of the nation's worth. For example, in France and Egypt in the late nineteenth and early twentieth centuries, the male architects of modern democracies advocated women's emancipation and participation in public life, particularly through education (although not yet the vote) as core to the construction of the modern nation and its values. Education (and the training of women as elementary school teachers, strongly pushed in France) was key not for women's own sake, but in order to better partner the modern husband and educate his sons.[9] In Kemalist Turkey, women's participation in the national project needed to be more complete: Turkish women obtained the vote in 1930, long before either French (1944) or Egyptian women (1956). This enfranchisement, however, came at a price—that of co-optation to the agenda of an increasingly antidemocratic state.[10] If women were to enter into modernity via their inscription within the public sphere, they were to do it on the state's terms or not at all. When it came to women *running* for public office, however, the male political class was less eager to welcome women into the national emancipatory project, adding to established arguments of scientific naturalism new ones of masculinist meritocracy.[11]

Such emancipatory politics, however, largely concerned the urban middle classes. Working-class women, even though they had, through working outside the home, been in the public sphere for some time, were of less concern in nation building, at least in the early decades of the century, than those whom Virginia Woolf called in 1938 the "daughters of educated men."[12] If working-class women mattered, it was largely through their participation in popular culture, especially as music hall entertainers, which placed them in a category more or less akin to the traditional *femmes publiques*. It was during the Second World War, in democratic Western nations, that blue-collar women workers suddenly became important as cultural emblems of the nation. Many of them worked, for example, in armaments factories, and Rosie the Riveter—along with the famous "We Can Do It" poster by Howard Miller featuring an overalled and headscarved female worker determinedly flexing her right forearm—became instruments of nationalist wartime propaganda in the United States long before they became feminist icons.[13] The appropriation of such imagery by second-wave feminists is problematic for that reason, even if the opening of nontraditional work opportunities has demonstrably been a somewhat ambiguous benefit of wars for women.

For conservative regimes, on the other hand, such as Thatcher's Britain, Reagan's or the Bushes' (senior and junior) United States, or Howard's Australia, and particularly Fascist regimes—Franco's Spain or Hitler's Third Reich—the publicly inscribed civic duty of women for the national good was not via their emancipation but through their reprivatization, often associated with a renewed incursion of religion into politics.[14] This was so even if they *also* worked in armaments factories (although in Nazi Germany this was largely taken care of by using Jews and other "undesirables" as slave labor). More or less explicit variants on the Nazi theme *Kinder Küche Kirche* (children, kitchen, and church) were adopted throughout the century by conservative regimes worldwide to redomesticate white women (the ones that mattered for nation building). They also featured strongly in opposition to various campaigns for women's rights in the public sphere, as is epitomized by the antisuffrage New Zealand cartoon in Figure 5.1. These conservative and backlash values were even famously, and very publicly, defended by female political leaders themselves in the later decades of the century, such as Britain's "Iron Lady," Prime Minister Margaret Thatcher, in the 1980s, or Australia's extreme-right leader Pauline Hanson, in the 1990s.[15]

In fact, in the more than a century that has now elapsed since women first attended a polling booth to cast their votes in a national election, it has become increasingly evident that control of women's *public* display of their *private* roles remains a national obsession, in practically any country one cares to name—notwithstanding the demonstrable differences between democratic and predemocratic regimes in terms of women's access to formal equality in the public sphere.[16] Even female politicians, that literal *embodiment* of women's enfranchisement as citizens and thus as electable to public office, have paid the price of access to public office through being indelibly marked by their female Otherness, to use a Beauvoirian concept.[17] They are so marked, first, through their clothing and makeup: even power-dressed—even lesbian, such as Sigurdardottir—they are still female. Thus, Sigurdardottir is dressed in tailored and elegant clothes befitting her female position within the elite, her hair is carefully styled, and she wears bright red lipstick. Second, they are marked by public associations with their private roles as wife and mother, or, in the case of a peculiar assimilation of lesbians in public life to heterosexual maleness (notwithstanding their feminized appearance), as a sort of lesbian husband. Thus, the partnership of former president of the Australian Medical Association, well-known lesbian icon, or "dykon," Kerryn Phelps, with former teacher Jackie Stricker is featured in a well-known book.[18] Failing a marriage or motherhood, public women may be characterized by their former feminine careers, such as the description, in the British press in particular, of Sigurdardottir as a "former air hostess." Little matter that it had been almost four decades since she had worked as one, or that, during that time, she had built a long and impressive career in both the trade union movement and politics.[19]

If women in public life (particularly, although not solely, politicians) conformed, then they were rewarded with media canonization as good girls; if they refused to conform in some way, willingly or through some sort of "failure," to live up to the prescribed model, then an array of other coded media representations was brought into play to demonize them in ways that foregrounded their femaleness: whore, princess, naïf.[20] In either case, cultural representations of women in public life have placed the accent on their sexualization: even with the keys to the City that their vote, and their electability represent, women have remained, again in Beauvoirian terms, Othered as (the) "sex." And nowhere have they been more so than when they have criticized male power: Beauvoir herself, on the publication of *The Second Sex*, was subjected to viciously sexualizing attacks, the most notorious of which came from François Mauriac. Mauriac told a colleague (who, like him, wrote for the journal *Les Temps Modernes* that Beauvoir had cofounded with Sartre and Merleau-Ponty in 1945) that he had now "learned everything about your boss's vagina."[21] The *femme publique* in the modern political sense remained for many *la femme publique* in the sexist vernacular sense.

"MARRIED TO A BUILDING FOR THE REST OF MY LIFE"[22]

The slogan "A woman's place is in the home," believed to have been coined in the United States in the mid-nineteenth century, has, in fact, been regularly deployed ever since—any time a woman has suggested her place might be elsewhere, in the polling booths or the workplace, for example, as the antisuffragist cartoon of 1893, as shown in Figure 5.1, exemplifies. The cartoon shows a role-reversed world where women have abandoned their wifely duties to become monstrous viragos, while men, emasculated, overwhelmed, face a house in disarray. The social fabric is unraveled by the transgressive female crossing the material and symbolic boundary between domestic and public space and by women's abandonment of the prescriptive "natural" role as it had been so copiously spelled out by Rousseau. This cartoon is disturbing not only in its overt antifeminism but in the clearly limited imagination of its creator William Blomfield: he paints a world where the only possibility is a sexual division of labor, space, and culture, along the polarized lines sketched by Perrot and cited at the beginning of this chapter. Throughout much of the twentieth century, this sexual division of labor was to remain codified in law and even when the laws changed, custom, and thus culture, were frequently slow to follow. For example, women either lost their jobs on marrying or were legally required to obtain their husbands' permission to continue to work (such a law remained on the statute books until 1962 in France). Restrictive laws that were often framed as protecting women, such as restrictions on night work (codified internationally in International Labour Organization Convention No. 4 of 1919), were mainly there to protect the husband's rights to domestic service and to ensure that his children also received it. Such measures were deemed necessary because, contrary to much popular propaganda, women *were* overwhelmingly involved in the urban workforce in many parts of the West, quite early in the century, but predominantly in blue-collar work, where their lower rates of pay were attractive to employers but where shift work was also the norm. They far outnumbered white-collar women workers until after 1945 (although the patterns vary considerably from one country to another).[23] During the 1930s Depression, however, even working-class married women were blamed, as they typically have been during times of recession, for stealing men's jobs and neglecting their families: in 1931 married women working outside the home were labeled "undeserving parasites" by New York State Assemblyman Arthur Schwartz.[24]

Even the Second World War imagery of emancipated, Western, wage-earning women outside Fascist or occupied countries soon disappeared once the war had ended. Postwar culture was filled with increasingly globalized American imagery of the dutiful wife and mother who wanted nothing more than to stay at home with her new household appliances. Once again, women became very publicly private: the modernity of suffragists and wartime riveters gave way, in the so-called free world of the Cold War years, to a carefully choreographed domesticity that just a decade earlier had been associated with Fascism (including the promotion of Mothers' Day). The public recodification of women as safeguarders of home and family served a multiple ideological purpose in a time of postwar economic growth. First, it ensured that European-background families of the (sub)urban middle classes would turn their attention to reproducing themselves in societies that not only had been depleted of their male populations by war but were also starting to come under migratory and demographic pressure from the postcolonized world. Second, it created a vast new market among newly affluent but bored stay-at-home wives: consumerism became an emotional and intellectual diversion among the "daughters of educated men" who were given little else to think about. Third, it created moral pressure on women who had started to join the white-collar workforce to return home, at a time when returning servicemen were after jobs and careers. If they did work outside the home, it was up until they married or had children, and it was in public-sphere extensions of their domestic role (secretary or "Girl Friday," nurse, elementary school teacher). Finally, it provided a useful antidote to the sorts of subversive ideas that had had cartoonist Blomfield so worried in 1893, and that in the postwar years were associated to some extent with feminism but most particularly with Communism—and the unionized working class. Rosie the Riveter suddenly became Olga the Ugly (although in the Soviet bloc, women were also being redomesticated).[25]

The very public push to return women to private domesticity was considerably helped within popular culture, not only by advertising and the expanding film and, soon, television industry, but also by the rise of two other powerful tools of propaganda: women's magazines and the child psychology industry. Women's magazines targeting domesticated women had in fact existed from the mid-nineteenth century: *Good Housekeeping* started publication in 1859; *Ladies Home Journal*, in 1883; and *McCalls*, formerly *The Queen*, in 1897. Along with the other four of the co-called seven sisters (*Better Homes and Gardens, Family Circle, Redbook,* and *Woman's Day*), all but *McCalls* continue today to sell millions of copies per issue. But it was in the years prior to, and especially following, the Second World War that these magazines became mass-culture instruments of fabricating modern femininity, targeting not only those already within the white middle-class but also those aspiring to it (which was practically everybody white and a good number of those who were not). Immaculately dressed, permed, made-up, and manicured housewives smilingly and effortlessly extracted spotless clothing from washing machines or family dinners and cakes from gleaming ovens, as the regulation husband, son, and daughter looked on, the whole taking place in houses that epitomized modern middle-class suburbia.

If the "seven sisters" focused on modernizing traditionalism, a new generation of magazines was to retraditionalize modernity. These magazines' appearance can be seen both as a response to the emergence of mass-produced ready-to-wear fashion from the 1920s and as part of the wider 1930s cultural fantasy factory associated with recovery from the Great Depression and distraction from the emergence of European extreme rights and movement toward another war. The French magazine *Marie Claire*, for example, started in 1937 as a sort of "poor woman's *Vogue*" with a print run of 800,000, and was, along with magazines like it, to train generations of women in appropriately gendered behavior, helping the French beauty industry along as it did so. These magazines were another example of the "My, how things have changed"/ *plus ça change* contradiction. They held out the promise of democratization and liberation for new generations of working-class and lower-middle-class women, yet kept them busy buying and donning clothing and makeup in order to catch a man, never delivering on the promise of real public participation. As Luisa Passerini puts it, recasting Frankfurt School style critiques of mass culture from a feminist perspective, there emerged a duality of cultural production which

> repeatedly feeds great hopes of change, only to provide answers in the end that correspond perfectly with respect for established order. This ambiguity results from historical conditions in which popular classes have gained access to public life; they become actors of this public life without at the same time being able to decide on how they will entertain themselves, think or imagine: the media have looked after it for them. These problems become more acute when it is women's history that is concerned.[26]

If fashion "adorned women in dreams," then women's magazines gave their readers the imagery and language of those dreams.[27] They colored in the banality of the day-to-day much as Metro-Goldwyn-Mayer Technicolor sepia-toned Kansas for Judy Garland's Dorothy as she stepped into the world of Oz.[28] With the postwar invention of a new cultural actor and consumer, the teenager, that fantasy began earlier and earlier, with yet another generation of magazines explicitly targeting this readership. The oldest of these, *Seventeen*, started in 1944 in the United States. But the fantasy, like the red shoes Dorothy inherited from the Wicked Witch of the East, always led back to the grey flatness of home in the end.

Alongside the popular-culture fairy floss of boyfriends and makeup and husbands and shining new Frigidaires, came another, more intellectual force for family conservatism, fueled by the development of psychology and psychoanalysis. One of the most influential names in this trend was of course Dr. Benjamin Spock, whose 1946 publication *The Common Sense Book of Baby and Child Care* was to become one of the world's all-time best sellers.[29]

Men became the experts on telling women how to mother and what little boys and little girls needed in order to grow up into appropriately gendered men and women. Even though Spock, who was a progressive in many other areas, revised his book some thirty years later, following protests from feminists, to make it less sexist, it had already left its legacy.[30] Generations of women not only received professional reinforcement for the cultural transfer of gender roles from one generation to the next but were given the added weight of responsibility, indeed, guilt, if their children were unhappy, perceived to be neglected, or otherwise "did not turn out all right." Another prejudice that was to be given "scientific" weight by much of the psychology profession was the idea of sex differences in ability: psychology was to pick up where the eighteenth-century discourse of "nature" and nineteenth-century positivism had left off.[31] Its impact endures to this day, as can be evidenced by the controversy over then Harvard president Lawrence Summers's remarks, in January 2005, that "innate differences between men and women" could account for the lower participation and success rate of women in science and mathematics careers.

The question, however, is necessarily begged: if such a lavishly public cultural arsenal was mobilized, in the middle decades of the twentieth century, to reprivatize women within the functions of pleasing men, marrying them, keeping their houses, and having and rearing their children, then men must have been very worried indeed that women may not, in fact, "naturally" gravitate toward such roles as the pinnacle of their life ambition.

NOT THE CHURCH, NOT THE STATE[32]

Some of the century's most heated political debates among men, whether progressive or conservative in party-political terms, concerned the regulation of women's sexuality and fertility. The more traditionally private the issue, the more ferociously public became the debate, perhaps nowhere more so than in the area of reproductive rights. On one level, reproductive rights were related to governmental obsessions with demographics that resulted at various times in the century in governmental financial incentives being offered to women to stay at home and procreate: so-called baby bonuses. The sums have, however, mostly been so derisory as to prompt one to wonder how, on their own, they would convince anyone to forgo a decent wage to stay home and have children. Whether women have children or not, and *which* women have children or not, was nonetheless a major preoccupation of governments throughout the century: birth control was opposed for white middle-class women but often encouraged for others, particularly in the United States; Depo-Provera and other forms of sterilization were used to target disabled, poor, black, and indigenous women and factory workers.[33] Yet, the main thrust of state opposition throughout the century to women's claiming of ownership of their own bodies in matters reproductive stemmed not from demographic concerns but religious ones. They fueled opposition in the 1910s and 1920s to contraception, championed by Margaret Sanger in the United States and Marie Stopes in the United Kingdom, and to campaigns for legal abortion from the late 1960s that continue to this day, including in the West (Ireland, for example, maintains strict restrictions to abortion).[34] They similarly fueled the Reagan administration's famous "global gag rule" of 1984 that barred any foreign organization receiving U.S. foreign assistance from performing abortions, advocating for its legalization or decriminalization, or providing information and referrals for abortion, even where it was legal.[35]

The campaign for abortion was characterized by spectacular public actions by both feminists and antiabortionists, often involving both violence (by antiabortion commandos) and arrests (of abortion campaigners and antiabortionists, including women, attacking or harassing women).[36] In France, two events were to become significant historical landmarks for the feminist movement. The first was the 1971 publication, in news magazine *Le Nouvel Observateur*, of the "Manifesto of the 343," also known as "The 343 tarts" (*les 343 salopes*), in which 343 women, including well-known intellectuals and politicians, attested to having had an abortion (some of them had not). The second, related event is the 1972 trial of a working-class single mother, Michèle C., for having helped her underage daughter, Marie-Claire, who had been raped, obtain an illegal abortion. Defense lawyer Gisèle Halimi, supported by Simone de Beauvoir, decided to make the case into a political trial and risked legal action against herself (and indeed disbarment) by publishing transcripts of proceedings, as did some journalists.[37] The trial became a public polemic not only about a woman's right to choose, legally framed as proprietorial rights over her own body (*libre disposition de son corps*), but also about the class barriers to women in France: women with more money were able to travel to England, among other places, to obtain abortions there. It also became about women's safety: Michèle C.'s daughter's backstreet abortion caused a hemorrhage, and many women suffered permanent physical (not to mention psychological) damage or died from such procedures. Successive abortion demonstrations at that time, in France as elsewhere, which brought tens of thousands of women into the streets, foregrounded these issues: the first one to take place in France, featured in Figure 5.2, was in Paris on November 20, 1971. The symbolic fire

FIGURE 5.2: Paris women demonstrate for abortion rights, November 20, 1971. Photographer Catherine Deudon.

lit in a coffin was to lament the harm done to "thousands of women every year [who are] victims of clandestine abortions in France."

The ferocity of continued opposition to abortion has demonstrated just how important control of women's sexuality and reproductive capacity remained to men, in both public and private spheres, even in the later and supposedly postfeminist years of the century. The abortion and contraception debates also highlighted the extent to which women of the twentieth century *embodied* modernity, claiming ownership of bodies that had for centuries been the property of fathers, husbands, sons, the church, the feudal lord, and/or the state.

"IT SIMPLY ISN'T DONE"

If women's rebellion in the name of reproductive choice was combated openly, other rebellions were easier to co-opt and channel, and nowhere more so than in the area of appearance. Modern urban women's style, and their newly public sexuality, became constructed by the fashion, culture, and advertising industries as something for men (and sometimes women) to desire and for women to aspire to. For these industries, women became not only a powerful yet co-optable mass of consumers with new liberties and new needs, but also newly available as hypersexualized commodities and accessories, selling everything from cars to cigarettes, from hosiery to holidays. The choices that women began to assert as "public women," seeking to turn their expressions of sexuality into an emancipatory value rather than a source of shame, had increasingly to be negotiated via a capitalist consumer machine and a normalizing culture that co-opted women's self-expression, once again, to suit the needs of the dominant classes of men.

I recall in the late 1970s an acquaintance commenting on the irony of those seeking to hold on to their individuality, their "difference," by doing something as superficial as changing their clothes. Yet throughout the century, women's negotiated expressions of modernity frequently took precisely that superficial route. At the same time, as we saw previously in the case of politicians, the extent to which such measures really *were* so superficial is debatable, for one is hard pressed to find any item of men's clothing that is so hotly debated by women as men have, throughout our modern era, debated the covering, uncovering, or re-covering, of women, and the manner in which that covering or uncovering is to be done—not to mention capitalized on. From the 1920s conceptualization of the thoroughly modern woman—the short-skirted flapper or the trousered garçonne—to 1960s miniskirts and bikinis, from the mythical bra burning of the 1970s[38] to the hijab debates of the following decades that continue to this day, women's appearance has been a barometer of the nation's modernity, moral fabric, economic growth, or simply its ability to control its women. Whether lauded as modernity or deplored as decadent immorality, whether praised as reflecting the proper values or condemned as markers of neoconservatism, how women look has been almost as important to the men of their modern societies as whether they work outside the home, practice contraception, or, indeed, vote.

In 1930 Australian lingerie company Berlei (registered on the Australian stock exchange from 1917 and transnationalized from 1923) released a cinema advertisement for one of its new "foundation" garments and in particular its new way of fitting individual female figures.[39] Clearly, the Depression was not going to stand in the way of underwear sales. The ad's title screen reads: "'It Isn't Done': Depicting the futility of careless dressing and the importance of correctly moulded figure lines beneath the New and Clinging gowns." It shows a scene of two women preparing for an evening out. The younger one, Barb—played, as it happens, by my aunt, Olive Lewis, who was a slender nineteen-year-old at the time—dressed in undergarments, despondently tells

Judith that her evening dress doesn't hang right. Judith replies that she needs "foundation," which is not a corset but "something much newer," and that it "simply isn't done" to go out without it. She then calls the Berlei specialist, who "scientifically" plots the young woman's measurements against the Berlei Type Indicator (which had apparently been produced with the aid of University of Sydney research); the garment arrives by courier shortly afterward.[40] Barb finds the garment "lovely," and of course, it makes her evening gown hang beautifully. She concludes: "I'll never forsake my Berlei: It Isn't Done!"

This ad is as fascinating for the high campery and bad acting of its delivery as it is for the message it communicates. In order to look publicly good in her evening gown, Barb must don complicated underwear that will remain hidden, thus private. Yet by virtue of being plastered across Australian cinemas, the garment and its wearer became very public indeed. The ad further communicates the message that to go out in public without the body-molding prosthesis under the dress "isn't done": it is inappropriate and somehow in bad taste. In any case, the garment is pretty and desirable and, as such, makes its wearer so as well. Finally, the ad gives a scientific veneer to the wearing by women of complicated and restrictive clothes: the Berlei foundation is both fashionable and at the cutting edge of modern science. This multilayered combination of science and sexuality in a public display of feminine privateness would be the tone of much undergarment and indeed personal hygiene and beauty advertising throughout the century. Never had women's intimate apparel and personal hygiene been so public; never had women's bodies been so regularly on public display outside pornography and prostitution. And, with surprising ease, their "emancipation" within modernity was constructed as obtainable only via the wearing of ridiculous clothes.

The most notorious example of co-optation of women's public entry into modernity was, however, through the promotion of self-harming behavior: the marketing campaign for Virginia Slims "cigarettes for women," begun in the 1960s, in which women were addressed as "baby" and told that they'd "come a long way."[41] Yet in some ways, the relatively innocent feminine modernity of the Berlei ad, the health-damaging "liberation" of the Virginia Slims campaign, and even the quasi-pornographic world of later lingerie ads were not so far apart. They all projected into the public domain an obsession with reconfiguring what men—and capital—wanted women to do as being "what women want."

The postscript of this episode is that my aunt, after her brief but relatively successful modeling career, married and "settled down" as they said then, becoming a dentist's wife and stay-at-home mother of three—anything else "simply wasn't done." At the time she married in the mid-1930s, she was slightly older than the median marriage age for Australian women and among roughly 55 percent of all women who were married, which was only slightly higher than the percentage of married women in 2001—although significantly lower than the baby boom high of 64 percent in the mid-1950s.[42] She had slightly above the famous 2.5 children per marriage that was already becoming the norm. So she was, in fact, statistically representative of only slightly more than half the population. Marriage "simply wasn't done" in the real world as much as the public imagery of women's redomestication within marriage would have had one believe.

One of the most public-private female garments of the century, however, and certainly among the most controversial, if not *the* most controversial, was—and still is—the modern version of the Islamic headscarf, or hijab (of which the original meaning is "curtain").[43] Hijab wearing or removal is directly connected not only with public harnessing of women's appearance and behavior to a national, religious, or ethnic project via the gendered assertion of values, but also to women's own assertion of identity, in terms of gender, class, ethnicity, religion—and indeed, modernity. For the hijab, even articulated as "traditional," is as thoroughly modern as the short skirts and bobbed hair of the Western 1920s or the Berlei girdle of the 1930s, whether we are speaking of the Muslim world or the West (although other, traditional forms of female head covering exist in both). Moreover, as surely as the public display of women in underwear (often used by pietist Muslims as an example of Western "decadence" with which the "modest" hijab is contrasted), it draws attention to women's sexuality, which is symbolized in monotheistic cultures by, among other things, their hair.[44]

For many women in the Muslim world, hijabization has meant upward mobility and an entry into the public sphere: it has enabled women to move into the respectable middle classes, get a job, or undertake study.[45] It has also become, for many, a status symbol: for pietist Western converts, overperformance of religious identity makes up for a lack of ethnic and cultural identity and personal history within that identity; for young Western nationals of non-Western origin, colorful hijabs combined with fashionable and often body-hugging clothing confer ethnic chic; or for young professionals of the modern urban centers of the Muslim world, the well-dressed hijabi is a symbol of both bourgeois aspiration and often, paradoxically, an entry into democratic modernity. One can see many of these last, for example, in Istanbul's hip Beyoglu district. Their long, flowing scarves, donned for an evening out on the town, replace the long, flowing hair of their Western equivalents, and combined with colorful clothes and glittering accessories, far from hiding their youthful female sexuality, display it. This is a peculiar paradox of the globalized, cosmopolitanized hijab: although necessarily and inextricably linked with current global debates on gender, Islam, and ethnicity, it had become by the end of the last century, just as inextricably linked with fashion and codification of women's overtly sexualized participation in the public sphere.

DROIT DE CITÉ: "FREEDOM OF THE CITY"

Discussions of the public/private divide, especially in relation to the West in the twentieth century, generally focus on urban middle classes. Rural women in most countries, for example, have worked, largely unwaged, in family-based and land-based businesses and subsistence economies; in some societies, they have even been the main worker in the family business. The public/private divide is not an irrelevant question for them, but public debates about women in the economy and the family, and women's appearance and sexuality, have largely not addressed their context.

Such debates are more likely to concern them, in the public political sphere at least, when it is a question of "traditional practices." Yet, even if it is demonstrably true that traditional acts of violence against women have been harder to combat within close-knit patriarchal communities that are relatively remote from urban centers, this is also true for both working-class and immigrant ghettos and elite enclaves in cities. The former were largely neglected by the state for most of the century as regards the provision of services, and male violence against women was essentialized as a working-class or "ethnic" phenomenon; whereas the latter, that is, the elite enclaves (at least outside the celebrity scandal circuit), had the means (and the patriarchal economic might) to keep their dirty linen far from public eyes.

In all cases, however, the feminist-led public breaking of silences did begin to have some knock-on effects that went from legislation to local initiatives to the use of cultural production, notably autobiography and cinema, to denounce male violence outside middle-class urban centers. For example, in 1987, the Australian feature film *Shame*, starring well-known actor Deborah-Lee Furness, denounced the silence and thus complicity of adults, including police, concerning rural cultures of male violence against teenage girls, in which the girls, predictably, carried the public burden of private shame.[46] Yet even here, it was the urban, liberated, motorbike-riding lawyer (played by Furness) who broke the silence. The film was largely ignored after its release, and when it did make it into a mainstream cinema, it was in urban centers and for a limited season. Another film, Anne Wheeler's Canadian film *Loyalties*, made the same year as *Shame*, also treats the public silencing of privatized violence against girls from an upper-class perspective. It tells the story of Lily, a wealthy upper-class woman whose husband's pedophilic rapes of girls have resulted in their exile from the United Kingdom to a remote rural area of Canada, where no one knows their history. Lily has remained loyal to her husband in keeping silent about the assaults, notwithstanding her obvious discomfort. In Canada, she develops a friendship with a local indigenous woman, Rosanne, whom she employs as her housekeeper. It is when Lily's husband tries to rape Rosanne's daughter that Lily must decide where her loyalties lie. Both films highlighted the continued domestication of violence, even after two decades of second-wave feminism, and the weight of silence carried by women and girls, whatever their class, ethnicity, or geographic location. They demonstrated that the private "sanctuary" of the home, even in the supposedly postfeminist late twentieth century, was rarely one for women.

Public space, however, has been equally ambiguous. In urban centers at the beginning of the twentieth century, the street was decidedly associated with *femmes publiques* in the common French sense of the term, as conveyed by the English expression *streetwalker*. It was a male province, and if a woman ventured into it unescorted by a man or a servant, she was either a servant herself (or some other working-class woman and thus by definition not "decent"), an eccentric bohemian oddity, or a prostitute. Rebecca West's celebrated 1913 comment could as easily have referred to her peregrinations as her sentiments: "I myself have never been able to find out what feminism is; I only know that people call me a feminist whenever I express sentiments that differentiate me from a doormat or a prostitute."[47]

As the century progressed and middle-class women began to participate in greater numbers in the workforce and other aspects of public life, they also claimed *droit de cité* in spatial terms, and without head covering. They claimed the street to go to work, shop, socialize, and vote, and they claimed it to express their anger about being refused it. Finally, they claimed the night, not as ladies of the night, not as "ladies" at all, but as women who wished to walk the streets free from men acting on the assumption that all women in public were prostitutable *femmes publiques*. Their response to governments and police who told them to stay at home when there was news of rapists or killers about became the demand that men stay home as they were the problem. In Britain, it was precisely such unhelpful police responses, and perceived police inaction, in the second half of the 1970s, concerning the murder of prostitutes by a serial rapist and killer who became known as the Yorkshire Ripper, that sparked the development of Reclaim the Night marches there.[48]

More generally, the street became, more and more throughout the twentieth century, a place to *demonstrate* one's commitment to a cause or support or opposition to actions of governments and other actors such as corporations, hence the name "demonstration." Feminists massively embraced this tactic, often creatively and theatrically (such as in chaining themselves to the railings of parliament). Feminist demonstrations were buoyant, performative, and creative; they played on strong symbolism. For example, on August 26, 1970, feminists placed a wreath at the tomb of the unknown soldier under Paris's Arc de Triomphe. With the wreath there was a placard: "There is someone more unknown than the unknown soldier: his wife." Figure 5.2, discussed previously, similarly shows the use of symbolism and street theater, as the women who died in backstreet abortions are symbolically "cremated."

Just as feminists were bringing stories of domesticated, privatized male violence against women out onto the streets, however, culture and advertising industries were transforming the hypersexualization of women and even celebration of violence against them into an art form, more or less in direct proportion to vocal feminist opposition to such violence and the increase in legal sanctions against it. "Liberation" became assimilated to generalized pornographic representations of women's sexuality and sexualization of violence against women in cultural and advertising industries, in a so-called postfeminist age, attracting new feminist critique, both of the practices and of women's embracing of them as "liberating."[49]

Women also interrogated inequities in allocations of public space, either physically or symbolically, what should or should not count as privileged or restricted semiprivate space in the public sphere, and who should decide. Men-only space in clubs and bars in some countries, for example, was challenged by women, and men presented counterchallenges to women's spaces such as women-only swimming baths or women-only feminist conferences or meeting spaces. In other areas, notably religious ones, traditional configurations of segregated space endured: privileged and larger for men and semiprivate and smaller for women, as in traditional synagogues or mosques, or in some evangelical groups; although in more progressive Christian and Jewish groups, women claimed equal space, including as pastors or rabbis. As public education became universally available to girls, co-ed schools maintained sex segregation in classrooms and in sport and recreational space, and many still do (although in France the opposite—*mixité*—was the norm). More generally, in public activities where women and men began to be assumed to participate equally, less space, both physical and symbolic, was often accorded to women: sporting activities being one obvious example in the West. Apart from debates throughout the twentieth century as to whether women should even play (some types of) sports, or whether women were as athletic as men, women's sports have continued to command less physical space, less media space, and less money. This resulted in some bizarre fund-raising activities with dubious partners, such as the controversial Virginia Slims funding of a women's tennis circuit, launched in 1970 after a campaign by well-known champion and out lesbian Billie Jean King (who also famously defeated tennis veteran Bobby Riggs in three straight sets in 1973, after Riggs boasted that no woman was a match for a man in tennis). An equally controversial fund-raiser was the nude calendar created by the Australian female soccer team the Matildas in 1999. (In a peculiar twist to the commodification of women's bodies to sell products, the tastefully and often rather coyly nude charity calendar became, at the end of the last century and turn of the current one, somewhat of a phenomenon, popularized in particular by the 2000 UK Women's Institute Calendar, subject of Nigel Cole's 2003 film *Calendar Girls*, which raised £2 million for leukemia patients.)

Another dimension of public and private space concerns its symbolic occupation by lesbians, who used public space to emerge symbolically from the closet of repression of their sexual identity, to literally *become visible*. In doing so, however, they also gravitated toward urban subcultures that have offered them some degree of protection, as they do to this day (this has also been true for some independent heterosexual women and gay men, although neither group has been as vulnerable as lesbians in public space). Early in the century in particular, they found *droit de cité* in bohemian literary and artistic circles in urban spaces, notably in Europe: Paris and Berlin being oft-cited examples. Paris in particular, in the early decades of the century, was home to what are now figures of lesbian legend, many of them expatriates from England or the United States: Gertrude Stein with her mannish looks and "wife," Alice B. Toklas; Renée Vivien, Natalie Barney, Djuna Barnes, and their affairs, salons, and public personae (purple is believed to have become "the lesbian colour" because it was Renée Vivien's favorite); Colette's famous liaison with the Marquise de Belboeuf, better known as Missy, and their performances of lesbianism on the stages of Montmartre's music halls; and dancer, choreographer, and theater lighting innovator, the *fée électricité* Loïe Fuller.[50] This bohemian *droit de cité* was also arguably the case for gay men, but men's presence in the streets at the time was already a given (even if certain effeminate forms of homosexuality were frowned on), so a distinct and visible lesbian presence was remarkable. Lesbians were to wait many decades before the streets of Paris and Berlin were to be as friendly to them again (even if, after the end of Fascism, they remained far more friendly than those of many Anglo cities or other parts of Europe). Yet, lesbian visibility and *droit de cité* have remained an issue into the twenty-first century. In Madrid in 2008, the theme of the national Gay Pride march was "lesbian visibility," which presupposes that such visibility remains a problem, whether in the gay movement or the broader community.

CONCLUSION: RECONFIGURINGS OF PUBLIC AND PRIVATE

Women's emergence into the public sphere and their challenging of public-private divides in the twentieth century not only transformed the public sphere but also created new interrogations of the idea of "privacy" and who has rights to it, when, and with whom, resulting in some of the most significant political debates and cultural transformations of the century. At the same time, private violence chased women into the public sphere, necessitating a new feminist vocabulary: *sexual harassment* was not a concept a century or even half a century ago and was not specifically named in legislation until the 1980s. Nor, for that matter, was *marital rape* or *domestic violence*. As women achieved criminalization of rape and domestic violence, however, new justifications emerged: the "she asked for it" defense being a perverse new configuration of the prostitutable *femme publique*, while the "nagging wife" became the private-sphere defense.

In negotiating their public/private existences, even the most publicly liberated women (on whomever's terms) were still constantly reminded of their "becoming woman" (to use yet another Beauvoirian concept). As Beauvoir herself wrote in 1949: "If I want to define myself, I first have to say: 'I am a woman'; all other assertions will arise from this basic truth. A man never begins by positing himself as an individual of a certain sex: that he is a man goes without saying."[51] At the beginning of this third millennium, women continue to be marked in their public representations by their allotted role in the private sphere: the modern twentieth century, for all its knowledge and progress, did not dismantle that dichotomy. If anything, it reinforced it: the price of women's colossal gains in formal rights and freedom of movement and action was a stronger cultural recoding of woman-ness on other levels. If changing the law regulating the public and private spheres has been a long and complicated process for women, changing the culture has proved to be even more so.

CHAPTER SIX

Education and Work

DEBORAH SIMONTON

The extent to which education, training, and the workplace became inextricably linked marked a significant cultural shift in modern women's experience. This had not been the case until primary education became increasingly compulsory from the late nineteenth century onward. Educational reform had roots in eighteenth-century Enlightenment debates, which received new impetus in the nineteenth century, growing in strength especially through middle-class women's claims for employment. The pressure for improved female education, and, especially, demands for access to higher education and to the same educational opportunities as males, formed central aims of the woman's movement. As higher education for young men progressed and formalized, and as social and economic demands came to place a value on such education, women too saw it as a positive good in itself, but explicitly as a route to other opportunities. While feminists argued for education to help young women, usually from the middle class, to get work, middle-class women argued that better education could help them contribute meaningfully to society. Increasingly, feminist demands had a vocational edge since professions and, ultimately, high-status white-collar jobs required higher education, while education became fundamental to claims for women's right to work and the battle for equal pay. Thus, the drive for education and training forged a direct link to employment.

Though women had always been important to Western economies through paid and unpaid work, by the modern era, two key changes affected cultural perceptions. First, employment became much more clearly perceived as paid work that could be counted. Seeing work as only activities taking place in formal workplaces with salaries and wages attached had the effect of devaluing the invisible or unwaged work in which women were concentrated. Second, important changes in the occupational structure had specific implications for women as many traditional jobs disappeared and new areas of work emerged in assembly and white-collar work. This chapter concentrates on the European experience, which reflected a relative cultural homogeneity of shifts in the educational and working worlds of women. It refers to other parts of the Western world where this experience often recurred, especially the United States, which increasingly influenced European ideas. The text attempts to draw a holistic picture of the issues of educational and employment experiences for women in the twentieth century, and thus the examples illustrate a broadly coherent picture. While cultural variance had a role to play, it cannot be fully explored here.

ACCESS TO SCHOOLING

From the end of the nineteenth century, a much clearer idea of girlhood emerged, combined with an important shift in the balance between work, education, and leisure. Going to work in the early teens had long marked an interim stage for girls, concluded by marriage. During the twentieth century, formal schooling shaped girlhood much more explicitly as it became compulsory; leaving ages rose, and more girls stayed on voluntarily. The speed of change depended on a number of factors including compulsory and postprimary education, rising standards of living, smaller family sizes, and changing expectations of adulthood.

By the beginning of the twentieth century, the perception of schooling as a public good meant that European nation-states had intervened to create state systems. Though Prussia made primary education compulsory for girls in 1812 and Denmark did in 1814, most Western countries did so from the mid-nineteenth century onward. By 1900, Europe, Australia, New Zealand, and most of the United States required primary school attendance, though the American South lagged behind until 1918. The biggest changes in access and opportunity came after the Second World War, and particularly in the 1960s. Virtually all North American and European girls attended primary school by the end of the twentieth century, and almost all stayed into secondary school. Girls' enrollments compared well with those of boys, and commonly they stayed on average longer than boys did. Secondary education became more available and free, while the democratic imperative, that educational opportunity was fundamental to the process of active citizenship, helped reduce disparities.

The growth of state education had important implications for girls because most countries took the view that education should be available, indeed required, for both boys and girls. In this way, education contributed to raising aspirations. Employment legislation had gradually restricted young people's workday and, by the interwar years, underpinned the common belief that paid work should not interfere with schooling. However, fighting for secondary academic education was sometimes necessary. In 1900, Karen Danielsen (Horney), a fifteen-year-old German girl, was delighted when after two years of resistance her authoritarian father relented and allowed her to attend the new girls' *Gymnasium* in Hamburg. But the whole family had to join forces to persuade him:

> Three of Mother's friends came one after the other yesterday, to work on Mother to send me to the Gymnasium. Mother spoke with Father afterward....Berndt [her brother] heard a lecture on "the woman question" by a Gentleman who greatly praised the Gymnasium for girls. Berndt had to tell Father the whole lecture. When he goes to Tante Clara she will work on him too....I believe more and more that I "must" get there.[1]

Karen's story was replicated in the thousands, as middle-class girls like Vera Brittain and working-class girls like Rose Naylor Gamble fought for the right to get a secondary education and progress to higher education. While Brittain's family could afford fees, Gamble managed only because her older sisters went to work and she gained a grammar school scholarship.[2] Most girls in the 1920s saw the leaving age (between eleven and thirteen years old) as the end of their girlhood, especially working-class girls for whom the next step was work. As one German girl reflected nostalgically, "The time came and I had to leave school, and I had to part from those I liked. Although it was very hard for me, I had to go, as the years of school were over."[3] However, after 1945, the legal leaving age lost its position as a marker of the onset of youth, as more stayed in school or chose further and higher education. In fact, adults returning to the classroom meant that far more than girls and boys attended school, including continuing and higher education.

CLASS AND ETHNICITY

This picture of progress, however, covered serious disparities of class and race, operating in attendance, completion rates, and progression. In the United States, racially segregated education affected girls at least as much as it did boys, while policies of selection and costs of continued schooling operated against working-class girls in Britain. Contemporaries are still battling for the rights of Native American women to education, while religious and ethnic differences affect girls across Europe. Cultural distinctions, like Islamic traditions, which kept women at home, contributed to restricting their continuation of schooling. Yet, Arab feminists saw education as the first step in gaining a semblance of equality during nationalist struggles against colonial powers. Frequently, like militant Egyptian Doria Shafik, they were well educated themselves. Rebuffed by the University of Cairo, Sorbonne-educated Shafik founded *Bint al-Nil* (Daughter of the Nile) in 1945, the first women's magazine in Arabic and targeting women's education. Language difficulties prevented many women in European immigrant communities full engagement with educational systems. Only later in the twentieth century, from the 1980s especially, have countries addressed these issues to strive for a comprehensive inclusion of girls and women in education. Political factors also came into play. While many of the earliest secondary and higher education students were Jewish, these women were explicitly excluded by many regimes. Russian pogroms, Nazi purges, and Fascist exclusions typified this overt racism before the First and Second World Wars. In contemporary France, controversy surrounded the social exclusion of impoverished immigrants, which created a two-tiered schooling that embedded ethnic difference into society. This left more than half of migrant women without qualifications, which led to their persistent high levels of unemployment or employment in the most menial jobs.[4] Sex and race have been entangled in the battles for girls' education in the United States. Officials at the National Women's Law Center, an advocacy group in Washington, D.C., argued that integration of education "is especially beneficial for female students, who suffer from negative stereotypes about their abilities in such male-dominated fields as math and science." Jennifer Brown, of Legal Momentum, a women's rights advocacy group in New York, further claimed, "Integrated schools also offer students of all races and genders a higher quality education than racially isolated schools. That is key for women and girls, especially those of color, because they are more likely than their male peers to grow up to be poor. Integrated education, in other words, helps lift them out of poverty."[5]

To some extent, differences between educational opportunities for working-class girls reflected the difficulties of families parting with daughters' labor, particularly when they perceived girls' main aim was to marry and help support households, not to develop careers. In 1945, John Newsom's report, *The Education of Girls*, explicitly expressed the prevailing view: "for the vast majority of women, the business of homemaking and early nurture of children is a dominant theme in their lives, while for men the equivalent...is to earn enough to support their wives and families."[6] Furthermore, working-class girls' families frequently did not have a tradition and therefore knowledge of how the systems worked, or what benefits might accrue. This was pronounced in the case of rural girls and their families. For example, in France in 1962, only 16 percent of farmers' and workers' children continued to upper secondary schools, while 75 percent of higher civil servants' children did.[7] Even though attendance requirements applied to girls, racial, social, and familial factors meant they were more likely to be absent from school. Education was not yet uniformly free, often placing burdens on families who had to decide which children to send. So even with rising legal leaving ages, working-class, especially rural, girls could be kept at home to help out, and truant officers were less likely to challenge this behavior.

Sociological interest in the working classes began to raise questions about social class differences in progression and achievement in the 1960s and 1970s. French and British working-class children experienced a sense of dislocation and isolation when they moved on to grammar schools or *lycées*, demonstrating that a range of hidden exclusions operated, including financial costs, but also difficulties of dealing with social and cultural differences. These girls also often felt uncomfortable with their families and disoriented when associating with their own peer group who did not attend. Susan Foley argued that the disorientation of rural girls partly explained why girls spearheaded the exodus to town from the 1960s.[8] Gradually, however, governments began to address class issues, largely in the 1980s, and generated targets to improve participation in order to address skill shortages in the workplace. Secondary schooling increasingly became free, and countries often provided financial support to poorer families to help offset costs. Though not aimed at girls, these measures had a spin-off effect. Legislation was nominally sex blind, and progression from elementary through secondary education came to be seen as normal. Thus, educational opportunity improved, even if some families, and authorities, retained a lax view of whether to force girls to attend, or whether they were expected to study after the school-leaving age.

GENDER AND THE CURRICULUM

The curriculum was not sex blind. Until the 1970s, Europeans were certain that girls and boys should study different subjects for different ends. Education for homemaking and motherhood took on new resonance at the turn of the twentieth century in the midst of concerns about population decline and eugenic

fears that the working classes and ethnic "others" would overwhelm and undermine the white middle-class consensus. The French government chastised
primary school *inspectrices* for not sufficiently emphasizing domestic values
and skills for the nation's wives and mothers.[9] This insistence on domestic
studies also reflected tension with middle-class demands for women's rights
and academic education, so that domestic values acted as a fight back for traditional norms. During the interwar years, it gained particular resonance as
Nazi Germany, Fascist Italy, and Franco's Spain—followed during the war by
Vichy France—reemphasized women's role as homemakers in nation building.
The Italian School Charter of 1939 explained: "The destination and social mission of women, being distinct in fascist life, have at their foundation different
and special institutions of instruction." Similarly, Dr. August Reeber-Gruber,
Consultant on Girls' Education, stated, "The task of our schooling... is simple:
the moulding of German girls as carriers of the National Socialist point of
view."[10] In France, home economics became compulsory in 1942, although the
dictum was problematic because insufficient teachers could teach the subject.
At the same time, Vichy banned competitive sports in favor of gymnastics and
swimming to produce flexible, balanced bodies for childbearing.[11] Not only
authoritarian regimes focused girls' education on domestic studies. The English Board of Education explicitly encouraged domestic science courses to

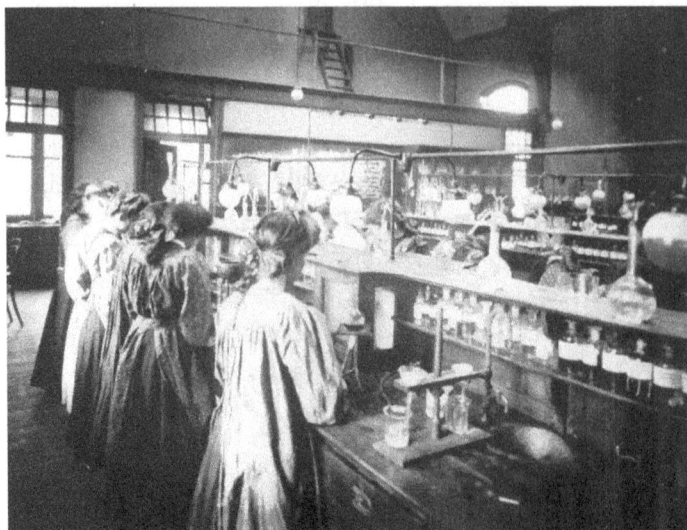

FIGURE 6.1: Girls in the chemistry lab, Manchester Girls High School,
1905.

provide housekeeping skills for girls, and many schools used Mabel Liddiard's *The Mothercraft Manual*, running to twelve editions between 1923 and 1956.

Domestic training retained its central role after the Second World War. It echoed many women's wishes to "put things back to rights" as one woman wrote to *Constanze*, a German women's magazine.[12] Promotion of domestic studies also reflected governmental priorities to foster stable nations and a traditional gender order ensuring full male employment. Employment was at the forefront of debates, since female wartime service had given women a wider sense of their potential. However, many, like Newsom, argued that a grammar school curriculum for a privileged few failed to meet the needs of most women whose primary role was as homemaker. Therefore, his influential report advised limited vocational training as preparation for shop assistants, clerical workers, and mothers by providing nutrition, housekeeping, basic accounts, sewing, and hygiene. State education limited the academic subjects available to girls. The Soviet Union was an exception, as its push for literacy also promoted girls' education and curricular options that could lead to university. Elsewhere, girls' schooling focused on "the three R's." Given the kinds of work largely available, such education contained a kernel of realism, but it also spoke to a gender difference in educational values and opportunities. It sent the message that personal and social betterment were not female goals. However, middle-class girls and their supporters challenged this central notion. Young people at Combelles in Normandy complained, "Girls don't have access to professional training and employment with the same opportunity as boys... because people have retained the old idea of 'the woman at home.'"[13]

During the first half-century, some girls gained access to academic education through private schooling, but state systems lagged behind, saturated by a belief in female intellectual inferiority. Serious education was seen as masculinizing, fostering unfeminine characteristics like competitive spirit. Some changes were implemented after the First World War when the loss of men and demands of national economies meant females needed to be trained to fill the gap. Many families also saw their savings eroded with inflation, meaning daughters with no dowries had to go to work. In France, for example, the *baccalauréat* was finally introduced into state schools after 1924, providing a normal route to careers. Germany, however, managed girls' secondary schooling with primary education, keeping the curriculum different from and inferior to boys' secondary education. In Scotland, authorities set lower targets for girls in mathematics and reading. Thus, there had been little real change.

A significant curricular shift came after the Second World War, due to a combination of social, economic, and political imperatives. The war had fostered a wider acceptance of liberal values and a sense of entitlement. The needs of national economies, which by the 1960s reached full employment, meant that women's labor was needed. The Soviet launch of Sputnik in 1957 acted as a wake-up call to western Europe and America, which had hitherto taken their technical and economic superiority for granted. By the 1950s, girls were better educated than their mothers because of increased access, they stayed at school longer because families had less need of their labor, and they had more personal freedom. Their aspirations had changed, and, though not rejecting marriage and motherhood, they envisioned rewarding work and careers. Parents also challenged the emphasis on practical subjects, as needlecrafts no longer offered a route to work with the decline in textile industries, and because they felt that crafts took time away from academic subjects so that girls risked failing by comparison with boys. By the 1960s, the cumulative effect of postwar changes and a shifting attitude that girls should strive for their full potential began to address the lack of confidence that pervaded girls' attitudes toward education. Nevertheless, many girls continued to be influenced by assumptions that they were intellectually inferior to boys and had different interests and abilities. They benefited from the new educational climate but faced gender distinctions in qualifying routes. French girls, for example, remained a serious minority of trainees in technical schools. A shortage of mathematics, physics, and chemistry teachers was coupled with many girls choosing arts and languages. Indeed, in 1959, twice as many British boys as girls took exams in mathematics, with a similar difference in physics and chemistry, while more girls took geography and history.[14] Class differences were noticeable despite shifting attitudes toward middle-class girls' education. The English Secondary Modern School with its vocational emphasis continued to provide integrated domestic science courses and to promote typing as appropriate for girls. There was circularity to the gendered curriculum in that only more girls taking the subjects to exam level could address the shortage of science and mathematics teachers—but there were not enough teachers to prepare them. Girls also needed to visualize realistic career options to warrant further study.

Real change came from the 1970s, what in Germany was called the *Fraüleinwunder* (girl miracle), a virtual revolution in female educational opportunities.[15] Evidence from across Europe showed girls caught up with and overtook boys in both participation and grades. Most significant was a dramatic shift in awareness and attitudes toward girls' education. The feminist movement of the 1970s pointedly argued that gender bias throughout the system had undermined girls' potential. Women criticized stereotyped images and language in textbooks. They pointed out that men's achievements were applauded while, in

Sheila Rowbotham's phrase, women were hidden from history.[16] Importantly they challenged the assumptions that girls should do domestic science and that they were better at arts and soft sciences, like biology.

Co-education changed the shape of girls' education after the war. Seen as the way to instill democratic principles in the minds of future voters, practicalities often required both sexes to share one school. Co-education was not new, since Stockholm *samskolen* introduced it in 1876, and the Dutch did at *Hogere Burgerschool* (citizen's high schools) in 1899. By 1919, more than a fifth of English secondary schools were co-educational, and by 1925, 92 percent of Dutch secondary school girls learned at co-educational schools. Many viewed co-education as a positive way to change the relationship between the sexes and recognize girls' potential. Ironically, however, feminist criticism, notably in Germany and Britain, claimed that it did not necessarily lead to equality. They argued that separate education enabled girls to establish their identities as young women and find success at school instead of competition and teasing from boys. Dale Spender's study of English secondary schooling showed that boys dominated discussions and more successfully commanded teachers' attention. Girls were more likely to ask questions of classmates because they were reluctant to express their viewpoints in front of boys. Such studies suggested that co-education further embedded gender roles and fostered gender inequality.[17] In contrast, in the United States, Title IX, of the Education Amendment Act of 1972 acted as an important counter to sex-segregated resources. It stated: "No person in the United States shall, on the basis of sex, be excluded from participation in, be denied the benefits of, or be subjected to discrimination under any education program or activity receiving Federal financial assistance." The act led feminists to fight explicitly against single-sex schools to gain and preserve equal opportunities for females at all levels of education.

After 1980, curricular change in girls' education was indeed a *Fraüleinwunder*. Curricular bias was eroded so that girls not only got better grades than boys but also did so in the sciences. Positive initiatives to encourage girls in science bore fruit. In Britain, the National Curriculum, for example, required students to participate in all three sciences and technology. In England and Ireland, boys were introduced to needlework, and girls gained greater access to competitive sports, including the male preserve of football. The picture and timeline was uneven across Europe as national differences inflected the emphases and initiatives, and some persistent cultural and religious traditions operated to produce a kaleidoscope of education structures and opportunities. For example, until recently, Irish boys' and girls' exam scripts were a different color. Yet, significantly, over time, the climate of opinion changed, males became more accepting of the changes, the educational environment became less gender biased, and girls became more confident and motivated.

HIGHER EDUCATION

The battle for higher education specifically had to counter perceptions of gender, usually laced with the physiological limits of females. At the turn of the twentieth century, some experts still claimed that excessive study brought on hysteria; others feared it would weaken women's maternal desires and become a first step in a dangerous reversal of sex roles. Families frequently had to be persuaded that it was relevant for daughters. French philosopher Simone de Beauvoir remembered:

> In my family milieu, it was considered peculiar for a young girl to pursue higher education; getting work implied social decline. Obviously my father was a vigorous antifeminist...he considered that a woman's place was in the home and in salons.[18]

Her family, however, was one of those whose financial resources had suffered during the First World War.

During the century, a combination of less elitism in universities, better secondary preparation, and greater social acceptance that girls could and often should continue to higher education reshaped their opportunities. Alongside expansion of secondary education, women gained access to teacher training during the nineteenth century, and most admitted women at the outset since teaching and caring for the young were seen as a natural female arena. Women gained access to universities from the mid-nineteenth century. Zürich was the first European university to open its doors to women, from 1865, and many aspiring women emigrated to study there. In 1870, Finland admitted women, and between 1870 and 1900, most European universities admitted women, though resistance to women's higher education remained, shaped by national cultural values. For example, French women struggled to gain access to prestigious and professional training at the *Grandes Écoles* because girls could not attend the preparatory courses, unofficial quotas operated, and teachers directed the best girls to "suitable" work in teaching. At Oxford, women received degrees only after the First World War in 1920, and at Cambridge after the Second World War, in 1946, virtually the last major university to do so. In Germany, as Patricia Mazón argued, the process also included a simultaneous decision about what kind of women to admit. Admission depended on the acquisition of the *Arbitur*, which remained rare for women and excluded foreign, especially Russian Jewish, women but not foreign men. Thus, formal admission of women reaffirmed a hierarchy based on sex, so that the first female students were less international and more elite than their male counterparts.[19]

Before the First World War, women comprised only 7 percent of the student body in Germany and France and 16 percent in Britain. Nevertheless, across the Western world, numbers of women at various colleges and institutions increased, and the 1920s flapper was likely to be better educated than her mother and more inclined to recognize new opportunities, like the new white-bloused work, discussed subsequently. After the Second World War, governments realized the wastage of potential as they reassessed priorities. Britain and Nordic countries, for example, recognized that existing systems excluded the best and the brightest because of growth in numbers of young people. The British Robbins Report of 1963 marked a cultural shift with the creation of grants and expansion of the university system. Where there had been twelve universities before 1945, by 1965 there were forty-nine, spread across the country. In Denmark, a similar democratization took place, increasing from two universities to eight between 1960 and 1985. Nordic women moved from constituting a third of university students in 1969, after reforms, to almost half in 1983, overtaking men by 1999. European women more than kept up in higher education enrollment and graduation rates; from virtual parity in 1991 at around 30 percent of the age group, they vastly overshadowed males in their increasing uptake and graduation from higher education. Nevertheless, gender differences between enrollments by academic discipline reflected the same debates as in secondary education, with obvious impact on employment opportunities. Yet, in the first decade of the twenty-first century, these disparities narrowed. Women comprised around half of science graduates, although still only 20 to 30 percent of engineers were female, while 75 to 80 percent of education and health care graduates were.[20]

THE WORKPLACE

As the previous discussion showed, education and employment were integrally related, especially in the twentieth century when education became more essential for the kinds of work available. Women's work altered in two ways: an increase in the number and proportion of women working, and a shift away from domestic service and industry to the tertiary sector, like shops and clerical work. These two generalizations disguise contradictory trends. Women's employment did not increase evenly everywhere, while shifts in the kinds and

locations of women's work were inconsistent, often hiding important conti-
nuities. The economic infrastructure of where women lived and their social
position frequently determined their experience of work as did their position
in the life cycle. The simple fact that work was increasingly defined as taking
place in specified workplaces and paid in specific ways underrecorded women's
laboring activities.

Instead of numbers, the shifting structure of work was the most important change in women's experience. A dramatic decline of domestic service
was exacerbated by the First World War, which provided an escape for many
disenchanted young women. Key areas of traditional female work in manufacturing, like textiles and homework, declined while light industries generated
employment in processing and assembling, like in electronics. Paid work for
women in the countryside also diminished, so the workforce increasingly consisted of unpaid family members, usually rural wives. The diminution of rural
opportunities and the decline in domestic service paralleled the rise of clerical
and retail employment so that the locations and shape of the workplace were
significantly different, with a wide range of apparently new opportunities in
teaching, office work, professions, and caring.

The work life cycle changed in three important ways. First, labor and educational legislation removed the youngest girls from the workforce. Second,
more single adult women workers chose to work as middle-class females came
to see work as appropriate, while the gap left by young girls created opportunities. Therefore, single women remained a major part of the workforce.
Third, married women had a greater tendency to stay in work or to return once
their children had grown. Married women often had worked at home, but in
the twentieth century, they were increasingly less likely to quit work on marriage itself—leaving the workplace was more common when children arrived.
Married women's input rose to unparalleled levels after 1945. The pool of
single women had shrunk because of earlier marriage, a rising school-leaving
age, and longer periods in higher education, encouraging employers to target
married women and mothers. Smaller families meant that child care responsibilities finished earlier. The rising divorce rate, accelerating in the 1960s, also
pushed more mothers into the labor market. In 1961, 20.5 percent of Belgian
married women worked, but 48.6 percent of divorced women did, matching
the participation rate of single women, 49.2 percent.[21] The creation of formalized part-time work from the 1960s also promoted increased employment of
married women. While reducing labor costs for employers, it benefited women
who needed flexibility. The disadvantage was that it was insecure, unrecognized as real work by officialdom, including pension schemes, and usually

poorly paid, though European directives are gradually altering this. Job-share was one solution, because "real" jobs were shared.

There is little doubt that the two world wars brought more women into the workforce temporarily through substitution or conscription. However, women did not drop other jobs and flood to the ranks. Their usual employment was hard hit. Many domestic servants chose war work, but others lost jobs, as the fall in demand for luxuries hit millinery and dressmaking. Some countries conscripted women, and female nurses, doctors, and other civilian workers "did their bit." The United States sent telephone operators, or "Hello Girls," to run military phone banks. A legacy of the First World War was the introduction of new working practices, especially assembly-line systems, particularly Taylorism or the Bedaud system, where a job was subdivided into individual operations that could be easily taught and performed. Often seen

FIGURE 6.2: Dora Miles and Dorothy Johnson, Douglas Aircraft Company, ca. 1940. Library of Congress, Prints & Photographs Division, FSA/OWI Collection (reproduction number, e.g., LC-USF34-9058-C).

as deskilling and undermining craftwork, these processes met with more resistance outside of wartime and were only applied to large-scale production, but employing women, virtual novices in engineering, created a precedent. Despite the backlash, longer term it was another tiny step in women becoming workers. Perhaps as important as the visibility of female war workers was the effect on women. Some went from their close-knit communities and rural milieu into a world of factories, joining women with different stories. A Scotswoman reflected on how this experience broadened their horizons, "Oh, we got up to all sorts!...and we came back knowing there was more out there than our little worlds." Women came to appreciate their own skills, gained confidence in their abilities, and acquired a sense of their right to work.

OLD WORK, NEW WORK

Farmwives assumed an increased share of tasks as hiring help became unprofitable, including men's traditional fieldwork and use of machinery. They also retained their usual work in the house and barnyard. They were "hidden" labor, least likely to be recorded, yet they were so central to farming that in Weimar, Germany, wives worked an average of 12 percent more hours annually than their husbands and 40 percent more than hired help.[22] While custom prohibited men from meddling in women's domains, women assisted in male terrains regularly. Peasant-worker strategies kept small farms viable, as men migrated either long term or seasonally to bring in much-needed income. Women became responsible for farms, as in Couto, Portugal, in 1979, where they comprised 74.2 percent of self-employed farmers.[23] In 1939 and 1949, Norwegian women worked on farms, while husbands often were fishermen or factory employees.[24] German and Basque men worked early mornings and late evenings on farms, commuting to jobs daily. Thus, a major postwar trend was the feminization of agriculture, more pronounced on part-time farms where women took over work previously performed by men. In some communities, women also took nonfarm work, and Danish, Norwegian, and Dutch women increasingly sought paid jobs. Danish women working off-farm increased from 6 percent to 26 percent between 1960 and 1975.[25] However, mechanization and increased reliance on migrant labor in North America meant that many African American families permanently left fields for factories.

Some farmwomen became countrywomen. They took on tasks removed from direct production, like bookkeeping, and managed household consumption: shopping, freezing, and storing became paramount activities. They ran *pensions*, or bed-and-breakfasts; set up country shops or teashops; or made and marketed rural crafts. They became mediators between the community and visitors, referring them to shops, events, and beaches, and filled the social welfare gap created by a relative lack of rural social services. Mutual support meant stepping in during crises, helping when a woman was ill, lending items for parties, or picking up shopping. This was important work for women and important for their communities.

Homework and sweatshops was largely urban work, attracting working-class and immigrant women in Europe and North America, often in localities where there were few other options. Public sensibilities were shocked by the New York Triangle Shirtwaist Company fire in 1911, where 146 immigrant women, mostly Jewish, died. But the need for income provided a ready workforce. In Europe, fashion changes forced a decline in home-based trades as garment making plummeted. In Glasgow, numbers dropped by 27.5 percent between 1901 and 1911.[26] However, women also left of their own volition, especially when clerical and shop work provided an alternative. Ultimately, the sector shrank but did not disappear. Immigrants formed a substantial part of this workforce, concentrated in the New York and London East End garment trades. In the latter part of the twentieth century, it became even more closely

FIGURE 6.3: Group of women in a New York sweatshop, 1908.

associated with ethnic minority and immigrant women. Frequently, sweated work was the only resort of women migrating to the West, seeking a place in the land of opportunity but ending up exploited by "sweaters" and human traffickers. The legacy of a European postcolonial world was that large numbers of women chose to work at home to avoid cultural and language differences, as well as discriminatory practices, and to meet the sheer need that many in these communities faced.

Manufacturing work shifted to new processes and light industries, in chemicals, electronics, food processing, pharmaceuticals, optics, and precision engineering. From the outset, these relied heavily on a female workforce, but men took the lion's share of new jobs, and openings were not rapid enough to replace traditional jobs. Yet, women appeared in increasing numbers across manufacturing, were no longer marginalized into female industries, and were less at risk from economic fluctuations and decline in single industries. Magneti Marelli engineering company in 1930s Milan, Perry Willson explains,

> was one of the first examples of a "modern industrial workforce" in Italy, fairly stable and employed in a highly mechanized and "scientifically organized" factory … but the two factors which are most important to explain this pattern were management strategy and the large numbers of women in the labour force.[27]

Management had a stake in tapping green labor, a workforce with little industrial heritage that was more likely to accept new processes and conditions

FIGURE 6.4: Södertøalje, Sweden, tobacco workers. Courtesy Göteborgs Universitetsbibliotek.

of employment. The belief that women were calmer and steadier made them an attractive labor force. Mechanized jobs required less strength and skill and therefore commanded a lower wage, so women remained cheap labor.

The preeminent nineteenth-century female job, domestic service, was seen as personally degrading and constrained by comparison with new opportunities. As long as service paid significantly better, the restrictions and inconveniences mattered less, but by 1914, other jobs paid more and offered more freedom. Political changes, pressures for female emancipation, and working-class movements contributed to a more independent spirit among servants. For most, an increase in personal freedom, daily contact with other young women, and greater opportunities to meet men were influential. More education also kept girls from service and gave them better skills and knowledge to improve their prospects. When young women had options, they left service, not always choosing better paid or higher-status work. The First World War sealed its fate. One munitions worker at the London City Exchange said, "I feel so pleased that the war's over that I'll take any old job that comes along," but when offered domestic service, she laughed it off with, "Except that!"[28]

Servants had long been migrants, from countrywomen traveling into local towns to long-range migrants from Brittany, Scotland, and Ireland. Ethnicity was also an issue. In the United States, Norwegian, Irish, and Slovakian women comprised large portions of the servant class, as did African Americans in both the North and South. The postwar world revised domestic service, frequently relying on ethnic minority immigrants to supply domestic services. Employers were often female workers themselves, who because of education and opportunity, could afford to hire migrant workers for their housework. In France, more than 50 percent of migrant women were domestic servants, usually non–European Union nationals. In addition, large numbers of unregistered women worked as servants, and many of these were under sixteen years of age.[29]

The twentieth century saw the creation of white-bloused work. Women had a long heritage in family firms, shops, and quasi-professions, and improved education enabled them to take on tasks requiring literacy and understanding. Many wanted "something better" than manual work, while the new middle-class workers were a vociferous and significant group. Much work was new, especially selling at counters, typing, and telephony, and many occupations were classed as female from the start. The first female office workers, factory inspectors, and professionals were drawn from middle-class women with good education, usually better than the men they worked with. The first sales assistants were modestly educated from lower-middle-class and working-class families. In white-collar work, gender shaped policies of hiring women and the kind of jobs available. Employing women meant employers could hire fewer men and offer them a career path, keeping women in lower paid jobs, since they assumed women would leave on marriage. A post office official in 1870 said that salaries that attracted only men of an "inferior" class were sufficient to attract ladies of a "superior" class.[30] White-bloused workers were involved in the transition of the workplace just as men, but they had fewer opportunities for higher-status work.

Retailing changed with the wider consumer economy and the emergence of chain and department stores. Instead of making up goods and building relationships with customers, assistants maintained stock, cashiered, sold, and displayed goods. However, new products and a greater range of merchandise required well-informed sales staff leading to in-house training. Clerical work expanded as offices demanded more records and correspondence. Initially, women joined smaller public sector offices and businesses associated with females, while banks, insurance companies, shipping firms, and big merchant houses hired them only for a narrow range of tasks. German banks entrusted fewer than half their female employees with banking, and the Prudential gave women documents for new working-class insurance to copy.[31] Yet, it was not certain that this would become a revolution. Anna Polak, director of the Dutch National Bureau for Women's Labour, wrote tentatively in 1902 that office jobs were "still new for women…[whether they would] open a desirable future, both financially and morally remained uncertain."[32] Often employed experimentally, as women demonstrated their aptitude, they gained other clerical and administrative jobs. After the First World War, civil services became the largest-scale employers of female clerks, first in telegraphy and telephony. The war gave women promotion opportunities, previously blocked by separate grading structures; some who had left on marriage returned. Afterward, many kept their jobs, and openings multiplied with the return of full male employment and continued expansion. After the Second World War, the number of white-bloused workers rose rapidly, surpassing men, a feature encouraged by the growth of welfare states, while far more married women stayed or returned to work as marriage bars fell. Unquestionably, female clerical workers became more visible. For example, in 1899, only 1.6 percent of Dutch clerks were female; by 1947, 38.8 percent were.[33] The public saw a new modern woman, ubiquitous in cities, depicted in films, and who became the symbol of young, working females in the interwar period.

Women proactively claimed white-bloused work, perceiving it as opportunity and independence. There were far more applicants than jobs. As new work, it avoided competition with men and promised respectable prospects for middle-class women. Strict discipline and sexually segregated employment were positive features, and they took considerable pride in their work. Jo Brouwer, a Dutch typist, exclaimed, "I was as happy as Larry... From that day, a new life had started, so very varied, so very satisfactory and at times so desperately busy, as few girls have ever lived."[34] Weimar shop assistants regarded themselves as "a cut above" factory workers who "did not know how to behave," while clerks and secretaries regarded themselves as above shop assistants because their work was more worthwhile and better remunerated.[35] Women's entry was contested, yet it is important that they perceived clerking as a positive option, that they were not "introduced," but that many female voices claimed it at a time when the workplace was undergoing radical redefinition.

Entering professions was far more contested, as men's desire to preserve exclusivity created structural and cultural barriers that limited access and promotion for women. The demand for paid work for middle-class women coupled with feminism and better access to education provided the impetus and means for women to become professionals. But gendered prejudices and prohibitive practices operated to protect the liberal professions. Broadly speaking, two sorts of profession emerged: those that always had a large female component, like nursing, teaching, and social work; and those that remained male dominated and controlled, like law, medicine, pharmacy, and management. Suzanne Borel entered the French Diplomatic Service with great fanfare but was not allowed to undertake consular duties abroad: "Few women are better placed than I to appreciate the cunning, often combined with treachery and persistence, employed by men to place obstacles in the path of those unfortunate women who stray from the beaten track."[36] Professional bodies used regulations to block women even if they had requisite educational qualifications. As Dame Margaret Booth described, "In 1903 Gray's Inn, having admitted Bertha Cave to its Honourable Society, probably by mistake, they refused to call her to the Bar simply because she was a woman."[37] Such prohibitions were not unique to law, and women faced restrictions to qualify and practice as doctors and pharmacists. Even when women gained entrance through their inventiveness, and sometimes audacity, they faced widespread prejudices. In 1961, Jerrie M. Cobb, the first woman to qualify as an astronaut for the National Aeronautics and Space Administration, was told that women could take less stress than men. When Aileen Clarke Hernandez was appointed to the U.S. Equal Opportunities Commission, created to police discrimination on the basis of race, color, religion, sex, or national origin, she was continually frustrated by the assumption that civil rights applied to men. The commission even booked a meeting in a private male club. She felt confronted by a "sea of male faces and derision about sex discrimination."[38] Thus, perceptions of what it meant to be female were joined with exclusivity of male professions to restrict not only women's entry but also their movement within them.

Teaching demonstrated the resilience of these gendered notions. Despite equal pay and grading, vertical segregation persisted. Across Europe in 2000, women made up between a half and two-thirds of all teaching professionals, but they dominated primary teaching, comprising between 80 and 90 percent of teachers. They made up about a third of secondary teachers and higher education lecturers. In 1980, they comprised more than half of Danish teachers at *folkeskoler* (schools for seven- to sixteen-year-olds), but only 4 percent of school principals. Higher education was more resistant. In 1934, only five French university professors were female. In the late 1960s, females comprised only 9 percent of full-time academic staff in British universities, and by 1992–93, they comprised only 22 percent, concentrated in lower grades, comprising only 5 percent of professors and 11 percent of readers and senior lecturers.[39] However, by the turn of the twenty-first century, women comprised 45.7 percent of tertiary educators. Clearly, the profession was more female, with implications for pay and status, and women had made gains, if not achieved parity, at the upper levels.

GENDERING WOMEN'S WORK

Work was contested on a number of levels. Although it was widely acknowledged that many women worked during their lifetimes, men identified themselves as workers, while women remained preeminently mothers, wives, and daughters. Men's work and women's were deemed different and separate— though often complementary. Thus, a deeply held gendered division of labor permeated culture, society, and workplaces, fostered by specialization and segregation. Five parameters shaped ideas about women's work in the twentieth century: appropriateness, type of product, skill, technology, and authority. These were interrelated, of course, and together shaped a gendered workplace. Movement took place within areas of work and in precise tasks, like the shift of clerical work from men to women, while a variety of factors like war experience, education, and feminism broke down or redrew many boundaries.

Underpinning employment policies and often women's decision making was what was appropriate for women to do while retaining gentility and the question of whether to work or not. So, while white-collar work was "suitable," particularly for middle-class women needing income, careful decisions were made about where they worked. For example, the French postal service did not place women in working-class areas, described as unsuitable for "naturally high strung" women.[40] For the same reason, they tended to cluster in textiles and service, both associated with feminine characteristics. During the century, the shift from domestic service to other forms of service, even secretarial work, continued this tendency to see particular forms of work as appropriate.

Medicine and teaching illustrate this point. Late nineteenth-century developments in medical knowledge created a medical discourse grounded in learning and special training, fostered by university education. Therefore, medicine developed two career structures with nurses positioned as doctors' auxiliaries. Initially perceptions of nurses reflected woman's maternal role, while doctors took responsibility for treatment. However, as the doctor's role became more clearly diagnostic, nurses undertook more duties, which by virtue of their transfer to women, became devalued. The journal *Hospital* explained in 1912:

> Nursing may be roughly defined as the care of patients under medical control. Such care or treatment is subsidiary simply in the sense that treatment is subsidiary to diagnosis...This principle of the proper division of labour defines the relation of medical men to nurses.[41]

Thus, despite the aims of nursing to establish a profession based on expertise, its subordination to medicine left nurses in a devalued, low-status, and poorly paid profession. Similarly, gendered ideas made it difficult for women to qualify in medicine and complicated their position with regard to nurses. Both of these have changed significantly since the 1970s, as more women qualified as doctors, though with differences in specialisms, and nursing created degree routes and upgraded professional qualifications.

Teaching, in contrast, developed a unified career structure from the outset, although vertical segregation existed, with men gaining greater access to training, certification, better pay, and higher status positions. Men were cast as "academics," and women as "caregivers," so that women were more successful in gaining primary posts whereas men secured secondary-level positions and taught academic subjects. Nevertheless, dedicated women strove to shift teaching from a vocation to a profession with professional respect and remuneration. Sarah Burstall, headmistress of Manchester High School for Girls, commented favorably in 1909 on the American treatment of teachers: "They belong to a profession which is respected and considered as a means of national defense, like the navy here." Yet she noted that women's position was no better: "The higher up the scale one goes, from the kindergarten to the university,

FIGURE 6.5: Nurses in Dronning Louises children's hospital, Copenhagen, 1895. Reproduction no. 840828F005. Courtesy of the Danish Museum of Nursing History.

the worse is the position of women. Organization, initiative, administration, government, are in the hands of men."[42] The efforts and determination of such women prevented teaching from falling into the same trap as nursing, while an influx of middle-class women helped upgrade it. Nevertheless, identification with caring rather than academic qualifications persisted, and women remained less likely to gain positions of responsibility, as we have seen.

Segregation was reflected in the products and industries in which men and women concentrated. Men were far more likely to produce certain goods or work in particular industries and women in others. In automobile manufacture at Coventry, England, and Boulogne-Billancourt, France, women workers were a tiny minority, as machinists sewing car trims, car cleaners, or canteen workers. Men made automobiles. Magneti Marelli expanded radio production, increasing recruitment of women, while men made accumulator batteries.[43] Women produced lighter, smaller articles, often in mechanized or automated settings, usually routine, boring, and part of a fragmented work process. That it was paid less than men's work is a virtual truism that had as much to do with the gender of the worker as the work.

Segregation was similarly a feature of white-bloused work. Within retail, men worked where training was required, where goods were expensive, or where work was rough and heavy; women predominated in light and untrained work with low pay. Men maintained strong continuity between the artisan and the new salesman, selling jewelry, gloves, and stockings, while women sold provisions and women's clothes. In 1910, the British National Union of Shop Assistants reported a "fairly clear line of demarcation" between men's and women's work, though the socially progressive union admitted that there was a place for women in some jobs requiring "skill, method and brains."[44] Women's growing experience and good record as managers during the First World War helped them gain higher status responsible posts, and in 1930s London, female buyers outnumbered men. Nevertheless, in the 1980s, men still held top jobs in management, training, and stock control, and they dominated departments with expensive or bulky consumables. Women, more visible on display counters, sold to women. The same vertical segregation operated in office jobs from the outset.

As these examples illustrate, segregation was a function of different jobs for different sexes but also fostered a hierarchy so that men tended to get and retain jobs with status and authority. Specialization helped to solidify hierarchical structures, restricting promotion between levels. It was common in manufacturing and typified white-collar work, while similar dichotomies existed in teaching and medicine and other professions. For example, shifts in clerical work helped to create significant distinctions between clerks, administrators, and managers. Tasks and ranks became more closely associated with different levels of education, and bridging gaps became more difficult. Vertical segregation was fostered by perceptions of men as supervisors and managers; the image of the *paterfamilias* was not far away. Pay scales and grading provided quite separate gendered hierarchies, preventing women from moving into administrative and higher-grade work. Even as women gained pension schemes and unified pay and promotion scales, men tended to retain senior posts with more responsibility and status. Although careers opened, "the glass ceiling" operated an unwritten rule preventing women from reaching the highest echelons.

Work regarded as skilled was carefully preserved for men, reinforced by segregated workplaces so that women did not appear to be threatening men's jobs or status. The view persisted that women did jobs requiring dexterity better than men, like pea picking and assemblage, but were unable to match them in jobs needing strength and stamina. So outside of "female" work, women were constrained to the most tedious and repetitive tasks and barred from specialized "skilled" ones where men retained a monopoly. Capitalist expansion is charged with creating specialization, leading to fragmented routinized work with a presumed loss of skill and status. Although frequently workers needed a limited range of specific skills, on an intellectual level, some grades and professions required quite complex understanding and skill. Arguably, work was "degraded" and not "deskilled" because women did it.

Technical expertise was brought into play to define skilled and unskilled work. The relationship of women to machines was not straightforward. On the one hand, mechanization supposedly allowed more women to be employed and to replace skilled, and expensive, men. On the other hand, women were not supposed to understand machines and were only there to tend and operate them. Yet machinery could be used to determine both "skill" and "deskilling" and often provided an opportunity to regender work. When Norwegian women telegraphers fought for equal pay in 1898, the director reported they were less competent than men, particularly on complicated equipment and in technical aspects, despite equal training, equal workloads, and overall better marks on training courses. One female telegrapher retorted, "The primary reason why female telegraphers manifest little interest in the technical aspects of their work is that our lords and masters, men, have since time immemorial regarded themselves as the only ones competent in this field."[45] Women did not get "technical" work, and specialist equipment and tools were kept for men, although machines frequently replaced men's higher-paid manual labor, tended by considerably lower-paid women. But where work was new, women replaced no one, like operating wrapping machines in the Dutch margarine industry. Indeed, further technical changes meant machines replaced women.[46] Men were associated with repairing and maintaining machinery, while women fed it, stopped it, and started it, but did not mess with it. In Armentières, men maintaining the factory heater were paid better than women operatives.[47] Indeed, women's work cannot be disentangled from their sex, since perceptions of what women could do were inextricably tied to what employers and male workers perceived women to be.

The vision of the woman worker as docile, malleable, unskilled, and ultimately dispensable, shaped the character of their employment opportunities. Importantly, natural differences ascribed to men and women are precisely that—ascribed. Women can and did do the same tasks as men; they were sometimes better at them. They were not frail, delicate, and weak. In fact, the history of women's work is about their strength, both physical and mental. It is also about claiming a place in the world of work, and sometimes about claiming an actual physical space, whether in fields or farmyard, office or shops, factories or workshops. A running debate was "equal pay for equal work," but where that was achieved, other forms of discrimination operated. Not the least of these was that women were still not perceived first as workers. Masculinity is tied up with men's work, while femininity is still tied to domestic "duties."

WOMEN'S VOICES, WOMEN'S CHOICES

A range of variables determined whether a woman went out to work. Much depended on the perception of their contribution to the labor market by family members, other workers, and employers, as well as their place in the life cycle. The belief that women did not work after marriage had tremendous purchase, which was very much alive when British Prime Minister Margaret Thatcher advised women to go back to their homes so that men could work during the dark years of the 1980s. Clearly, the workplace was a gendered context in which women often encountered a hostile environment. But self-perception and needs, familial or personal, played a significant role.

The way women related to work reflected a range of choices and decisions they made based on complex considerations. Often women chose the work they wanted to do. They left agriculture, particularly when they could migrate to towns. Women valued off-farm work for the money, but also for social contact and positive feedback. As Irish women commented: "it is a great feeling knowing you are doing something useful and getting paid for it," and "you are more your own person."[48] Many were enthusiastic about the higher wages and increased freedom that factory work represented. They found "more life" there, had money to spend, and took pleasure in the collective experience; a young Belfast woman said, "We were happy... You stood all day at your work and sung them songs."[49] In contrast, however, some wished to work only until marriage and saw factory work as boring and temporary.

Many women believed that working from home gave them control over their work and time. Homeworkers, working in jobs where they had trained, often saw themselves as self-employed. They claimed greater choice and could sometimes utilize a pricing structure that compensated for overheads, holiday, and sick pay. Yet most worked to a pattern and rhythm dictated by employers and their own need for income. The division of labor left homeworkers discretion over only trivial parts of their work, while employers ruled over rates of pay, quality standards, and how much work was distributed. Women had to accept the conditions or go elsewhere, and for many this was not an option. Women also tended toward "self-exploitation" in that if rates of pay dropped, they worked harder to make the same amount of money, thus producing goods cheaper.

Women might choose to marry or to take up work in factories or home-work. They demanded education, created voluntary work and social work, and claimed shop and office work. They shaped their own context, worked for their own reasons, and enjoyed it. The effect was that women became more employment oriented and less inclined to live their lives in separate phases. Women were agents in the conception of their work experience and in fashioning themselves as workers with an identity based in the workplace, not as women who happened to be working.

CHAPTER SEVEN

Power: Women, Politics, and Power in Europe after 1920

JUNE HANNAM

This chapter will focus on European women's engagement in politics in the period after 1920 and their attempts, both individually and collectively, to bring about changes in women's social, political, and economic position. It will ask how far, and in what ways, women were able to exercise political power and influence. Power in this context can be conceived of in a broad sense as "the ability of an individual or group to influence the course of events in the direction they desire, even against resistance by others."[1] Until the twentieth century, women were excluded from access to formal political structures at a national level. And yet, as feminist scholarship has shown, if a wide definition of politics is adopted to include "any public actions intended to change or shape political, social or economic conditions," then it can be argued that women played an extensive role in political life from the nineteenth century onward.[2] They took part in antislavery campaigns, established and managed philanthropic organizations, and joined trade unions, as well as forming their own pressure groups to demand reforms in women's unequal social position.

In the twentieth century, women continued to organize in a variety of ways to achieve social change; for example, some sought to exert influence within established political parties, often by forming separate women's organizations within them, while others established groups that provided services to women outside male-dominated structures, including rape crisis shelters and self-help health facilities.[3] They also had different ideas about what they hoped to achieve for women. These could be affected by class, political ideology, party loyalties, race, and sexual orientation.[4] Cutting across these divisions were debates about what equality might mean for women and how far women's difference from men should be emphasized and acknowledged.[5] The intention here is to discuss the complex strategies and demands that were put forward by those interested in achieving change in women's social, political, and economic position after 1920. It will be suggested that the aims and objectives of different groups can only be understood in relation to the prevailing ideological assumptions about appropriate gender roles, and the interaction between family structures and relationships and the public domain, in specific historical contexts.

One key change in the twentieth century across most of Europe was that women finally gained the right to vote. This gave them access for the first time to the formal sphere of parliamentary or representative government, although the timing of their enfranchisement was varied. Scandinavian countries were among the first to enfranchise women, and this was interrelated with nationalist struggles; Finland and Norway included women in the franchise just before the First World War, while Denmark and Iceland soon followed suit. There was a spate of enfranchisement after the war itself, including in Britain, Germany, Czechoslovakia, the Netherlands, and Sweden. France and Italy, however, waited until after the Second World War, while Switzerland was one of the last liberal democracies in Europe to enfranchise women, in 1971. In some countries, women enjoyed the vote for only a brief period before a change of regime brought authoritarian governments that denied voting rights to all members of the population. In Spain, for example, women were enfranchised in 1931 when the new republic introduced constitutional reform. Defeat in the Spanish Civil War saw the end of the republic, and women lost the right to vote under the dictatorship of General Franco, only regaining the franchise in 1976 with the restoration of a democracy.[6]

Political parties were unsure about the potential impact of the new woman voter. Magazines, newspapers, and the cinema in the 1920s were full of images of the young single woman who had greater personal freedoms than previous generations. Described as a flapper in Britain, a *garçonne* in France, and a *maschietta* in Italy, she wore knee-length dresses, bobbed her hair, and was evident in the streets and cafés of large cities.[7] Married women, however, were still associated with family life and domesticity despite the fact that, with the exception of Britain, an increased proportion were recorded as engaged in paid employment in the years between the two world wars.[8] The young woman voter might have seemed like an unknown quantity, but political parties also had contradictory views about the potential impact of the married woman's vote. Parties on the left assumed that the housewife, bounded by her domestic world, was more likely to be conservative in her politics. The fear that women were under the sway of the priest and sought the return of the monarchy prevented many republicans in France from giving support to women's suffrage.[9]

For most of the first half of the twentieth century, the evidence suggests that women did give support to more conservative political parties. In Weimar Germany, where women outnumbered men in the electorate, and also in Austria, "the religiously affiliated parties of the Centre and Right profited most from women's votes."[10] In Britain, when women over twenty-one finally gained the franchise in 1928, the Labour Party argued that younger women voters were likely to support a party standing for social reform. Nonetheless, an analysis of constituency electoral results for the period of the mid-1920s to the 1930s suggests that the political crisis of 1931 undermined the Labour Party's efforts to mobilize the female vote and drove many working-class women to vote for other parties.[11] This remained the case for the period 1945–66, when it has been argued that there was a "strong preference" for Conservatives among female voters. Ina Zweiniger-Bargielowska suggests that this was encouraged by the Conservative Party's critique of postwar austerity and their aim of directing propaganda to the female consumer by promising to end rationing and shortages.[12] A similar trend could be seen in the rest of Europe. A survey of women's political participation in Europe in 1955, undertaken on behalf of the United Nations Educational, Scientific, and Cultural Organization (UNESCO), indicated that women were most likely to vote for moderate conservative parties.[13]

Women were usually faced with the choice of voting for candidates from existing political parties that tended not to give priority to issues that addressed gender inequalities, or even to social welfare that would improve women's lives. Women did, however, take an active part in the mainstream political parties. In contrast to the conservatism of female voters, women joined social democratic parties in large numbers. In Britain, for example, there were 250,000 members of the women's sections in the late 1920s, and women formed just over 40 percent of all individual members of the Labour Party by the early 1930s, while in Germany in 1928, women made up 21 percent of the 867,671 members of the Social Democratic Party (SPD) and 17 percent of the 130,000 members of the Communist Party (KPD).[14] In Austria and Holland, just over a third of Social Democratic Party members were women, while in Norway and Sweden the figure was 16 percent and 14 percent, respectively. Nonetheless, it was difficult for women to make their voices heard in organizations that were dominated by men, and they were underrepresented in leadership positions and at conferences, where female delegates rarely numbered more than 10–15 percent.

Although the rhetoric of parties on the left supported women's rights in the workplace, the image most often conveyed in party propaganda was that of domesticity. In Britain, for example, Martin Francis argues that the Labour Party was willing to see its values represented in feminine as well as masculine terms, but this conception was narrowed to the suffering working-class wife and mother.[15] Women's identification with the home was a key feature of political and social culture from the interwar years to beyond the Second World War and was shared by all political parties. Nonetheless, the nature of that domestic world was depicted differently over time. In the 1930s, the economic depression encouraged the view that married women should devote their time to homes and children, but attention was focused on the difficulties faced by the working-class mother in carrying out domestic tasks when faced with poverty, unsanitary housing, and poor health facilities. In this context, social welfare demands were paramount. In the 1950s, the emphasis on women's domestic role continued despite the fact that married women were entering the labor force in larger numbers. With a rise in the standard of living, women were identified with consumerism and expected to use the new labor-saving devices to create a congenial environment for husbands and children.[16] Research by psychologists and psychiatrists also reinforced the importance of the full-time presence of the mother within the home to ensure the emotional health of children and to prevent juvenile delinquency and problem families. For example, the findings of John Bowlby's influential book *Child Care and the Growth of Love* (1953) were disseminated widely in the media. His research was based on children in institutional care who had had little contact with their mothers, but his term "maternal deprivation" was then used to apply to situations where mothers were not constantly with their children.[17]

It was difficult for women to gain election to their national representative bodies. In most countries, the number of women who were preselected to stand as candidates for national parliaments and representative assemblies was small, and even fewer were successful in gaining election up to the last two decades of the twentieth century. In Britain, for example, where there had been a strong suffrage movement, women members of Parliament (MPs) represented less than 5 percent of all MPs in the House of Commons until the late 1980s, when the figure still did not rise above 10 percent. In Norway in the interwar years, women held only 3 out of 150 seats in the national parliament, the

Storting, and this did not rise significantly until the 1970s, while in France the proportion of women MPs was still only 6 percent in the 1990s.[18] In Italy, 21 women from three parties were elected to the Constituent Assembly in 1946, 3.7 percent of the total. As the hopes and expectations of the immediate post-war years began to fade, the numbers declined so that by 1968 there were only 17 women.[19] Weimar Germany had the highest proportion of female members; between 1919 and 1933, approximately 8 percent of Reichstag members were women, and they numbered 112 in total across the period.[20] This compares well with Britain, where a total of 32 women became MPs in the interwar years. There was a peak in 1931 when women comprised 2.5 percent of all MPs.[21] In contrast to female voting patterns, the majority of women elected to national parliaments were members of social democratic parties—in the Reichstag in 1920, for example, 22 female members were social democrats out of a total of 39 spread across six parties.[22]

There were both structural and ideological barriers to women's participation in national politics.[23] It was difficult to gain preselection as a candidate at all, let alone for seats that were winnable, and if they were successful, women had to cope with an unfamiliar space. Brian Harrison's description of the House of Commons as "The Men's House" sums up some of the issues—the facilities in representative assemblies, the style of debate, and the conduct of business could all be off-putting to women.[24] As Gisela Kaplan suggests, "It is not at all easy to be assertive and vocal in an environment (of politics) that tightly encapsulates expectations of traditional norms of female conduct, of submissiveness and 'niceness.'"[25] Women were often more comfortable taking part in local politics where they thought they could get something done. Ruth Dalton, for example, was elected to the British House of Commons at a by-election in 1929. She stood as a candidate as a stopgap measure until her husband was available to contest the seat at the general election held a few months later. In his memoirs, he claimed that she only stood to help him and never wanted to be an MP since she preferred her work on the London County Council.[26] There was also hostility in many countries to women's attempt to enter the formal political arena. In Italy, for example, Anna Rossi-Doria claims that ordinary party members remained suspicious of women as voters; Communists and Socialists feared the influence of the church on women, while the Christian democrats worried about its effect on family life. When women did take part in national politics, they faced prejudice from other members and from the media. When one woman took the floor in a foreign policy debate, the journalists "were overcome by a compelling need to go for a coffee or a smoke in the lobby, reappearing now and then to exchange muttered witticisms about the pots the speaker had neglected to put on the stove and the socks that she was no doubt incapable of darning."[27]

Both opponents and supporters of women's suffrage had assumed that women would use their votes to pursue "women's issues." These can be defined as "public concerns that impinge primarily on the private (especially domestic) sphere of social life," in particular values associated with caregiving roles and with children.[28] It was difficult for women who were elected to national parliaments, however, to know whether they should be emphasizing questions that might be of particular interest to women or giving priority to the policies of their respective parties. Even if they were committed feminists, they could be reluctant to confine themselves to what were seen as women's issues—the British MP and feminist Ellen Wilkinson, for instance, wanted to become involved in questions of finance and foreign policy, as well as social welfare issues. In 1924, in an interview with the press, she claimed that although she was the only Labour woman MP "and have women's interests to look after, I do not want to be regarded purely as a women's MP since most of the voters in Middlesborough are men."[29] In an electoral system in which MPs were chosen by voters of both sexes and different classes, the question of what it meant to be a representative, and who should be represented, was a complicated one to resolve. In Weimar Germany, however, women from across the political spectrum tended to confine themselves to taking up, and speaking on, what they considered to be women's issues, in particular social policy questions and legal reforms for women. Claudia Koonz argues that men and women delegates of all parties welcomed this traditionalism, although women did not just want to replicate a masculine style of debate and male priorities. The Reichstag deputy Marianne Webber wrote, "It is our responsibility to infuse all life with our special blend of feminine and humane influence."[30] Women often acted together across party lines on a number of questions, in particular protective legislation for female workers and civic equality for women, where they were able to influence policy outcomes. For example, when the upper house, the Reichsrat, vetoed a law that enabled women to serve on juries, women deputies from the Reichstag were so indignant that they reintroduced the measure and the veto was rescinded.[31]

In Britain, too, despite their differences on party politics, women did act together in the 1930s on questions such as the women's nationality debate in 1930 and the payment of pensions to spinsters after the age of fifty-five.[32] In Italy, women deputies in the Constituent Assembly worked together to ensure that women's rights were inserted into the text of the postwar constitution. Rossi-Doria argues that this established principles on which women could draw over the next few years as they began to obtain equal civil rights in the family and in the workplace. This suggests that when women exerted pressure as a distinct block, they could gain positive results. In some circumstances, individual women elected to office could also make a difference. The Russian revolutionary Alexandra Kollontai, the Spanish anarchist Federica Montseny, and the French politician Simone Veil were all ministers of health and worked to legalize abortion in their respective countries.

Alternatively, there could be fundamental policy differences among women from different political parties. Even if they put the interests of women at the forefront of their activities, they did not necessarily agree on what those interests were. Koonz's analysis of women deputies in the Reichstag provides an interesting case study of this position. She found that Socialist women emphasized the rights of women as workers, as well as their responsibilities as parents. They called for protective legislation at the workplace but also for changes in family and labor laws so that they could have full equality and the ability to become active citizens. Conservative, Catholic, and liberal women also advocated women's emancipation but aimed to increase women's power within their traditional domain of the family. They then argued that the values that they developed there, in particular moral values, should be used to transform the political sphere.[33]

Women also used other public and political spaces in order to get their voices heard. They organized themselves in a range of groups that involved women working together with other women. Some of these were explicitly feminist organizations that continued to be active after the First World War. Where women still did not have the vote, as in France, the focus was on the women's franchise. The French Union for Women's Suffrage, for example, extended its organization beyond Paris and into the provinces so that by 1929 it had 100,000 members. Where women already had the vote, as in Britain and Germany, feminist organizations turned their attention to demands for equal rights in other areas. In Britain, for instance, the program of the Six Point Group, whose main focus was the professional middle-class woman, included equal pay for teachers, equal employment opportunities in the civil service, and equal guardianship of children. Along with other groups, they also campaigned to extend voting rights from women over thirty years of age to all women over the age of twenty-one. An equal franchise with men was finally achieved in 1928.[34]

Members of other feminist groups such as the National Union of Societies for Equal Citizenship (NUSEC), led by Eleanor Rathbone, had different priorities. They emphasized the importance of social reform to improve the position of women within the home and, alongside equal rights, sought to gain greater recognition for motherhood and the fulfillment women experienced from this role. Rathbone spent many years, as the leader of NUSEC and as an MP in the 1920s and 1930s, campaigning for family allowances as a way to provide greater economic independence for mothers. Lady Rhondda, Winifred Holtby, and others in the Six Point Group were critical of this program and argued that it detracted from the key objectives of feminism, which were equality and status for women.[35]

The other groups in which women acted together to achieve improvements in their lives—women's auxiliaries in political parties and women's organizations that did not accept the label feminist—appealed as their main constituency to wives and mothers and shared, with more overtly feminist groups, a social welfare program. Women organizers who sought to encourage working-class housewives and mothers to join the auxiliaries of social democratic parties emphasized how politics, in particular policies concerning education, housing, and health, was inextricably linked to the home and everyday life. Women's section meetings often combined sewing circles and the organization of social events with discussions about social welfare questions and practical advice on birth control. Women members raised money for their party but, at the same time gained personal confidence for themselves and could be mobilized on behalf of campaigns to improve their own lives and those of their children.[36] In Britain, the members of Labour Party women's sections played a key role in supporting miners' families during the lockout of 1926—they raised money, distributed food and clothing, and spoke in support of the miners' cause at public meetings.[37] Working-class women's activism was significant since, in the face of skepticism from parties that emphasized the importance of the male worker, it showed that women in the home did take an interest in political issues and that politicization did not have to come just from the workplace.

Other women's groups that appealed to housewives and mothers were independent of political party affiliations. In Germany, it has been argued that the Bund Deutscher Frauenvereine (BDF), which had once been a radical organization, had become far more conservative in the interwar years when it focused on the family and led campaigns to oppose the liberalization of sexual morality that was associated with Berlin and the Weimar Republic.[38] In Denmark, too, liberal and conservative lower-middle-class women joined housewives guilds that emphasized women's traditional roles and condemned birth control, abortion, and married women's work.[39] However, Caitriona Beaumont suggests that although some women's organizations explicitly refused the label feminist, they should still be seen as an important part of the movement to improve women's social and economic position. In Britain, the Women's Institute and the Townswomen's Guild sought a range of social reforms in the 1930s to enhance women's position in the home, while some members had the courage to speak out in favor of contraception and abortion. They encouraged women to use their new voting rights and attempted to educate the new "woman citizen." Beaumont argues that by distancing themselves from feminist organizations, they were able to attract a large number of housewives and mothers who would otherwise have been put off by negative publicity, and that in the process, they did seek to challenge gender inequalities.[40] Housewives' associations that largely represented middle-class women reached a peak in the 1940s and 1950s in most countries and were often able to gain representation for their groups in the official committee system. Nonetheless, by this stage, there was little sense that these groups were part of a collective movement that questioned traditional gender roles or that they were willing to take direct action to achieve their goals.[41]

Most women's organizations in this period, whether self-proclaimed feminists or not, campaigned for welfare reforms to improve the health and welfare of women and children, including maternity clinics, better housing, and education. Some also campaigned on issues that had the potential to give women greater autonomy and control over their lives, in particular access to birth control information and economic assistance to families in the shape of family allowances. They did not, however, always agree on how the allowances should be financed or what they hoped to achieve by them. In Norway, liberal feminists saw child allowances as a way in which mothers could pay for child care and therefore continue with paid employment, whereas Socialist women wanted a mother's wage financed through the tax system and therefore freeing them from outside employment.[42] Women also faced the difficulty that an interest in maternity and family welfare was shared by a wide range of groups in the period, in particular those concerned with pro-natalism and eugenics. Thus, feminist arguments could easily become lost in a more general discourse about national health and welfare, while the detailed provisions of any reforms that were introduced might work against rather than for women's interests. In France, for example, fears about population decline led to increasingly severe penalties for disseminating birth control information or carrying out abortions in the interwar years, while family allowances were provided by employers who used these to control wages rather than to ensure economic independence for mothers.[43]

By focusing on women's needs as mothers rather than on their rights as women as a basis on which to demand reforms, there was a danger that they would simply confirm, rather than challenge, women's identification with the home. As Geoff Eley notes, "maternalism could either disable women politically, by fixing them in the domestic role; or it could empower them by constructing particular sites of activity and validating women's participation."[44] Most social democratic parties, including those in Germany and Belgium, placed emphasis on protecting the working-class family, and they viewed women as agents of family moralization rather than as independent political subjects.[45] Although social welfare questions such as maternal and child health formed a significant element of party programs, there was far less interest in addressing issues relating to women's rights.[46] As noted previously, women were rarely in positions of influence in parties that placed the male industrial worker at the center of political theory and practice. They were also underrepresented in leadership positions, both locally and nationally, or took on "administrative posts such as union treasurer rather than assuming policymaking positions."[47] Thus, they had restricted political influence, and their separate organization could reinforce both their marginality and their gender roles.

Women faced considerable resistance when they raised the more controversial issues of birth control and family allowances. In Britain, Socialist women such as Dorothy Jewson and Dora Russell tried to get support from the Labour Party for their demand that municipal clinics should give birth control advice to working-class mothers. They highlighted the class injustice of denying this right to working-class women when their wealthier counterparts could visit private clinics and also emphasized the health and economic benefits that working-class families would enjoy if they could control the number of births. Fear of losing the Catholic vote, however, coupled with the assumption that this was a private rather than a political issue, meant that by 1928 it was clear that the party would not adopt the issue as official policy. Similarly, with family allowances, the Labour Party only took the matter seriously when it was raised as part of a Living Wage campaign launched by the affiliated Socialist group, the Independent Labour Party, but the opposition of trade unionists, who saw this as a threat to the male family wage, ensured that yet again the party did not take it further.[48]

In Scandinavian countries, however, women did play a part in actually shaping the social welfare measures that were introduced in the 1930s. In Sweden, where social democrats played an important part in gaining political and civil rights for women in the 1920s, Socialist women were able to ensure that birth control and welfare issues were placed high on the agenda. A package of reforms was introduced that did not simply fix women in their maternal role. These included job protection for pregnant women, the legalization of

contraception, and maternity benefits paid to mothers, and they were not accompanied, as in Britain, by an attack on married women's employment.[49] A
variety of women's groups came together to support these reforms across party
and class lines. The trade unions did not object to women's demands since a
very segregated labor market meant that there was little competition between
men and women at the workplace, while the idea of the "People's Home" created a space to look at policies around housing, maternal health, and reproduction that brought women's rights together with the national interest. Eley
argues that social democratic feminists then had an important influence on the
Commission on Married Women's Work and Population policy, 1935–38, that
came up with progressive policies in those areas.[50] In Norway, however, where
political and civil rights had been gained in the nineteenth century, there was
little cooperation between Socialists and liberal feminists, and the social democrats actually introduced a marriage bar.[51]

It is difficult to determine how far women's campaigns were responsible
for the welfare reforms that were introduced. It was easier for them to make
gains when their aims coincided with those of the parties in power or with
other pressure groups. When social democratic parties in countries such as
Denmark, Sweden, and Norway, for instance, introduced welfare reforms,
they aimed not just to benefit women but also to redistribute income through
direct taxation. It was far less likely, however, that birth control and abortion
rights would have been introduced unless women had been active in raising
the issue, although some members of the medical profession also gave support. Women benefited from the more liberal climate in many countries after
the First World War when contraception was discussed more freely and a
number of birth control clinics and advice centers, either supported by local
authorities or run privately, were established in Norway, Sweden, Holland,
Belgium, Germany, and England. Although their campaign to ensure that municipal clinics would give free birth control advice failed initially in Britain,
women did ensure that the issue was discussed widely in the 1920s. Labour
Party women such as Dorothy Jewson and Jessie Stephen were active in the
Workers' Birth Control Group, while Stella Browne, a Socialist and feminist,
who saw birth control as an aspect of sexual self-determination, established
the New Generation League to campaign on this single issue. Members of
both organizations traveled the country speaking to Labour Party women's
sections, branches of the Women's Co-operative Guild, and adult education
classes. They introduced resolutions at Labour Party conferences and persuaded sympathetic MPs to raise the issue in Parliament.[52] This facilitated the
decision made by the Labour government in 1930, when it was no longer able

to control how local councils allocated funds, to send a memorandum to local health committees giving them the right to offer birth control advice to married women "in cases of medical necessity."[53]

Abortion rights were far more difficult to raise and to achieve. For a brief period after the Bolshevik Revolution in Russia, there was an emphasis on sexual freedoms and new relationships within the family, expressed in the writings of Alexandra Kollontai, and legislation was introduced on birth control, divorce, and abortion. In the late 1930s, abortion based on a restricted set of criteria was also introduced in Sweden and Denmark. Nonetheless, there were also losses as well as gains; access to birth control information was restricted in Nazi Germany and Mussolini's Italy after 1926, while abortion was recriminalized in the Soviet Union in 1936.[54] As Stalin drove forward industrialization in Russia, the traditional family was seen as a source of stability, and women were expected to take part in waged work and to produce more children. In this context, divorce laws were tightened and abortion outlawed.[55] Feminists were themselves divided on abortion rights. In Switzerland, the suffragist Anna Löffler-Herzog opposed attempts by Socialists to decriminalize abortion on the grounds that a woman would be "depreciated in her quality as creator and guardian of life" and would be unable to fulfill her civilizing mission.[56]

Disagreements between women activists could hamper their ability to achieve changes for women. In Britain, there were splits in feminist organizations over whether the focus of campaigning should be equal rights or the welfare needs of the working-class mother, and a further conflict arose in the 1920s between feminist groups and Labour Party women over protective legislation for female workers. While NUSEC and the Six Point Group wanted to remove protective legislation on the grounds that it hampered women in competition for work and placed artificial constraints on the labor market, Labour women wanted to extend such legislation to include men and were not prepared to see any reduction in the protection enjoyed by women workers before this was achieved.[57] Members of feminist groups were often suspicious that women who campaigned within mixed-sex political parties put loyalty to class and party above feminist concerns whenever there was a disagreement with the male-dominated leadership, a view that has been echoed by historians of the interwar years.[58] Nonetheless, Pat Thane argues that Labour women did manage to make a difference within their party. They wanted women to have real choices in their lives, put welfare on the Labour Party's agenda, brought more women into public life, and helped to improve local services.[59] The latter was most likely to happen when local women activists joined with their male colleagues to press for reforms that were seen as in the interests of the Labour

Party as well as of women.[60] In the 1930s, for example, the Labour Party's policy agenda shifted to a greater emphasis on welfare reforms, including maternity, education, and housing, and this in turn influenced the priorities of party activists at the grass roots.

In the difficult economic and political context of the interwar years, feminists also sought to use international groups to push forward their demands. After the First World War, organizations such as the Women's International League for Peace and Freedom and the International Woman Suffrage Alliance lobbied the League of Nations to accept women as delegates and to open up employment to them in the secretariat. There were conflicts over protective legislation that mirrored those in individual countries, in particular in Britain and the United States, and therefore it was difficult to gain agreement on whether feminists should try to obtain a treaty on equal rights within the framework of the League of Nations. There was cooperation over other issues, however, such as equal nationality rights for married women, and these were debated in depth by the league in 1931. Toward the end of the decade, women's groups convinced the league that the social position of women should be given international attention, and the league established an inquiry into the rights and status of women. Although this was interrupted by the outbreak of war, it laid the foundations for postwar developments when the United Nations established a Commission on the Status of Women. It was accepted at this stage that women's rights needed to be seen as an integral part of human rights.[61]

In the aftermath of the Second World War, women gained equal voting rights in many countries that had excluded them from the franchise in the early 1920s, including France, Bulgaria, Italy, Hungary, Romania, and Belgium. Women took advantage of this period of liberation to press their claims for full civil rights. In France, for example, prewar suffragists, resistance workers, and Catholics joined together to pressurize politicians to ensure that the new constitution would include a clause on sexual equality in all areas of life, including family law.[62] In Norway in 1945–46, women's organizations mobilized alongside similar groups in Sweden and Denmark to seek a change in the law on citizenship so that individual rights would supplant communal or family rights. Ida Blom suggests that the persistent campaign of the women's movement lay behind the new law that was passed in 1950 when it was decided that marriage would not interfere with women's citizenship.[63] In practice, however, in many countries women's economic, political, and social position was slow to change. In France, married women remained legal minors until 1965, and husbands were considered heads of household until 1975. In Italy and Ireland, women were subordinate to male relatives within the family and, in the 1950s and 1960s, suffered from discriminatory legislation relating to divorce, adultery, and abortion.[64]

Fears of social instability after the upheavals of war led governments in western Europe to emphasize the importance of a traditional gender division of labor in the family, which underpinned social welfare policies, while the image of the full-time housewife permeated the media. A growth of conservative politics, reinforced by the Cold War, created a difficult context for women to challenge inequalities and discrimination. And yet there was a tension between the realities of women's daily lives and prevailing images of the contented housewife. Young women took advantage of a growth in educational opportunities, while married women entered the labor force in larger numbers. They were clustered in part-time and low-paid work that prompted extensive public debates and government inquiries into gender inequalities at the workplace, many of which resulted in legislation. In Norway, for example, the principle of equal pay was adopted in 1958, and a new taxation system for married couples was introduced, weakening the male breadwinner system.[65] There may not have been a mass movement for women's rights in the 1950s and 1960s, but women's groups continued to exert pressure on employers and governments to improve women's position in the workplace and in the home. In Britain, for example, women within trade unions mounted an equal pay campaign in the 1950s that prepared the ground for strikes in the 1960s.[66]

In the Communist regimes of Eastern Europe, women were in a different position. Where women were needed to participate in the labor force, social measures were introduced to support this. In East Germany, this included paid maternity leave, nurseries, and affirmative action in favor of vocational training, while abortion was also made legal in the 1950s.[67] Women could ensure the continuation of these gains from their position in representative institutions. In Bulgaria, Czechoslovakia, East Germany, Hungary, Romania, and the USSR, women comprised between 15 and 25 percent of parliamentary representatives in the 1960s compared with less than 5 percent in most countries in the rest of Europe, with the exception of Scandinavia.[68] Conversely, women in Eastern Europe were unable to undermine patriarchal power within the family, where social attitudes remained conservative, and they were expected to shoulder a double burden of paid employment and domestic labor.

In western Europe, it was the collective actions of women themselves that were to bring the greatest changes in their position. Women participated in the civil rights movement in the United States in the 1950s and 1960s and in protests against the Vietnam War, but found that they were often excluded from decision-making powers and that their concerns were marginalized. Inspired by the demonstration against the Miss World contest in Atlantic City in 1968, women were mobilized across Europe, especially in France, Germany, Britain, the Netherlands, and Italy, and drew attention to their grievances in what has come to be known as the Women's Liberation Movement. They not only called for equal rights legislation and the end of discriminatory practices, but also challenged the dominant norms and values in everyday society.[69] Through consciousness-raising groups, the Women's Liberation Movement encouraged women to develop an awareness of their position and to take control over their own lives and aspirations.[70] As they talked about the frustrations encountered in their private lives, women came to realize that their difficulties arose from social conditions that were shared by others. Thus, they highlighted the interconnections between personal life and political and social structures—for example, they noted how consumerism and advertising used women's sexuality to sell goods and then, by promoting an ideal body shape, fed into anxieties that could lead to eating disorders. For some women, the challenge to existing hierarchies meant that they set up new groups that would empower women outside of established institutions, for example, self-help health groups, tenants associations, and battered women's homes.[71]

Others sought to use legislation to remove legal, political, and social inequalities and also to gain rights for women that would ensure their autonomy. Control over reproduction through free contraceptive advice and the introduction of the Pill was central to women's autonomy. It is hardly surprising, therefore, that throughout Europe a key demand of the Women's Liberation Movement was for abortion rights. Rather than using the tactic of pressure-group lobbying, women staged mass protests to achieve their aims, with more than half a million women in each country (West Germany, France, Italy, and Britain) taking to the streets in marches for abortion rights.[72] In this context, women demanded individual choice, but in the case of domestic violence, they sought greater state intervention to protect women in the private sphere of the home. They asserted their right to be free of male violence in all areas of life and, in 1977, staged a series of Reclaim the Night marches to assert women's right to be in public spaces in safety after dark.

The women's liberation movement posed a challenge to the divisions made between formal politics and personal lives. In a survey conducted in Belgium in 1987, women were asked what they considered the three most positive changes that had occurred in women's lives in the twentieth century. Seventy percent cited the significance of the contraceptive pill, while 29 percent thought the right to vote was the next most important, and 28 percent named the washing machine.[73] As Kaplan notes, these represent the body, the public domain, and the private domain, or, expressed differently, the biological (reproductive), the political (the vote), and the economic (domestic labor). Changes in all of these could contribute toward greater autonomy.[74]

What did women manage to achieve? In most countries, the movement contributed toward legislation that aimed to enhance women's position, including equal pay, sex discrimination laws, and, most important of all, the legalization of abortion. In Scandinavian countries, "the explosion of feminist movements" was accompanied by an increase in the number of women in political assemblies. Mira Janova and Mariette Sineau suggest that parties responded to feminist pressure to have large numbers of women on their electoral lists and would have been punished by the female electorate if they had failed to do so. Women then made alliances of different kinds across party boundaries to advance women's position.[75] In Sweden, for example, a new policy for equal pay and equal opportunity was introduced in 1980, while in Finland in the late 1970s and 1980s there was a spate of legislation pertaining to work and child care, including changes to the tax system, which enabled child care expenses to be tax deductible.[76] Perhaps of even greater importance, however, was changing the terms in which "the woman question" was debated.[77] Thus, feminists showed that domestic violence and rape were not just the actions of violent individuals but were embedded in social structures and expectations about male and female roles. The women's liberation movement raised awareness of how all-pervasive sex discrimination was and encouraged women to think differently about themselves. In many instances, it empowered women to speak up against the use of sexist language and discriminatory practices.

There still, however, continued to be a gap between formal equality and everyday practice that needed to be challenged. As the Women's Liberation Movement lost momentum in the 1980s, this had to be done by individual or pressure-group action. Girls and women took full advantage of an increase in educational and employment opportunities and began to make inroads into positions of power in many organizations. Working through political parties, trade unions, and the professions, feminists attempted to influence policies affecting the lives of women, in particular in the area of social welfare. In Ireland, for instance, women took an active part in the referenda in the 1980s on abortion and the removal of the constitutional ban on divorce.[78] Without a strong feminist movement behind them, women did not necessarily use their positions of power and influence within such organizations to challenge gender inequalities. They were more likely to press for social welfare reforms to improve women's health or their housing conditions rather than to focus on

empowering women to take control over their lives. The subversive, question-
ing side of feminism, therefore, appeared to be lost.[79]

In the hostile political climate of the 1980s, in which there was a move to
the right, there was a new emphasis on the importance of the traditional family
and attacks on some of the gains made by women, in particular abortion rights.
In Eastern Europe, women did not necessarily make gains from the political
upheavals after 1989 when Communist regimes were replaced. They found that
many of the social rights they had enjoyed were threatened, while, increasingly,
they were expected to take up new roles as dependent wives and mothers rather
than as independent workers. The proportion of women in political assemblies
also declined, making it even more difficult for women to find a voice.[80]

Across Europe, women did find other spaces in which to challenge prevailing norms about femininity and to gain recognition for their achievements.
They focused on "educational, cultural and creative projects," including the
development of women's studies courses in higher education and the establish-
ment of feminist journals and publishing houses.[81] There were also moments
when women could be mobilized in larger numbers. In Britain, for example, a
women-only peace camp was set up at the Greenham Common nuclear base in
1981. In the following year, more than 30,000 women encircled the base and
left personal items such as photographs or children's clothes tied to the fence.[82]
This provides a good example of how informal networks could be effective
in leading to the organization of a large-scale protest. Similarly, in the United
States, three-quarters of a million women were still prepared to march on
Washington in 1992 when abortion rights were under threat.

Women also continued to exert pressure at an international level within
the European Union and the United Nations to ensure that gender inequalities
would remain high on the agenda. The proportion of women in the European
Parliament (35 percent in 2011) was higher than in most member states, and
efforts were made to "extend women's rights policies from those rooted in their
status as worker to ones which relate to reproduction and sexual violence."[83]
The European Parliament also presents some examples of women working effectively together across party and national boundaries. The high profile given
to gender inequalities by the women's movement in the 1970s also brought
more attention to their cause within the United Nations. Hertta Kuusinen from
Finland proposed to the UN Commission on the Status of Women that there
should be an International Women's Year. This was held in 1975 and was followed by the Decade for Women, 1976–85. The UN called on governments
to improve health, employment, and educational levels for women under the
banner of equality, development, and peace.

Women made even greater efforts to exert their collective influence through representative bodies. Women's groups, parliamentarians, party activists, and civil servants all exerted pressures on political parties to increase the number of women candidates. They were assisted in this by the UN conference of women in Beijing in 1995, which encouraged states to address the underrepresentation of women, while in 1997 an EU directive asked member states to prepare action plans on equal opportunities, which gave the issue a high profile. Individual countries adopted different measures to promote this. In Britain, for example, the all-women short list in the Labour Party for prospective parliamentary candidates was responsible for the rise of women MPs in 1997 to break the 100 barrier for the first time, while in Germany a quota system was used at national and local levels. Where women were able to achieve a critical mass of MPs—as in Britain in 1997—it was found that they did make a difference by bringing an alternative set of values to issues affecting women's equality.[84] When questioned, women MPs themselves thought that they had made a difference by voicing women's concerns on issues such as domestic violence and by making links with women's organizations in the constituencies.[85]

By the end of the twentieth century, therefore, there had been changes in the extent to which women could exercise at least some control in their lives, in particular over fertility and reproduction. Broad social and economic changes, as well as women's own pressure, had led to legislation that provided women with rights within the home and in the workplace. Young women in particular enjoyed greater access to education and had the freedom to express sexual desire and to have relationships outside marriage without social stigma. But there were still paradoxes in their position since violence against women and exploitative advertising were still endemic. In practice, women workers did not enjoy equal status with men, while an emphasis on the importance of fulfillment through both work and family meant that they often faced a double burden. An EU report of 1997 found that in all the member states, poverty mainly strikes women: 70 percent of the 36 million Europeans living in poverty are women. They make up 55 percent of the long-term unemployed; 90 percent of single parents, who live in still greater deprivation; and 80 percent of part-time workers, mostly employed in flexible and insecure jobs not eligible for employment protection and social benefits.[86] The report concluded that structural economic changes and cultural traditions reinforced discrimination in employment and in everyday life.

Faced with the persistence of gender inequalities, women in the twenty-first century continue to use their collective and individual power and influence to bring change. After well over a century of women's campaigns, they can draw on the experience gained of using different tactics and a variety of spaces in which to make their claims. It is likely that debate will continue over aims and objectives and over what is meant by women's best interests, but this should not prevent women from acting collectively to challenge gender inequalities and to gain greater power to influence decision making within the societies in which they live.

CHAPTER EIGHT

Artistic Representation: From Cinema to the Interactive Screen

JANELL HOBSON

In this chapter, I explore how artistic representations of women reflect the cinematic framework that undergirds much of our visual culture of the twentieth century. In describing this visual apparatus as cinematic, I refer to the ways that artists respond to this visual paradigm framed by the photographic construct. I also explore how the intersections of gender, race, nationality, and sexuality shape the cinematic gaze and mise-en-scène. In connecting photography with cinema, I call attention to the literal construction of cinema as motion picture, a collection of photographs that give the illusion of movement. At once illusory and realist, the cinematic image has become the predominant visual language for modernity. Moving from the modern to the postmodern and, later, to the digital revolution, I further examine how feminist artists, in particular, reframe cinematic language to articulate new meanings of gender and its myriad constructions, especially with emerging new media. Within a global and contemporary context, these artworks enable an alternative visual vocabulary to interpret women's representations in film.

CONSTRUCTING A CINEMATIC WORLDVIEW

One of the more peculiar images from the missing footage of the iconic science fiction film *Metropolis* (1927) depicts a feverish vision in which the seductive cyborg, doubling as our virtuous white heroine Maria, fuses with spectral images of an "African primitive" and an Asian woman. This Maria double, unleashed as a veritable Salome, whose "exotic dance" lures a party of male attendees to their destruction, is thus associated with hypersexual femininity, blackness, and Orientalism. As lethal as this presence of Otherness might be, the film's climactic witch burning of the cyborg Maria (or lynching as the case may be) suggests nonetheless that a medieval response to modernity is just as destructive. This provocative image speaks to the film's fascination with and fear of technology and modernity, which are curiously linked to the body of the Other—female, nonwhite, and non-Western—a body that is often viewed in opposition to modernity, indeed as primitive, as nature. The cyborg's seduction is thus one of deception as it pretends to be a premodern body.

As heavy-handed in its moral message as it is technically accomplished, Fritz Lang's 1927 silent film masterpiece expands on existing tropes of femininity and foreignness that were magnified by the proliferation of photographic imagery. While the film criticizes modern advancements, which morally corrupt and enslave the masses, it is indebted to modernity for its artistic vision. Of all the inventions of the modern era, cinema is perhaps the most pronounced and the most influential medium in visual culture. Through mirrors, light, and optical illusion, it creates both fantasy and a vision of reality. In still or motion pictures, a received image captures our dreams and our myths, as well as projects our worldview. And embedded within this worldview is a conventional portrayal of gender, race, sexuality, and nationality.

Analyses of women in film have grown more complex since the emergence of feminist film theory during the 1970s, when such theorists as Laura Mulvey pronounced the inevitable masculinist view of the movie camera as the "determining male gaze [that] projects its fantasy onto the female figure…[which is] coded for strong visual and erotic impact so that [women] can be said to connote *to-be-looked-at-ness*."[1] Over time, feminist critiques have revealed how this male gaze is also raced and nationalistic in its view of the world from a white imperialist perspective. Such postcolonial feminist theorists as Ella Shohat have expanded feminist film theory to address "cinema's geographical and historical constructs as symptomatic of the colonialist imagery generally but also more specifically as a product of a gendered Western gaze…that reflects the symbiotic relations between patriarchal and colonial articulations of difference."[2]

As Shohat reminds us, it is no coincidence that photographic technologies emerged alongside Western imperialism during the mid-nineteenth century and flourished at the height of modernity in the twentieth century. Not long after their inventions, the earliest photography and motion pictures were utilized both for ethnographic depictions of nonwhites and pornographic spectacles of the female body. Via the photographic body, global white imperialism combined with male dominance to display the power and control over these marginalized subjects. In some instances, these visual tropes combined in ethnographic nude portraits of women of color, as documented in a collection of nineteenth-century photographs preserved by Deborah Willis and Carla Williams.[3]

One of the more disturbing photographs from this era features a young South Australian Aboriginal woman called "Ellen," who is positioned as a naked specimen for scientific study with her arm outstretched and measured while her breasts and private parts are on full display in this frontal pose. As Willis and Williams observe, "What had been presented as documents of new and unexplored cultures were in fact carefully constructed manifestations of previously held European notions of the 'primitive savage.' One element in the picture-making process was undoubtedly the titillation of the photographers themselves, who were at least temporarily freed from the moral restrictions of their Western cultures."[4] Indeed, this photographic spectacle of black female nudes would later be reframed by the National Geographic Society, founded in 1888, which created, as Carla Williams argues, "the 'National Geographic' aesthetic... [which introduced] generations of American males and females to 'primitive-style' nudity. Countless examples of bare-breasted or totally nude women of color have appeared in *National Geographic*. Thus, presenting unclothed African [and other nonwhite] bodies to a Victorian audience... could be condoned."[5]

Because racialized and scientific discourse allowed photographers and filmmakers to survey these bodies beyond Western codes of decency and to proliferate these images to a wide audience through the guise of scientific and anthropological "education," the black female body exists outside Mulvey's definition of women's "strong visual and erotic impact." This attention to race in analyzing women in film thus requires that feminist film theory, as Jane Gaines argues, move beyond theorizing the white female body "in terms of objectification, fetishization and symbolic absence" and complicating the black female body as the "paradox of non-being."[6] Here, Gaines references Hortense Spillers who famously described black female sexuality as the site for unrecognizable femininity, "unvoiced, misseen."[7]

Alluding to an oppressive history of slavery, colonialism, and legal segrega-tion, Spillers intersects race and gender to articulate the silences around this (mis)representation of black women's bodies, which are simultaneously hyper-feminine in excessive displays of nudity and defeminized in white suprema-cist language that denies their beauty and desirability. The 1879 ethnographic portrait of Ellen is a prime example of how such spectacles submerge the aes-thetic and erotic treatment of black female bodies while nude pictures of white women are either hidden in the secretive texts of stag pornography or given license for sexual display through non-Western contexts. As Shohat describes of the latter:

> The gender and colonial discursive intersections in Hollywood…exploit the Orient, Africa, and Latin America as a pretext for eroticized images, especially from 1934 through the mid-1950s when the restrictive code forbade "scenes of passion" in all but the most puerile terms…Exoticiz-ing and eroticizing the Third World allowed for the imperial imaginary to play out its own fantasies of sexual domination.[8]

This dichotomy between West and non-West helped shape a cinematic lan-guage in which these geographic spaces collide fantasy and the realism of the photographic image. The colonizing male gaze thus reflects the colonizing mis-sion of subjugating both land and the female body in the realist fantasy realm represented by cinema.

As the camera surveys both land and bodies, it also serves as a "travel-ogue," as Alison Griffiths documents in her research of turn-of-the-century cinema. Anthropology and ethnography combined with popular culture to turn cinema into a "civic educator and tool of colonial propaganda."[9] Because of this developing role of cinema, it comes as no surprise that, within European art practices, painters resorted to impressionistic, expressionistic, and abstract art, leaving the more realist portrayal of the body and the world to photogra-phy and cinema. *Metropolis*, debuting at the close of the silent film era, would offer a glimpse of cinema, less as ethnography and more as expressionist art, before the more theatrical and ethnographic components offered in film would dominate with the oncoming era of sound technology. Nonetheless, art bor-rows from these realist images constructed from cinema to create a compelling conversation around gender and racial tropes.

The subject of race and its interplay with gender has constituted cinema's modern advancements and contributed to film's complex storytelling. Not only do we find racial subjects in the plot of D. W. Griffith's 1915 *Birth of a*

Nation (the film is celebrated for its novel display of film editing and montage, editing techniques also utilized as a storytelling counterpoint in Oscar Micheaux's racially subversive 1920 *Within Our Gates*) they also undergird the first "talkie," Alan Crosland's 1927 *Jazz Singer*, in which Al Jolson dons blackface and belts out the melodramatic ballad, "Mammy," in the musical spectacle. That these cinematic advancements simultaneously emphasize racial politics and gender relations (the threat of interracial sexual relations in Griffith's silent film, the caricatured mother–son relationship in Crosland's talkie) underscores how critical these factors are in shaping national narratives and the body politic.

In the wake of cinema's sound technology, other national cinemas emulated Hollywood through the spectacle offered in the musical. French cinema employed their celebrated American émigré and entertainer Josephine Baker to headline films that emphasized her racial "difference" and libidinal dancing, which required her to function as a "stand-in" for France's colonial subjects— such as an Antillean in *Zou Zou* or an African, unleashed by the "tom-tom drums," in *Princess Tam Tam*. Indeed, the spectacle of racial difference became so performative that white bodies could also appropriate the same cultural signifiers, as demonstrated in the performance of "Hot Voodoo" by international German star Marlene Dietrich, who donned a blond "Afro" and emerged from a gorilla suit in *Blonde Venus*.

While Western movie musicals collapsed cultures and blurred the national lines of entertainment through the spectacle of the female body and colonialist tropes of Orientalism and primitivism, other film industries, such as in India, utilized the musical to highlight culturally specific music and dances with links to an earlier mode of Hindi storytelling. In particular, Hindi cinema allowed for a space in which audiences recognized playback singers, like Lata Mangeshkar—who were reduced to a small number in the industry in the wake of Partition in 1947—in their own right and not as a submerged identity shared with the film's stars.[10] While a playback singer could hold such cultural and national resonance in one context, in another context, such as in Hollywood, a playback singer may not even be recognized in the closing credits, so eager were film producers to maintain the illusion that the voice and the body emanated from the same source. What we have then, in this early history of sound cinema that laid the foundation for different cinematic practices, is the boundary markers between fantasy and reality, with the body as contested space for gendered, raced, and nationalist meanings. It is a modern history that feminists would return to and rewrite in their own postmodern narratives.

CONTESTING CINEMATIC HISTORIES

These differences in cinematic practices complicate how women's bodies are interpreted on-screen and offscreen. In Hollywood cinema, women's bodies are what film scholar Gwendolyn Audrey Foster describes as "substitutable fragmented constructions" in which a face, a hand, a body double, or an offscreen voice can be edited together to create a "whole" woman on-screen.[11] This cinematic framing becomes a point of contention in filmmaker Julie Dash's 1983 film short, *Illusions*.

In this work, Dash repositions the black female body to contest black women's invisibility in mainstream Hollywood cinema. The plot unfolds on a 1940s Hollywood set in which two black female protagonists are placed front and center in the narrative. One character, Ester Jeeter, functions as a playback singer, who is hired to overdub a musical voice-over. Through her juxtaposition of Ester, emerging from the dark in the backdrop as she provides sound to the image of the singing white woman on-screen, Dash refocuses the camera on the black female body, in particular through the camera close-up on Ester. The effect here is ironic, even comical, as it becomes quite obvious that the black woman in full view is lip-synching to the film soundtrack. While pointing to the fabricated constructions of Hollywood femininity, Dash uses her own film to reproduce and, thus, expose this artificiality.

The other black female character in this film short is Mignon Dupree, an executive assistant at the film studio who is light enough to "pass" for white. Her motives for passing, however, differ significantly from those of other "passing" characters in Hollywood films like *Imitation of Life* and *Pinky*. Whereas these passing-for-white heroines transgress the color line for love and acceptance in the white social world, Mignon passes in order to participate in the power structure of the film industry. Hers is not the goal of choosing the limited role of passive yet desirable white female. She is portrayed working side-by-side with the Hollywood "powers that be," even rebuffing the sexual advances of white men. In these ways, Mignon becomes a stand-in for the black feminist filmmaker Dash as she delivers an accusatory monologue at the film's end: "Your scissors and your paste methods have eliminated my history, my participation in this country." It becomes rather evident that, through this film short, Dash resolves to correct this erasure through filmmaking.

This momentum in the 1980s for feminist artistic revisions echoes the postmodern preoccupation with deconstruction and signification. Dash also reflects the postcolonial impulse utilized in the work of anthropologist and filmmaker Trinh T. Minh-ha, who rewrites and reassesses the colonial gaze to "learn how to un-write and write anew."[12] This goal is brilliantly coded in the images and sound she literally reassembles in her 1982 film short, *Reassemblage*. In this ethnographic "film about Senegal," Trinh consciously challenges her audience to question the meanings that each image and sound should convey about the African subject. Deliberately confounding the "National Geographic aesthetic," Trinh constructs a discordant film in which the visual and the sound do not match, in which they are not synchronized to convey a recognizable "story about Senegal." Her soft-spoken, accent-heavy English voice-over muses more than it authorizes. When she nonchalantly observes, for example, that a U.S. Peace Corps volunteer (who is not shown on-screen) has traveled to this rural village in Senegal to "teach" villagers about agriculture, Trinh renders his colonial narrative laughable by the continuous display of hardworking rural women engaged in the multitask demands of food production and labor. As Trinh remarks, "It took only forty years to label millions of years of culture as 'underdeveloped.'"

The more controversial element of Trinh's film is her close-up depictions of women's nudity. Her camera does not shy away from these extreme close-ups of Senegalese women's breasts, as if she is saying: I know you (Westerner) watch these films just for the nudity; I will shove it in your face. Indeed, Trinh cites a British man confessing that he feels he has watched "pornography" when viewing a travelogue on Africa. We may argue that Trinh has also reobjectified the black female body in a similar manner; however, she strategically questions the positioning of such nudity in the contexts of ethnography when similar nude images of white women are immediately recognizable for their erotic function and titillation.

These disruptive feminist narratives of cinema create a critical space for interrogation of the racial and sexual politics that shape how women's bodies are filmed. Following in a similar trajectory is the work of Australian Aboriginal filmmaker and artist Tracey Moffatt, who borrows from this postmodern and postcolonial mode of thinking. Her 1987 film short, *Nice Coloured Girls*, specifically juxtaposes the colonial narrative of "discovery" and sexual conquest with the contemporary scene of Sydney, Australia, and Aboriginal women's place within it. Moffatt contrasts the voice-over narrative of a British explorer, reading from a historical account of his exploits of the native women, with the subtitled narrative of three young Aboriginal women. These women also chronicle their own present-day "exploits" of white men, who are called "Captain" in an intergenerational recognition of the legacy of these racialized and imperialist sexual relations. Through this multilayered narrative, Moffatt challenges the dominant script by reframing documentary-style filmmaking through oppositional storytelling.

Here, the written language of history is given oral expression while the oral interviews of the young women are given textual authority in the English subtitles: a role-reversal in which written language, rather than create such women as "objects of study," re-presents them as authoritative subjects with the power to subvert the limited positionality of the white male voice heard offscreen. Even the film's title gets rendered ironically with the film's music soundtrack, which includes Vanity 6's "Nasty Girls" and Aretha Franklin's "Evil Woman." This intertextual and transnational discourse between women of color prompts us to redefine the amoral actions of the women on-screen—who deliberately intoxicate a "Captain" before stealing from him and "leaving him for dead"—as those of resistance. Beyond these small acts of resistance, Moffatt closes the film by pulling back from the scene and panning over the wide expanse of Sydney's harbor, while the British explorer's voice-over continues in its naïve construct of the "innocent" and "nice coloured girl." This white naïveté, coupled with Aboriginal women's crafty ingenuity, is undercut by the larger context of a white dominant landscape revealing the urban development that has since displaced First Australian land and peoples.

These subtle politics of indigenous feminist resistance and postcolonial critique became mobilized in Moffatt's first feature-length film, *Bedevil*. This film debuted in 1993, the same "year of the Indigenous" people, occurring a year after the quincentennial celebrations of Christopher Columbus's "discovery" of the Americas. This is also the same year that New Zealand filmmaker Jane Campion received international acclaim for her Oscar-nominated *The Piano*, which, as Caroline Brown argues, "becomes the ultimate colonizing project, appropriating Maori culture as a site of radical and quirky difference. Despite the cleverness of their presence in the film—their humor, the fact that they speak their own language, their boldness—the Maori... are also perhaps too easily reincorporated into a host of earlier cultural stereotypes."[13] These cultural stereotypes, based in premodernity, hypersexuality, or "noble savagery," are posited as cinematic romance in Campion's film, which is resisted in Moffatt's *Bedevil*, a film that not only complicates indigenous representations but also interweaves multiracial narratives and interjects historical storytelling and its shaping of the present. Indeed, through its presentation of three "ghost stories," the subject of "bedevilment" to which the title alludes, Moffatt "repeatedly makes the point that land development has also led to the destruction of people and land."[14]

Like Campion, Moffatt's film incorporates lush visual scenes—in particular, a hypervisualized set of the outback in the second story, "Choo Choo Choo Choo" (in which Moffatt portrays the young version of her mother, while actress Auriel Andrews portrays the mature version)—and sweeping shots of the developed landscape of modern Australia that mirror promotional tourist imagery. These stories—including the first installment, "Mr. Chuck," and the final installment, "Lovin' the Spin I'm In"—narrate the hauntings in both faux-documentary style and caricatured performances. There is an element of falsity and absurdity, and not just because the stories involve ghosts. Moffatt seems to parody Western fixations, especially within the Hollywood horror genre, on haunted "Indian burial grounds," hence the literal grounding of each story within the land itself. In "Mr. Chuck," the construction of a movie theater is interrupted by the ghost of an American Second World War soldier in a nearby swamp, as well as by the vandalism of an Aboriginal boy, who is subject to abuse. We are introduced to this character, first as a middle-aged incarcerated man, who laughs hysterically at his childhood fears of this haunting. His narrative, which cryptically remarks, "I hated that place!" is juxtaposed with a stereotyped well-to-do white Australian, who comments, "I loved that place." Her delivery is one of melodramatic overacting, which inclines the audience to already discount her version of the story. In this dichotomous construction of Aboriginal disgust and white Australian nostalgia, Moffatt invites us to question what exactly accounts for such "bedevilment," and curiously, how cinematic constructs—literally represented in the unfinished movie theater—fail to camouflage deeper hauntings and historical tragedies that "stank worse than shit," through its superficial tales of romantic histories.

These nuanced presentations of personal and national histories also frame "Choo Choo Choo Choo," which recalls the haunting of a blind girl in the outback, where she was run over by a train. As with the unfinished movie theater, these train tracks were also left uncompleted by this tragedy. This story, told to Moffatt by her mother, Ruby, bridges the personal and the communal as Moffatt pans over various townsfolk who gesture a number of hand signals. We later learn that this mysterious sign language tells the tale of this haunting, while the mature Ruby cheerily reminisces about her experiences as a young woman with this supernatural being. Moving between the past and the present, the story unfolds in a complex multilayered telling. The present-day Ruby has gathered with some of her friends at the same site, abandoned and decrepit, to enjoy a day of eating and leisure. Through a clever and wry feminist sensibility, Ruby takes her time in telling us the story, just as Moffatt takes her time in piecing the puzzle of this ghost story—interjecting scenes of the "haunted house" with contemporary scenes of Ruby talking directly to the camera, even mimicking Julia Childs and the concept of "civilized dining" through her explanation of the "bush cuisine" she is preparing and her translation of the

Koori women's dialogue. In perhaps the most jarring and hilarious moment, she breaks down the imaginary fourth wall by walking up to the camera to wipe dust off from the filter in front of the lens. This moment prevents any "male" or "colonizing" gaze from framing her as an object of study or desire. It instead pulls the viewer into the drama, subjecting us to *her* gaze as this moment of maternal interference renders Ruby as the one in full control of both image production and historical storytelling.

The final story—"Lovin' the Spin I'm In"—involves the haunting of the only Aboriginal ghosts in the film, and these ghosts not only have more presence but also become fully embodied. Their tragedy as lovers, who married against betrothal law, and who become entrapped in a violent end, continues to haunt a warehouse, which is targeted by business developers with ambitions to open an offshore casino on the site. The developers' attempts to evict the few marginal tenants who reside there—including the mother of one of the lovers and a transgender Frida Kahlo impersonator—place them in opposition to the marginalized and the disempowered. Having been spooked by these ghosts, the developers run off, only to drive off in a continuous right-turn spin that prevents their escape.

The ghost lovers also haunt yet intrigue their next-door neighbor, a young Greek boy who is an outcast among his peers. The dancing silhouettes, which opened the film, thus parodying the exoticized images that opened the James Bond film *Dr. No*, take on a fuller presence in the red-lit warehouse where our ghostly dancers enchant us with a stunning *pas de deux* reenacting their contentious relationship. Like all ghosts, history insists on remembrance and continued storytelling, and Moffatt uses her film and the numerous ways that different languages—sign, dance, visuals—get mobilized in these retellings. In keeping with a postmodern and postcolonial feminist vision, Moffatt utilizes cinema's conventional sights and sounds to relearn these visual and aural codes. She has, much like Dash and Trinh, learned to "un-write and write anew."

In the wake of postmodern and postcolonial feminist productions of cinema, emerging artists have expanded the genre in progressive and innovative ways. With emerging media flourishing during the digital revolution, our visual culture continues to evolve. One artist who has creatively interrogated the filmic experience is Lorna Simpson, a gifted photographer and videographer, who mounted a video installation in 2003, titled *Corridor*. In this work, Simpson combines two video projections to create a double narrative of black women within domestic space. One narrative is set in 1860, in which our "house slave" resides in a dark, candlelit home where she has little time to herself; whereas the other narrative is set in 1960, in which our heroine (played by the same actress) is immersed in luxury, modernity, and ennui. This juxtaposition of the two scenes, which function as a hybrid "silent film"—no dialogue with the exception of a soundtrack that expertly mixes classical music with dissonant echoes of modern jazz—reflects what Simpson describes as "the psychological disposition of the characters portrayed."[15] Utilizing the house as metaphor, while crossing different timelines—detected through costume and architecture—Simpson presents the interior dimensions of both psyche and geography to comment on confinement and freedom.

What is particularly striking about this "film" is the way the characters appear to be in their most private realm. This image is uncommon, as black women in film are rarely depicted within their own space and rarely shown at leisure. This is especially true with the portrayal of the "house slave" (and even here, we only accord this identity onto the nineteenth-century black woman, who could be a free subject) whose only labor depicted is that in which she bathes herself. The other action portrayed is of her writing in an upstairs room. Indeed, the 1860 black woman seems more driven and with purpose in comparison to the 1960 black woman whose only actions about the house include personal grooming, preparing a meal—presumably for a date—and conversing on the phone. In her intimate moments, she too seems to have little time for herself except to contemplate her relationship to others. She is in a lovely modernist home, and yet, she seems more oppressed by its surroundings than the 1860 woman.

This provocative silent film art engages the politics of cinema to contest the "paradox of non-being," or what Lorraine O'Grady argues about black women's visual representation: "To name ourselves rather than be named we must first see ourselves. For some of us, this will not be easy. So long unmirrored, we may have forgotten we look."[16] The motif of mirrors and windows in *Corridor* suggests that Simpson is involved in a project of naming, of becoming, of mirroring new possibilities of seeing black women in film. In these ways, we may recognize how feminist artists and filmmakers are utilizing the cinematic impulse of visual culture to disrupt, dismantle, and reassemble the myriad meanings attached to women's bodies.

EMERGING CINEMA, EMERGING ART

One arena in which cinema emerges in new forms involves digital technology. The digital revolution, combining computer technology with photographic/filmic technologies, has shifted our relationship to visual "screen." Nowhere is this more evident than the Internet, which has evolved from windows to

e-mails to websites to interactive, multimedia Web 2.0. As with early cinema, the Internet projects itself as a "travelogue," via its World Wide Web.
As Lisa Nakamura argues, the Internet invokes a "technologically enabled
transnationality…that directly addresses the first-world user, whose position
on the network will allow him to metaphorically go wherever he likes."[17] In
addition, it has also mobilized the technology for greater access to women's
bodies with the proliferation of Internet porn sites, which also occurred with
the invention of still and motion pictures and, later, with the invention of video.

While new media seem to perpetuate old ideologies of race and gender,
certain feminist artists have reconfigured these tools for critique. Artist Roshini
Kempadoo, who develops digital multimedia art, is one such feminist who
began some of the earlier criticisms of the power and domination of cyberspace. In her 1996 web-based series, *Sweetness and Light*, Kempadoo explores
the legacies of colonialism and imperial power using her digital photo-texts.
Through her self-portrait in an image from the *Head People* segment, Kempadoo positions herself as a waiter in white blouse and tie serving up a computer
on a silver platter, which depicts on its screen the head of a white colonial
supervisor leading a military group of nonwhite soldiers. Against this image
is a backdrop of a balustrade, along which are depicted nude African women
in ethnographic postures, with rulers in between each subject, thus alluding
to the scientific legacy of reducing black subjects to their bodies, while white
representations of order and imperial power dominate on-screen.[18] In the same
series, Kempadoo constructs another image that fuses a landscape picture of
a Jamaican plantation with a faded photograph of a computer keyboard, thus
suggesting that cyberspace presents a new frontier of discovery, conquest, and
settlement. A third image from the *Great House People* segment presents a
historic black-and-white photograph from the British colonial period depicting two white men with a partially nude black woman seated on one of the
men's laps. Overlaid on a picture of a wooden entrance gate to an estate or
plantation, and accompanied by the written text "whichever way the eye is
turned, it is regaled with an endless variety of pleasing prospects," this image
lays bare the sexual history of conquest and empire that equates black female
bodies with colonized lands. Through this series, Kempadoo makes explicit
the sexualized arena of the Internet, which provides access to women's bodies
on a global scale—whether through cyberporn, e-mail–order brides, or other
forms of Internet sex trafficking.

This consumption of female bodies has prompted other digital artists of
color to utilize the Internet for artistic critique. Artist Prema Murthy constructs
two different websites that signify the information architecture of pornography,

in the case of "Bindi Girl," and search engines, in the case of "Mythic Hybrid." In "Bindi Girl," Murthy parodies both the ethnographic and the pornographic as the website features a quote from the Karma Sutra—that ancient Indian text that has captivated Western audiences with an Orientalist appetite for Indian culture and exotica—and the mark of the bindi, the red dot marked on the South Asian female body. An audio featuring a Lata Mangeshkaresque singer blares from the site in an attempt to overwhelm the user with these markers of Indian femininity. Curiously, or one should say deliberately, Murthy employs the mark of the bindi to deny users sight of the revealed pornographic body by placing it in strategic locations that cover up the nude women. It also features a warning message about the content of pornography—thus inviting associations between its subversive critique of Internet porn and actual porn sites—and an absurdist chat room dialogue between a "woman" and "man" simulating a sex fantasy. Mobilizing cinematic bodies—through brief glimpses of famous Bollywood female stars and the sound of its playback singers—Murthy critiques the cinematic construct of both the Internet and the text of pornography.

"Mythic Hybrid," on the other hand, presents the title of the artwork in the space of a "search box," which has already yielded a series of terms and topics pertaining to information about South and Southeast Asian women workers in computer hardware factories who provide the invisible labor of the digital age. Such terms include "ASIAN WOMEN," "Labour experiences," and "Power, Identity, and Exchange in Cyberspace"—thus defining to the Internet user what these women's bodies and labor mean in the realm of digital technology. Replete with audio, video, and written testimonials pertaining to information about South and Southeast Asian women workers in computer hardware factories, Murthy effectively "informs" her readers about the intrinsic role women of color play in shaping our technologies while also presenting the multimedia possibilities in which text, video, audio, and still images combine in the latest interactive art. The women presented in Murthy's multimedia narrative are both "mythic" (the invisible producers of the digital revolution) and "hybrid" (fusing their subaltern realities into the global information superhighway).

This imaginative approach in presenting the website as interactive performance art subverts information, the main driving force behind the Internet and our information age. It also gestures toward the interactivity of new media in shaping the future of art and cinema. Another artist, Cao Fei, has immersed herself in these recent expressions of emerging art, even emerging cinema. The film industry, much like the music industry, has had to incorporate the trends of digital technology to stay relevant, while pornography and video games have stayed ahead of the curve. One of these trends combines the Internet with social networking and gaming, such as *Second Life*—an avatar-driven social network site—which Cao Fei has mobilized for her artistic vision, including the designing of artwork as her Second Life avatar, China Tracy.

Machinima is the latest in movie and digital production, which relies on avatar creations that are assembled for movie and video making. Fei as China Tracy, constructed her machinima, *I.Mirror* (also available on YouTube), based on her own interactions within the Second Life virtual world. Exploring the fluid boundaries between real and fantasy, between freedom of information and corporate limitations, Tracy's machinima interrogates how identities, bodies, and nationalities are constituted via digital technologies.

In part one of *I.Mirror*, Tracy surveys the virtual landscape of Second Life, which is presented as "land for sale," thus reinforcing the precepts of consumerism and property while simultaneously promoting ideas of freedom from the real world. Tracy presents these contradictions, using her virtual body to literally fly beyond the national borders—represented by the numerous flags on display—while situating her identity within China. She may transcend the limitations of the physical and national body, but even within this virtual fantasy, she allows "reality" to intrude by depicting an industrial cesspool that threatens the environment. The careful details of this toxic waste dump signify crucial issues for the next era of our hi-tech world, which has perpetuated these toxic tech sites in the avaricious demand for the latest technologies and global developments. If Second Life is a mirror, then Tracy uses it to reflect what *is* and what *could be*.

Part two depicts her interactions and chats with a fellow Second Life user, Hug Yue, who accompanies China Tracy on her virtual travels across urbanscapes and rain forests. They also make music together, each taking turns on the piano and guitar. Hug Yue, who appears to be a young, dashing blonde and tuxedoed avatar, reveals that he is in his sixties, thus reflecting his comments that Second Life is about "youth, beauty, and money...it's all an illusion." Hug Yue, however, presents a different avatar closer to his age, thus showcasing how these aspects of self can be altered at one's will. China Tracy herself, who keeps to a standard body most likely representing her real self—long black hair and slender body—views the virtual space as an alternate reality, her avatar an alter ego of her true self, even when she confuses "RL and SL." Constantly presenting her body as afloat in space, Tracy depicts a suspended reality in which she loses herself. This perception of the simulated environment is in keeping with Jean Baudrillard's assertion that the "hyper real" creates a world "where there is more and more information, and less and less meaning."[19]

This, of course, is the ultimate illusion in which, as Coco Fusco sardonically comments, the Internet offers a "'virtual promised land' where 'we' don't need to be concerned with the violent exercise of power on bodies and territories anymore."[20] Tracy questions this conceit in part three by cataloguing the different raced, gendered, and national avatar bodies (even hybrid animal and alien bodies) one can access in Second Life, as well as the different sexual practices one can engage in through various interactions with others in this virtual world. The problem that Tracy showcases is how hegemonic these constructions are since women's bodies are rather pornographically designed, and the different "skins" one can try on for their avatars are limited in melanin choices and body types (thus suggesting that no users would fantasize themselves as very dark-skinned or as heavyset). These normative constructions underlie how, even within fantasy, not everybody has a place in it. Or, more to the point, these bodies still adhere to a white supremacist, sexist, and ageist worldview. Through these critical interrogations, Tracy reveals the limits of our imaginations and the possibilities for unmasking what she concludes to be "human beings behind hollow digits, all those lonely souls."

While Tracy ends her machinima with a wish for digital media that can provide a "new force which [transcends] this mortal coil," her documentation of "lonely souls" reaching out for shared experiences—even via virtual fantasies—speaks to the ways that the digital revolution continues to blur the boundaries between the private and the public. These narratives, which have evolved in the public sphere from cinema and television to the Internet, promise to expand media in more innovative and progressive ways. The work of filmmaker Ayoka Chenzira comes to mind, who has developed what she calls "tangible cinema." The first of these narratives, *Flying over Purgatory*, installed at the Georgia Institute of Technology, includes an original screenplay that Chenzira based on transcripts from South Africa's Post-Apartheid Truth and Reconciliation Commission. Two monitors depicting these testimonials were embedded within a wooden sculpture, thus inviting users to view sculpture—an old-school version of visual culture—alongside the digital interface.

Chenzira's second narrative installation, *CrazyQuilt Sightings: Surviving Broken Levees and Katrina*, also incorporates three-dimensional art through different fabrics, representing the quilting element alluded to in the title, and the computer interface, which includes varied oral testimonials and images relating to the Hurricane Katrina aftermath in New Orleans. Using a multitouch tabletop panel, Chenzira allows users to "build their own crazy quilt as they move items into a position and trigger a connecting video clip."[21] Through her visionary work, Chenzira demonstrates how digital technologies not only shape art but also encourage communal physical interactions (not just virtual ones) and shared memories. Such tangible approaches to cinema and art present future possibilities that expand women's participation and representation in new territory and a new imaginary.

CONCLUSION: FUTURE CINEMA, FUTURE ART, FUTURE FEMINISMS

Taken together, these modern developments illuminate the transgressive ways that women shape each new invention within our visual cultures. The cyborg in *Metropolis* may have been portrayed as a threat to our freedoms, our morals, and our traditions, but she has since evolved to serve as a mirror of our gendered, raced, and nationalist reality. More than that, she can be mobilized as counterpoints to white imperialist patriarchal narratives. Indeed as Donna Haraway has argued, cyborgs "require regeneration, not rebirth, and the possibilities for our reconstitution...[of a] world without gender."[22]

Even so, our imaginaries tend to limit these possibilities for reconstitution, perhaps because our visual culture has already been contained by a limited lens looking out on the world and on our bodies. The invention of cinema and other photographic technologies might move in concert with hegemonic systems, but feminist narratives exist to showcase another possibility and another world—based in reality or in fantasy—so that we can interrogate the roles we have been assigned pertaining to gender, race, class, nationality, and sexuality. Because of these counternarratives, we might be able to envision a future that is just as malleable and emergent as each new digital gadget that promises new and exciting ways to personalize and share our art and our mediated lives.

NOTES

Introduction

1. See Stephen Kern, *The Culture of Time and Space 1880–1918* (Cambridge: Harvard University Press, 1983); Jonathan Crary, *Techniques of the Observer: On Vision and Modernity in the Nineteenth Century* (Cambridge: MIT Press, 1994); Wolfgang Schivelbusch, *The Railway Journey: Trains and Travel in the Nineteenth Century*, trans. Anselm Hollo (Oxford: Basil Blackwell, 1980).

2. Tani Barlow defines "vernacular sociology" as "[s]ocial theory published in the mass media that presumes the existence of the social contract, introduces psycho-social dynamic theories of subjectivity, or invokes a 'social question.'" See Tani E. Barlow, "Buying In: Advertising and the Sexy Modern Girl Icon in Shanghai in the 1920s and 1930s," in *The Modern Girl Around the World: Consumption, Modernity, and Globalization*, ed. Alys Eve Weinbaum, Lynn M. Thomas, Priti Ramamurthy, Uta G. Poiger, Madeline Yue Dong, and Tani E. Barlow (Durham: Duke University Press, 2008), p. 299.

3. Marilyn Lake and Henry Reynolds, *Drawing the Global Colour Line: White Men's Countries and the Question of Racial Equality* (Melbourne: Melbourne University Press, 2008), p. 6.

4. Kern, *Culture of Time and Space*, p. 145.

5. Lake and Reynolds, *Global Colour Line*.

6. Lake and Reynolds, *Global Colour Line*, p. 23.

7. Julie Evans, Patricia Grimshaw, David Philips, and Shurlee Swain, *Equal Subjects, Unequal Right: Indigenous Peoples in British Settler Colonies 1830–1910* (Manchester: Manchester University Press, 2003), p. 3.

8. See the discussion in Rita Felski, *The Gender of Modernity* (Cambridge: Harvard University Press, 1995), p. 3; Kalpana Ram and Margaret Jolly, eds., *Maternities and Modernities: Colonial and Postcolonial Experiences in Asia and the Pacific* (New York: Cambridge University Press, 1998); Marylu Hill,

Mothering Modernity: Feminism, Modernism, and the Maternal Muse (Garland: New York, 1999).

9. See Kerreen Reiger, *The Disenchantment of the Home: Modernizing the Australian Family, 1880–1940* (Melbourne: Oxford University Press, 1985).

10. Kathy Peiss, *Cheap Amusements: Leisure in Turn-of-the-Century New York* (Philidelphia: Temple University Press, 1986), p. 4.

11. Felski, *Gender of Modernity*, p. 146.

12. Weinbaum et al., eds., *The Modern Girl Around the World*.

13. Kathy Piess, "Girls Lean Back Everywhere," in Weinbaum et al., *Modern Girl Around the World*, p. 350.

14. Patrice Petro, *Joyless Streets: Women and Melodramatic Representation in Weimar Germany* (Princeton, NJ: Princeton University Press, 1989).

15. Felski, *Gender of Modernity*, p. 4.

16. Scott McQuire, *Visions of Modernity: Representation, Memory, Time and Space in the Age of the Camera* (Sage: London, 1997), p. 22.

17. David Levin situates the commencement of modernity with "the 'discovery' of perspective and the rationalization of sight in the Italian Renascimento of the fifteenth-century" (*Modernity and the Hegemony of Vision* [Berkeley: University of California Press], p. 2).

18. Martin Jay, *Downcast Eyes: The Denigration of Vision in Twentieth Century French Thought* (Berkeley: University of California Press, 1994), p. 63.

19. Kern, *Culture of Time and Space*, p. 34.

20. Angela Woollacott, "White Colonialism and Sexual Modernity: Australian Women in the Early Twentieth Century Metropolis," in *Gender, Sexuality and Colonial Modernities*, ed. Antoinette Burton (Routledge: London, 1999), p. 50.

21. Janell Hobson, *Venus in the Dark: Blackness and Beauty in Popular Culture* (New York: Routledge, 2005), p. 46.

22. McQuire, *Visions of Modernity*, p. 55.

23. Picture postcards emerged in the late 1890s but not until 1902 were they made available in Britain with divided backs for messages and postal addresses. See Christine Cane and Niel Gunson, "Postcards: A Source for Aboriginal Biography," *Aboriginal History* 10, no. 1 (1986): p. 171.

24. Tony Hughes-D'Aeth, *Paper Nation: The Story of the Picturesque Atlas of Australasia 1886–1888* (Melbourne: Melbourne University Press, 2001), p. 191.

25. Peter Conrad, *Modern Times, Modern Places: Life and Art in the Twentieth Century* (London: Thames and Hudson, 1998), p. 9.

26. See Elizabeth Wilson, *The Sphinx in the City: Urban Life, the Control of Disorder and Women* (London: Virago Press, 1991).

27. Judith R. Walkowitz, *City of Dreadful Delights: Narratives of Sexual Danger in Late-Victorian London* (Chicago: University of Chicago Press, 1992), p. 46.

28. Felski, *Gender of Modernity*, p. 72.

29. William Leach, "Strategists of Display and the Production of Desire," in *Consuming Visions: Accumulation and Display of Goods in America 1830–1920,* ed. Simn J. Bronner (New York: W.W. Norton, 1989), pp. 99–132.

30. Fiona Paisley, *Glamour in the Pacific: Cultural Internationalism and Race Politics in the Women's Pan-Pacific* (Honolulu: Hawai'i University Press, 2009).

31. Heather Goodall, *Invasion to Embassy: Land in Aboriginal Politics in New South Wales 1770–1792* (Sydney: Sydney University Press), p. 4.

32. This is the argument passionately sustained in Heather Goodall's history of dispossession in New South Wales. Goodall, *Invasion to Embassy.*

33. Evans et al., *Equal Subjects*, pp. 190–91.

34. Evans et al., *Equal Subjects*, p. 182.

Chapter 1

Regarding the oral histories: the author undertook interviews with the following people in a way that conformed to the ethical standards of the Flinders University Social and Behavioural Ethics Research Committee:

Natasha, July 23, 2004.

Julie Mackey, August 9, 2004.

Margaret Kevin, August 29, 2004.

Amanda Collinge, December 20, 2004.

I wish to thank the women named here for sharing their stories.

1. This phrase is borrowed from Susan Magarey who has used it to describe the Australian Woman Movement of the late nineteenth century, which she argues was "not only born modern but a force for modernism," in part highlighting the absence of a local tradition and therefore the possibility of the movement defining itself entirely in a modern context and as an expression of the nation's modernity. Susan Magarey, "History, Cultural Studies and another look at First Wave Feminism in Australia," *Australian Historical Studies* 106 (1996): 96–110, p. 110.

2. Bronwyn Fredericks, "Australian Aboriginal Women's Health: Reflecting on the Past and Present," *Health and History* 2 (2007): 93–113, p. 98.

3. Fredericks, "Australian Aboriginal Women's Health."

4. It is worth noting that national birthrates have been measured in a way that includes women who have not become mothers, so the birthrate as it has applied exclusively to mothers has been higher than the rate for all Australian women.

5. Subsequent scholars of fertility rates have learned from the shortcomings of the 1903 inquiry. By 1971, for example, a major study led by John Caldwell, aiming to understand declining fertility, involved two-hour interviews with thousands of women from rural and urban Australia. John C. Caldwell, Christabel Young, Helen Ware, Donald Levis, and Anh-Thu Davis, "Knowledge, Attitudes and Practice of Family Planning in Melbourne, 1971," *Studies in Family Planning* 3 (1973): 47–59.

6. Gordon A. Carmichael, "Colonial and Post-colonial Demographic Patterns," in *Gender Relations in Australia, Domination and Negotiation,* ed. Kay Saunders and Raymond Evans (Sydney: Harcourt, Brace Jovanovich, 1992), p. 128.

7. In 1934 Australian women were averaging just over two births during their reproductive life cycles and many postponed marriage due to financial burden; in

1945 they averaged closer to three births and in 1961, the year the contraceptive pill became available, the figure was closer to four. See Carmichael, "Colonial and Post-colonial Demographic Patterns," pp. 128–29.

8. For example, the 1961 census showed Dutch Catholic women to have very high numbers of children and, in the 1970s, Southern European women were having especially large families. In the late 1970s and in to the 1980s, high fertility was most notable among women from Middle Eastern countries. Mohammad Jalal Abbasi-Shavazi and Peter McDonald, "Fertility and Multiculturalism: Immigrant Fertility in Australia, 1977–1991," *International Migration Review* 34 (2000): 215–42, p. 219.

9. Abbasi-Shavazi and McDonald, "Fertility and Multiculturalism," pp. 234–35.

10. John Caldwell quoted in Alison MacKinnon, "From one *Fin De Siecle* to Another: The Educated Woman and Declining Birth-Rate," *Australian Educational Researcher* 3 (1995): p. 84.

11. MacKinnon, "From one *Fin De Siecle* to Another," p. 75.

12. Jan Kociumbas, *Australian Childhood, a History* (Sydney: Allen and Unwin, 1997).

13. Diana Gittens, *Fair Sex: Family Size and Structure 1900–1939* (London: Hutchinson, 1982). Quoted in Kociumbas, *Australian Childhood*, p. 77.

14. Kociumbas, *Australian Childhood*, p. 77.

15. Kociumbas, *Australian Childhood*, p. 77.

16. Gordon A. Carmichael and Peter McDonald, "Fertility Trends and Differentials," in *The Transformation of Australia's Population: 1970–2030*, ed. Siew-Ean Khoo and Peter McDonald (Sydney: UNSW Press), p. 55.

17. Bob Birrell, *People and Place* 2 (2000), pp. 34–35.

18. Lois Bryson, Stephanie Strazzari, and Wendy Brown, "Shaping families. Women control and contraception," *Family Matters* (*Australian Institute of Family Studies*) 53 (1999), pp. 31–38.

19. Kociumbas, *Australian Childhood*, p. 150.

20. Kociumbas, *Australian Childhood*, p. 150.

21. Janet McCalman, *Sex and Suffering, Women's Health and a Women's Hospital* (Melbourne: Melbourne University Press, 1998), p. 96.

22. McCalman, *Sex and Suffering*, pp. 29–31.

23. Milton Lewis, "Maternity Care and Puerperal Fever in Sydney," in *Women and Children First, International Maternal and Infant Welfare 1870–1945*, ed. Marks Fildes and Marland Fildes (London: Routledge, 1992).

24. Kociumbas, *Australian Childhood*, p. 151.

25. Lewis, "Maternity Care and Puerperal Fever in Sydney," p. 30.

26. Philippa Mein Smith gives an example of such strategies when she notes that during the 1920s and 1930s the Victorian Baby Health Centres Association instructed nurses to urge expectant women to visit a doctor and if a patient had failed to do so a month after such urgings, to refuse to see them again. See Philippa Mein Smith, *Mothers and King Baby: Infant Survival and Welfare in an Imperial World: Australia, 1880–1950* (London: Macmillan, 1997), p. 203.

27. An account of this campaign is contained in Catherine Kevin, "Great Expectations: Episodes in a Political History of Pregnancy in Australia since 1945," in *Feminism*

and the Body, Interdisciplinary Perspectives, ed. Catherine Kevin (Newcastle Upon Tyne: Cambridge Scholars Publishing, 2009).

28. Bruce Mayes, *Medical Journal of Australia,* April 14, 1956, p. 597.
29. See, for example, New Zealand Obstetrics and Gynaecology Association, *The Expectant Mother* (Wellington: Whitcombe and Tombs, 1953), p. 87.
30. Garry Linnell, "Too Little, Too Soon," *Good Weekend (SMH),* August 11, 2001, pp. 22–31.
31. Mein Smith, *Mothers and King Baby,* p. 194.
32. Mein Smith, *Mothers and King Baby,* p. 212.
33. This figure is based on a the results of a 1935 survey carried out by Dr. Ethel Dunham of the U.S. Children's Bureau in six obstetrics hospitals.
34. Linnell, "Too Little, Too Soon," p. 25.
35. McCalman, *Sex and Suffering,* p. 244.
36. McCalman, *Sex and Suffering,* pp. 244–45.
37. *Medical Journal of Australia,* June 7, 1969, p. 1169. See also, for example, "The First Year of Life," *Medical Journal of Australia,* January 5, 1963. This article also emphasizes the importance of antenatal care for the neonate.
38. However, it is important to note that, as Leslie Cannold's work suggests, the historicity of viability is not its only contingency. A fetus considered viable in most Australian hospitals may not have been viable had it been born in parts of Pakistan or India, or in a remote Indigenous Australian community. Varying access to neonatal facilities throws the concept of viability into flux from yet another angle. See Leslie Cannold, *The Abortion Myth, Feminism, Morality and the Hard Choices Women Make* (Sydney: Allen and Unwin, 1998), p. 33.
39. In South Australia, for example, the percentage of total births to women aged thirty-five and over rose from 6 percent to 21 percent between 1985 and 2008. See Pregnancy Outcome Unit, Epidemiology Branch, *Pregnancy Outcomes in South Australia, 2008* (Adelaide: SA Health, 2008), p. 85.
40. Yueping Alex Wang, Georgina M. Chambers, Mbathio Dieng, and Elizabeth A. Sulliva, *Assisted Reproductive Technology in Australia and New Zealand 2007, Assisted Reproductive Technology Series 13* (Canberra: Australian Institute of Health and Welfare, 2009), p. ix.
41. Wang, Chambers, Dieng, and Sulliva, *Assisted Reproductive Technology,* p. 6.
42. Sheryl de Lacey, "Parent Identity and 'Virtual' Children: Why Patients Discard Rather Than Donate Unused Embryos," *Human Reproduction* 6 (2005): 1661–69; "Patients' Attitudes to Their Embryos and Their Destiny: Social Conditioning?" *Best Practice and Research Clinical Obstetrics and Gynaecology* (2006): 1–12; "Decisions for the Fate of Frozen Embryos: Fresh Insights into Patients' Thinking and Their Rationales for Donating or Discarding Embryos," *Human Reproduction* 6 (2007): 1751–58.
43. de Lacey, "Parent Identity and 'Virtual' Children," p. 1666.
44. de Lacey, "Parent Identity and 'Virtual' Children," p. 1666.
45. Janet McCalman, "To Die Without Friends: Solitaries, Drifters and Failures in a New World Society," in *Body and Mind, Historical Essays in Honour of F. B. Smith,* ed. Graeme Davison, Pat Jalland, and Wilfrid Prest (Melbourne: Melbourne University Press, 2009), pp. 173–94.

46. Janet McCalman, *Struggletown: Public and Private life in Richmond, 1900–1965* (Melbourne: Melbourne University Press, 1984).

47. McCalman, "To Die Without Friends," p. 181.

48. Marilyn Lake, "The Politics of Respectability: Identifying the Masculinist Context," *Historical Studies* 86 (1986): 116–31; Christina Twomey, "'Without Natural Protectors': Responses to Wife Desertion in Gold-Rush Victoria," *Australian Historical Studies* 108 (1997): 22–46.

49. McCalman "To Die Without Friends," p. 189.

50. McCalman, *Struggletown*, p. 48.

51. McCalman, *Struggletown*, p. 55.

52. McCalman, *Struggletown*, p. 59.

53. McCalman, *Struggletown*, p. 62.

54. Barbara Falk, "Rosanove, Joan Mavis (1896–1974)," *Australian Dictionary of Biography*, vol. 16 (Melbourne: Melbourne University Press, 2002), pp. 125–26.

55. Jill Waterhouse, "Holt, Beatrice (Bea) (1900–1988)," *Australian Dictionary of Biography*, vol. 17 (Melbourne: Melbourne University Press, 2009), pp. 542–43.

56. The account of this family is taken from oral histories given during interviews with the author by Julie Mackey on August 9, 2004, and Margaret Kevin on August 29, 2004.

57. Oral history with Margaret Kevin, pp. 1–2.

58. Oral history with Julie Mackey, p. 3.

59. Oral history with Julie Mackey, p. 35.

60. Oral history with Margaret Kevin, p. 10.

61. Oral history with Julie Mackey, p. 36.

62. Vanessa Gorman, *Layla's Story, a Memoir of Sex, Love, Loss and Belonging* (Camberwell: Penguin Books Australia, 2005) and *Losing Layla* (Dir: Vanessa Gorman, 2001).

63. Susannah Thompson, "'Awakened by Angels': Personal Narratives of Perinatal Death in Late Twentieth-Century Western Australia and Their Effects on Hospital Policies and Programmes," *Studies in Western Australian History* 25 (2007): p. 168.

64. Kerreen Reiger has explored the relationship between other aspects of the maternal reform movement and mainstream feminism in *Our Bodies, Our Babies: the Forgotten Woman's Movement* (Melbourne: Melbourne University Press, 2001).

65. Leslie J. Reagan, "From Hazard to Blessing to Tragedy: Representations of Miscarriage in Twentieth-Century America," *Feminist Studies* 2 (2003).

66. These arguments about miscarriage are pursued in more detail in Catherine Kevin, "'I Did Not Lose My Baby...My Baby Just Died', Historicising Twenty-first Century Discourses of Early Miscarriage," *South Atlantic Quarterly*, "Death Scenes" (David Ellison and Katrina Schlunke) 4 (2011): 849–65.

67. Lisa, "Reflections on Pregnancy Loss," The Miscarriage Association website, http://www.miscarriageassociation.org.uk/ma2006/support/reflections/index.htm (accessed June 15, 2009).

68. Lisa, "Reflections on Pregnancy Loss," p. 3.

69. Kate Evans, "Miscarriage: The Loneliest Grief of All," *The Independent*, January 27, 2009, http://www.independent.co.uk/life-style/health-and-families/features/miscarriage-the-loneliest-grief-of-all-1516750.html (accessed June 10, 2009).

70. Catherine Ryan, "Lost," *Overland* 192 (2008): 44–48, p. 46.

71. Monica Dux, "Time to End Secrecy and Face the Anguish of Miscarriage," *Sydney Morning Herald*, January 19, 2009.

72. Natasha, interview with author, July 23, 2004.

73. This case study is also explored in Catherine Kevin, "Forming Families on the Reproductive Technology Frontier," *Griffith Review* 10 (2005): 89–102, and in Kevin, "'I Did Not Lose My Baby...My Baby Just Died.'"

74. Amanda, interview with author, December 20, 2004.

Chapter 2

1. Betty Dodson, *Liberating Masturbation: A Meditation on Self-Love* (published by the author, 1974).

2. Betty Dodson, "Getting To Know Me," *Ms. Magazine*, August 1974, pp. 106–9.

3. Betty Dodson's website runs the by-line: "A second wave feminist liberating women one orgasm at a time." http://dodsonandross.com/blogs/betty-dodson (accessed 23 September 2010).

4. Sheila Jeffreys, *Anticlimax: A Feminist Perspective on the Sexual Revolution* (London: The Women's Press, 1990), pp. 233–38.

5. For example, Jane Gallop has argued in relation to the general "re-discovery" of the clitoris post-Masters and Johnson and post-women's liberation, that other forms of female sexuality—including those that favor vaginal stimulation—were made peripheral. Jane Gallop, *Thinking Through the Body* (New York: Columbia University Press, 1988), pp. 71–87.

6. See Ariel Levy, *Female Chauvinist Pigs: Women and the rise of Raunch Culture* (New York: Free Press, 2005), for her influential critique of the after-effects of "sex-positive feminism," namely raunch culture which she argues merges and co-opts the vocabularies of sexual liberation and feminist radicalism to produce a new insidious form of heterosex.

7. Michel Foucault, *The History of Sexuality Vol. 1*, trans. Robert Hurley (Camberwell: Penguin, 2008). (Originally published in translation in 1978.)

8. Annie Potts, "Coming, Coming, Gone: A Feminist Deconstruction of Heterosexual Orgasm," *Sexualities* 3 (2000): 55–76, p. 59.

9. For an overview of debates about twentieth-century sexual revolutions see Stephen Garton, *Histories of Sexuality* (London: Equinox, 2004), pp. 210–28.

10. Jocelyn Bosley, "From Monkey Facts to Human Ideologies: Theorizing Female Orgasm in Human and Nonhuman Primates, 1967–1983," *Signs: Journal of Women in Culture and Society* 35, no. 3 (2010): 647–71, p. 647.

11. Jeffrey Weeks, *Sexuality: Third Edition* (London: Routledge, 2010), p. 1.

12. Foucault, *The History of Sexuality*, p. 24.

13. Adrienne Rich, "Compulsory Heterosexuality" (1980) in *Sexualities: Critical Concepts in Sociology*, ed. Ken Plummer (London: Routledge, 2002), pp. 98–123.

14. For example, Alissa Levine's research into popular advice books and magazines in the 1998–2001 period, across a range of countries, reveals that "popular discourse appears unable to come to terms with the centrality of clitoris to sexual response." She suggests that the "discovery" of the G-Spot in the 1980s confused rather than clarified the role of the clitoris in female orgasm. Alissa Levine, *The Social Construction of Female Orgasm: A Cross-cultural Study* (unpublished PhD thesis, Department of Sociology, McGill University, Montreal, 2001), p. 134.

15. William H. Masters and Virginia E. Johnson, *Human Sexual Response* (Boston: Little, Brown and Company, 1966), p. 7.

16. Van de Velde described the stages of heterosex as "Prelude, Loveplay, Communion, Epilogie or Afterglow." Th. H. Van de Velde, *Ideal Marriage: Its Physiology and Technique* (1928; London: William Heinemann, 1971), p. xiii.

17. Doris Lessing, *The Golden Notebook* (1962; New York: Harper Perennial Modern Classic, 1999), p. 206.

18. American Psychiatric Association, *Diagnostic and Statistical Manual of Mental Disorders*, 4th ed. (American Psychiatric Association: Washington D.C., 2000), as cited in Cynthia A. Graham, "The DSM Diagnostic Criteria for Female Orgasmic Disorder," *Archive of Sexual Behaviour* 39 (2010): 256–70, p. 258.

19. Graham, "The DSM Diagnostic Criteria for Female Orgasmic Disorder," p. 258.

20. Marie Bonaparte originally published the preliminary results of her research into clitoral-vaginal variance and "clitoridal-vaginal reconciliation" in *Bruxelles-Medical Journal* in April 1924. A summary is offered in her best-known work *Female Sexuality* (London: Imago Publishing, 1953), pp. 150–52.

21. For a rich history of Marie Bonaparte's legacy see Alison Moore, "Relocating Marie Bonaparte's Clitoris," *Australian Feminist Studies* 24, no. 60 (June 2009): 149–65.

22. Josephine Singer and Irving Singer, "Types of Female Orgasm," *The Journal of Sex Research* 8, no. 4 (1972): 255–67, p. 259.

23. Beatrix Campbell, "A Feminist Sexual Politics: Now You See It, Now You Don't," *Feminist Review* 5 (1980): 1–18, p. 6.

24. Nancy Tuana, "Coming to Understand: Orgasm and the Epistemology of Ignorance," *Hypatia* 19, no. 1 (Winter 2004): 194–232.

25. Garton, *Histories of Sexuality*, p. 117.

26. Garton, *Histories of Sexuality*, p. 127.

27. Jonathan Margolis, *O: The History of the Orgasm* (London: Arrow Books, 2004), p. 314.

28. For an insightful summary of historiographical accounts of sexual modernity, and sexual modernity in general, see Stephen Garton, "Normalising Sexuality," in *Histories of Sexuality*, pp. 189–209, p. 192.

29. Annamarie Jagose, "Counterfeit Pleasures: Fake Orgasm and Queer Agency," *Textual Practice* 24, no. 3 (2010): 517–39, pp. 526, 530.

30. Cindy Patton, "Hegemony and Orgasm—or the Instability of Heterosexual Pornography," *Screen* 30 (1989): 100–110, p. 104–5.

31. See Ariel Levy, *Female Chauvinist Pigs: Women and the Rise of Raunch Culture* (New York: Free Press, 2005).

32. Rachel P. Maines, *The Technology of Orgasm: "Hysteria," the Vibrator, and Women's Sexual Satisfaction* (1999; Baltimore: John Hopkins Press, 2001), p. 5.

33. Sigmund Freud, "Some Psychical Consequences of the Anatomical Distinction between the Sexes (1925)," in *The Essentials of Psychoanalysis*, trans. James Strachey (London: Vintage, 2005), pp. 402–11.

34. Thomas Laqueur, *Making Sex: Body and Gender from the Greeks to Freud* (Cambridge: Harvard University Press, 1990), pp. 1–24, p. 3.

35. Laqueur, *Making Sex*, p. 236.

36. See Sigmund Freud, "Lecture 33: Femininity" (1933) in *The Essentials of Psychoanalysis*, pp. 412–32.

37. Sigmund Freud, "The Question of Lay Analysis," in *The Essentials of Psychoanalysis*, pp. 5–75, p. 32.

38. Freud's daughter, editor, and fellow psychoanalyst, Anna Freud, for example, praised her father for breaking down the taboo around sex at the beginning of the twentieth century and for bringing some relief to his patients when he encouraged them to speak about their sexual experiences. She also drew attention to his theorizing of child sexuality, a field in which she would become a leading figure. See Anna Freud, "Introduction to Human Sexuality," in Freud, *The Essentials of Psychoanalysis*, pp. 271–76.

39. Weeks, *Sexuality*, p. 77.

40. Foucault, *The History of Sexuality*.

41. Anna Clark, *Desire: A History of European Sexuality* (New York: Routledge, 2008), pp. 156–57.

42. Angus McLaren, *Twentieth-Century Sexuality: A History* (Oxford: Blackwell, 1999), p. 111.

43. Paul Rutherford, *A World Made Sexy: Freud to Madonna* (Toronto: University of Toronto Press, 2007), p. 46.

44. Joy Damousi, *Freud in the Antipodes: A Cultural History of Psychoanalysis in Australia* (Sydney: UNSW Press, 2005), p. 1.

45. McLaren, *Twentieth-Century Sexuality*, p. 122.

46. For example, Betty Friedan, *The Feminine Mystique* (New York: W.W Norton, 1963).

47. McLaren, *Twentieth-Century Sexuality*, p. 114.

48. Freud, "Lecture 33: Femininity," p. 417.

49. Freud, *The Essentials of Psychoanalysis*, p. 271.

50. Freud, *Three Essays on Sexuality III*, p. 357.

51. McLaren, *Twentieth-Century Sexuality*, p. 119.

52. Laqueur, *Making Sex*, p. 236.

53. Laqueur, *Making Sex*, p. 234.

54. Freud, "Introduction to Human Sexuality," p. 275.

55. Jacqueline Rose, "Femininity and Its Discontents," *Feminist Review* 80 (2005): 24–43, p. 33.

56. Maines, *The Technology of Orgasm*, pp. 9–10.

57. M. H. Colson, "Female Orgasm: Myths, Facts and Controversies," *Sexologies* 19 (2010): 8–14, p. 9.

58. Rutherford, *A World Made Sexy*, p. 59.

59. McLaren, *Twentieth-Century Sexuality*, p. 122.

60. Hera Cook, as cited in Clark, *Desire*, p. 175.

61. Jane Gerhard, "Revisiting 'The Myth of the Vaginal Orgasm': The Female Orgasm in American Sexual Thought and Second Wave Feminism," *Feminist Studies* 26 (Summer 2002): 449–76, pp. 454–56.

62. Gerhard, "Revisiting 'The Myth of the Vaginal Orgasm,'" pp. 458–59.

63. Jonathan Ned Katz, *The Invention of Heterosexuality* (New York: Plume, 1996), p. 83.

64. Clark, *Desire*, p. 174.

65. Clark, *Desire*, p. 168.

66. Atina Grossman, "The New Woman and the Rationalization of Sexuality in Weimar Germany," in *Desire: The Politics of Sexuality,* ed. Ann Snitow, Christine Stansell, and Sharon Thompson (London: Virago Press, 1984), pp. 190–211.

67. McLaren, *Twentieth-Century Sexuality*, pp. 46–49.

68. Clark, *Desire*, p. 175.

69. Van de Velde, *Ideal Marriage*, 1928, as cited in Campbell, "A Feminist Sexual Politics," p. 6.

70. McLaren, *Twentieth-Century Sexuality*, p. 51.

71. Margolis, *O: The History of the Orgasm*, p. 358.

72. Michael Edward Melody and Linda Mary Peterson, *Teaching America about Sex: Marriage Guides and Sex Manuals from the Late Victorians to Dr Ruth* (New York: NYU Press, 1999), p. 123.

73. Van de Velde, *Ideal Marriage*.

74. Van de Velde, *Ideal Marriage*, p. 131.

75. Dr. Helena Wright, *The Sex Factor in Marriage* (1930, revised 1947), cited in Margolis, *O: The History of the Orgasm*, p. 320.

76. Lynne Segal, *Straight Sex: Rethinking the Politics of Pleasure* (Irvine: University of California Press, 1994), p. 87.

77. Wright, *The Sex Factor in Marriage* (1947), cited in Campbell, "A Feminist Sexual Politics," p. 8.

78. Campbell, "A Feminist Sexual Politics," p. 9.

79. Natalie Angier, *Woman: An Intimate Geography* (New York: Anchor Books, 2000), p. 67.

80. Levine, *The Social Construction of Female Orgasm*, pp. 175–90.

81. Levine, *The Social Construction of Female Orgasm*, p. 161.

82. See Gail Hawkes and John Scott, eds. "Appendix 2: Key Thinkers in Sexology," *Perspectives in Human Sexuality* (South Melbourne: Oxford University Press, 2005), pp. 304–9.

83. Veronique Mottier, *Sexuality: A Very Short Introduction* (Oxford: Oxford University Press, 2008), p. 33.

84. Clark, *Desire*, pp. 154–55.

85. Mottier, *Sexuality*, p. 35.

86. Mottier, *Sexuality*, p. 91.

87. See http://www.kinseyinstitute.org/research/ak-data.html#Scope (accessed October 10, 2010).

88. Annie Potts, *The Science/Fiction of Sex: Feminist Deconstruction and the Vocabularies of Hetero-sex* (London: Routledge, 2002), p. 26.

89. Garton, *Histories of Sexuality*, p. 203.
90. Kinsey (1953), cited in Potts, *The Science/Fiction of Sex*, p. 26.
91. As cited in McLaren, *Twentieth-Century Sexuality*, p. 147.
92. Segal, *Straight Sex*, pp. 89–92.
93. Potts, *The Science/Fiction of Sex*, pp. 26–27.
94. Janice Irvine has noted the reception to *Human Sexual Response* was "remarkably similar" to the Kinsey Report, at least in terms of sales: the first printing sold out within three days, and the book was soon no. 2 on the *New York Times* nonfiction best-seller list. Janice Irvine, *Disorders of Desire: Sexuality and Gender in American Psychology* (Philadelphia: Temple University Press, 2005), p. 56.
95. As with Kinsey, Masters and Johnson would be attacked for their sampling method, which was later revealed to include prostitutes who they had actively recruited. These results were later eradicated from the published findings, which emphasized voluntary participation from the "respectable" suburbs where the studies were conducted. Irvine has suggested that the prostitutes who cooperated with the study were "sexologists in their own right" who knew as much about sexual technique and behavior as the scientists and undoubtedly influenced the outcome of the research. Irvine, *Disorders of Desire*, p. 57.
96. Masters and Johnson, *Human Sexual Response*, p. 135.
97. Masters and Johnson, *Human Sexual Response*, p. 45.
98. Masters and Johnson, *Human Sexual Response*, p. 129.
99. Irvine, *Disorders of Desire*, p. 62.
100. Segal, *Straight Sex*, pp. 97–98.
101. McLaren, *Twentieth-Century Sexuality*, p. 171.
102. McLaren, *Twentieth-Century Sexuality*, p. 172.
103. McLaren, *Twentieth-Century Sexuality*, pp. 177–79.
104. Irvine, *Disorders of Desire*, p. 65.
105. Mottier, *Sexuality*, p. 58.
106. Segal, *Straight Sex*, p. 223.
107. Statistic and terms referred to in a profile of Canadian sex researcher Lori Brotto in the weekend magazine of the *Sydney Morning Herald*, the *Good Weekend*, July 10, 2010, pp. 27–28.
108. Anne Koedt, "The Myth of the Vaginal Orgasm" (1970), in *A Reader in Feminist Knowledge*, ed. Sneja Gunew (London: Routledge, 1991), pp. 326–34.
109. Segal, *Straight Sex*, p. 35.
110. Gerhard, "Revisiting 'The Myth of the Vaginal Orgasm,'" pp. 449–76.
111. Alix Shulman, "Organs and Orgasms," in *Woman in Sexist Society: Studies in Power and Powerlessness*, ed. Vivian Gornick and Barbara K. Moran (New York: New American Library, 1971), pp. 292–303, p. 302.
112. Paula Bennett, "Critical Clitoridectomy: Female Sexual Imagery and Feminist Psychoanalytic Theory," *Signs* 18, no. 2 (Winter 1993): 235–59, p. 256.
113. Thomas Lacqueur, *Solitary Sex: A Cultural History of Masturbation* (New York: Zone Books, 2003).
114. Mottier, *Sexuality*, p. 65.

115. The G-Spot, a zone located in the front of the vagina, close to the urethra, which had been described as playing a determining role in vaginal orgasm, is named for gynaecologist Ernst Grafenburg, who originally published his findings in 1950. In the 1980s, interest in the G-Spot was revived following the publication of *The G-Spot and Other Recent Discoveries about Human Sexuality* by Alice Kahn Ladas, John Perry, and Beverley Whipple. See M.H. Colston, "Female Orgasm: Myths and Controversies," p. 10.

116. Campbell, "A Feminist Sexual Politics," p. 15.

117. Lynne Segal, "Sensual Uncertainty, or Why the Clitoris Is Not Enough," in *Sex and Love: New Thoughts on Old Contradictions*, ed. Sue Cartledge and Joanna Ryan (London: Women's Press, 1983), pp. 30–48.

118. Campbell, "A Feminist Sexual Politics," p. 16.

119. R. W. Connell, *Masculinities* (St. Leonards: Allen and Unwin, 1994).

120. Anthony Giddens, *The Transformation of Intimacy* (Cambridge: Polity Press, 1992), p. 2.

121. Jane Gaines, "Feminist Heterosexuality and Its Politically Incorrect Pleasures," *Critical Inquiry* 1, no. 2 (Winter 1995): 382–410, p. 384.

122. Virginia Braun, Nicola Gavey, and Kathyrn McPhillips, "The 'Fair Deal'?: Unpacking Accounts of Reciprocity of Heterosex," *Sexualities* 6 (2003): 237–60.

Chapter 3

1. There is a "death of God" theology that emphasizes the nonpersonal nature of the divine, but the phrase has been more widely used in the sense that society is increasingly secular, as in Steve Bruce, *God Is Dead: Secularization in the West* (Malden, MA: Blackwell, 2002). The term was widely circulated following the publication of Bishop John Robinson's controversial book *Honest to God* (London: SCM Press) in 1963.

2. Callum G. Brown, *Religion and Society in Twentieth-Century Britain* (Harlow: Pearson Longman, 2006), p. xv.

3. Samuel Huntington, "The Clash of Civilizations?" *Foreign Affairs* (Summer 1993), http://www.foreignaffairs.com/articles/48950/samuel-p-huntington/the-clash-of-civilizations (accessed June 3, 2010).

4. Giselle Vincett, Sonya Sharma, and Kristin Aune, "Introduction: Women, Religion and Secularization: One Size Does Not Fit All," in *Women and Religion in the West: Challenging Secularization,* ed. Kristin Aune, Sonya Sharma, and Giselle Vincett (Aldershot: Ashgate, 2008), p. 4.

5. Nikky-Guninder Kaur Singh, "Translating Sikh Scripture into English," *Sikh Formations* 3, no. 1 (2007): 33–49.

6. Karen Armstrong, "Man vs. God," *Wall Street Journal*, September 12, 2009, http://online.wsj.com/article/SB10001424052970203440104574405030643556324.html (accessed November 12, 2009).

7. Peter van der Veer, *Imperial Encounters: Religion and Modernity in India and Britain* (Princeton, NJ: Princeton University Press, 2001), p. 26.

8. Ross McKibbin, review of *Religion and Society in Twentieth-Century Britain*, by Callum Brown, *English Historical Review* 122, no. 499 (December 2007): 1464–68.

9. T. Jeremy Gunn, "The Complexity of Religion and the Definition of 'Religion' in International Law," *Harvard Human Rights Journal* 16 (2003): 189–215.

10. *Report of the Special Rapporteur of the Commission on Human Rights on Freedom of Religion or Belief*, UN (2001), supra note 81, cited in Gunn, "The Complexity of Religion," p. 215.

11. Alison Jasper, "Feminism and Religion," in *The Routledge Companion to Feminism and Postfeminism*, ed. Sarah Gamble (London: Routledge, 1998), p. 158.

12. Joan Wallach Scott, *The Politics of the Veil* (Princeton, NJ: Princeton University Press, 2007).

13. Sean Gill, *Women and the Church of England: From the Eighteenth Century to the Present* (London: SPCK, 1994), p. 234. Gill is quoting from a radio interview with Anne Widdicombe, then Social Services minister.

14. For some background on the rise of identity issues and identity politics in the later twentieth century, see Nancy Fraser and Axel Honneth, *Redistribution or Recognition? A Political-Philosophical Exchange* (London: Verso 2003); and for the wide scope of religious feminism, see the excellent journal *Feminist Theology*, http://fth.sagepub.com/.

15. Amira Hassan Nowaira, "Arabic Autobiography," in *The Encyclopaedia of Life Writing*, ed. Margaretta Jolly (Chicago: Fitzroy Dearborn, 2001), pp. 45–47.

16. Ibid.

17. Irshad Manji, *The Trouble with Islam: A Muslim's Call for Reform in Her Faith* (New York: St. Martin's Press, 2004); and http://www.irshadmanji.com/about-irshad.

18. An excellent overview of traditional secularization theory and its more recent challenges is given by Philip S. Gorski in "Historicizing the Secularization Debate: An Agenda for Research," in *Handbook of the Sociology of Religion,* ed. Michele Dillon (Cambridge: Cambridge University Press, 2003), pp. 110–22.

19. William Safran, ed., *The Secular and the Sacred: Nation, Religion and Politics* (London: Frank Cass, 2003).

20. *Daily News*, June 14, 1928, quoted in June Purvis, *Emmeline Pankhurst: A Biography* (London: Routledge, 2002), p. 354.

21. Purvis, *Emmeline Pankhurst*, pp. 352–53.

22. Timothy Larsen, *Christabel Pankhurst: Fundamentalism and Feminism in Coalition* (Woodbridge: The Boydell Press, 2002), p. 19.

23. Purvis, *Emmeline Pankhurst*, p. 344.

24. Larsen, *Christabel Pankhurst*.

25. Christabel Pankhurst, *Seeing the Future*, pp. 165–66, cited in Larsen, *Christabel Pankhurst*, p. 48.

26. Larsen, *Christabel Pankhurst*, pp. 139, 142.

27. Callum Brown, *The Death of Christian Britain* (London: Routledge, 2001), p. 58ff.

28. Ibid., p. 68.

29. Ibid., p. 195.

30. Ibid., p. 179.

31. Klaus J. Bade, *Migration in European History*, trans. Allison Brown (Malden, MA: Wiley-Blackwell, 2003), pp. 276–77.

32. A good starting point on this subject is Vron Ware, *Beyond the Pale: White Women, Racism & History* (London: Verso, 1992). See also Kumari Jayawardena, *The White Woman's Other Burden: Western Women and South Asia During British Rule* (London: Routledge, 1995).

33. Willfried Spohn, "Multiple Modernity, Nationalism and Religion: A Global Perspective," *Current Sociology* 51, no. 4 (2003): 265–86.

34. Afsaneh Najmabadi, "Gender and Secularism of Modernity: How Can a Muslim Woman Be French?" *Feminist Studies* 32, no. 2 (Summer 2006): 239–55.

35. Jayawardena, *The White Woman's Other Burden*, p. 206.

36. Malcolm Hamilton, "An Analysis of the Festival for Mind-Body-Spirit, London," in *Beyond New Age: Exploring Alternative Spirituality*, ed. Steven Sutcliffe and Marion Bowman (Edinburgh: Edinburgh University Press, 2000), cited in Dick Houtman and Stef Aupers, "The Spiritual Revolution and the New Age Gender Puzzle: The Sacralization of the Self in Late Modernity (1980–2000)," in Aune, Sharma, and Vincett, eds., *Women and Religion in the West*, p. 101.

37. Houtman and Aupers, "Spiritual Revolution," p. 111.

38. Stef Aupers and Dick Houtman, "Beyond the Spiritual Supermarket: The Social and Public Significance of New Age Spirituality," *Journal of Contemporary Religion* 21, no. 2 (2006): 201–22.

39. John P. Newport, *The New Age Movement and the Biblical Worldview: Conflict and Dialogue* (Grand Rapids, MI: Eerdmans Publishing, 1998), p. 290.

40. Ronald Hutton, *The Triumph of the Moon: A History of Modern Pagan Witchcraft* (Oxford: Oxford University Press, 1999), p. 117.

41. Hutton, *Triumph of the Moon*, pp. 205–40.

42. Owen Davies, *Witchcraft, Magic and Culture 1736–1951* (Manchester: Manchester University Press, 1999), p. 75.

43. Cited in Newport, *New Age Movement*, p. 290.

44. Hutton, *Triumph of the Moon*, p. 345.

45. Ibid., p. 346.

46. See http://www.starhawk.org/ (accessed June 3, 2010).

47. Paul John Eakin, *How Our Lives Become Stories* (Ithaca, NY: Cornell University Press, 1999).

48. Paul Heelas and Linda Woodhead, with Benjamin Seel, Bronislaw Szerszynski, and Karin Tusting, *The Spiritual Revolution: Why Religion Is Giving Way to Spirituality* (Malden, MA: Blackwell, 2005), pp. 2–3. Heelas and Woodhead take the words "massive turn" from Charles Taylor, *The Ethics of Authenticity* (Cambridge, MA: Harvard University Press, 1991), p. 26.

49. Heelas and Woodhead, *Spiritual Revolution*, p. 6.

50. Ian Hacking, *Rewriting the Soul: Multiple Personality and the Sciences of Memory* (Princeton, NJ: Princeton University Press, 1995).

51. Jens Brockmeier, "Autobiography, Narrative, and the Freudian Concept of Life History," *Philosophy, Psychiatry, & Psychology* 4, no. 3 (1997): 175–99.

52. Letter to Marie Bonaparte, as quoted in *Sigmund Freud: Life and Work* (1955) by Ernest Jones, vol. 2, pt. 3, chap. 16.

53. Diane Jonte-Pace, review of *Freud on Femininity and Faith*, by Judith van Herik, *Theology Today* 43, no. 1 (1986): 123–25.

54. Jasper, "Feminism and Religion," in *The Routledge Companion to Feminism and Postfeminism*, ed. Sarah Gamble (London: Routledge, 1998), pp. 158–67.

55. Agnes Bosanquet, "Luce Irigaray's Sensible Transcendental: Becoming Divine in the Body," *Transformations*, no. 11 (2005), http://www.transformationsjournal. org/journal/issue_11/article_01.shtml (accessed May 21, 2010).

56. Ann Loades, review of *Sexing the Trinity: Gender, Culture and the Divine*, by Gavin d'Costa, *Theology Today* 60, no. 3 (2003): 413–15; and Graham Ward, *Theology and Contemporary Critical Theory* (Basingstoke: Macmillan, 2000), pp. 18–26.

57. Penny Long Marler, "Religious Change in the West: Watch the Women," in Aune, Sharma, and Vincett, eds., *Women and Religion in the West*, p. 48.

58. Linda Woodhead, "'Because I'm Worth It': Religion and Women's Changing Lives in the West," in Aune, Sharma, and Vincett, eds., *Women and Religion in the West*, p. 148.

59. Karen Armstrong, *Jerusalem: One City, Three Faiths* (London: HarperCollins, 1996.)

60. It is a commonplace that "every generation must rewrite history in its own way," a quote sometimes attributed to the philosopher R. G. Collingwood.

61. Eeva Sointu and Linda Woodhead, "Spirituality, Gender, and Expressive Self-hood," *Journal for the Scientific Study of Religion* 47, no. 2 (May 2008): 259–76. The authors cite as the source of the term "stalled gender revolution" Arlie Russell Hochschild, *The Commercialization of Intimate Life: Notes from Home and Work* (Berkeley: University of California Press, 2003).

62. Sointu and Woodhead, "Spirituality," p. 266.

Chapter 4

1. Francisco A. R. Garcia, Karen M. Freund, Michelle Berlin, Kathleen B. Digre, Donald J. Dudley, Rose S. Fife, Geralde Gabeau, et al., "Progress and Priorities in the Health of Women and Girls: A Decade of Advances and Challenges," *Journal of Women's Health* 19 (2010): 671–80.

2. Chloe E. Bird and Patricia P. Rieker, *Gender and Health: The Effects of Constrained Choices and Social Policies* (Cambridge: Cambridge University Press, 2008).

3. Bird and Rieker, *Gender and Health*.

4. Thompson Prentice, "Health, History and Hard Choices: Funding Dilemmas in a Fast-Changing World," presented at "Health and Philanthropy: Leveraging Change," University of Indiana, August 2006, http://www.who.int/global_health_ histories/seminars/presentation07.pdf (accessed August 10, 2010).

5. World Health Organization, *The World Health Report 2003—Shaping the Future*, http://www.who.int/whr/2003/overview/en/print.html (accessed August 10, 2010).

6. James C. Reilly, *Rising Life Expectancy: A Global History* (Cambridge: Cambridge University Press, 2001).

7. Lois M. Verbrugge, "Pathways of Health and Death," in *Women, Health and Medicine in America: A Historical Handbook*, ed. Rima D. Apple (New Brunswick, NJ: Rutgers University Press, 1990), pp. 41–79; U.S. Centers for Disease Control, "Public Health and Aging: Trends in Aging—United States and Worldwide," *MMWR Weekly* 52, no. 6 (February 14, 2003): 101–6, http://www.cdc.gov/mmwr/preview/mmwrhtml/mm5206a2.htm (accessed July 13, 2010).

8. Verbrugge, "Pathways of Health and Death," p. 42.

9. George Rosen, *A History of Public Health* (Baltimore, MD: Johns Hopkins University Press, 1993).

10. James C. Reilly, *Poverty and Life Expectancy: The Jamaica Paradox* (Cambridge: Cambridge University Press, 2005).

11. U.S. Centers for Disease Control, "Achievements in Public Health, 1900–1999: Control of Infectious Diseases," *MMWR Weekly* 48, no. 29 (July 30, 1999): 621–29, http://www.cdc.gov/mmwr/preview/mmwrhtml/mm4829a1.htm (accessed July 13, 2010).

12. U.S. Centers for Disease Control, "Achievements in Public Health, 1900–1999: Healthier Mothers and Babies," *MMWR Weekly* 48, no. 38 (October 1, 1999): 849–58, http://www.cdc.gov/mmwr/preview/mmwrhtml/mm4838a2.htm (accessed July 13, 2010).

13. Sylvia Noble Tesh, *Hidden Arguments: Political Ideology and Disease Prevention Policy* (New Brunswick, NJ: Rutgers University Press, 1988).

14. Paul Starr, *The Social Transformation of American Medicine* (New York: Basic Books, 1982).

15. U.S. Centers for Disease Control, "Achievements: Healthier Mothers and Babies."

16. U.S. Centers for Disease Control, "Leading Causes of Death in Females, United States," http://www.cdc.gov/Women/lcod/ (accessed August 10, 2010).

17. William J. Blot and Joseph K. McLaughlin, "Response: Re: Are Women More Susceptible to Lung Cancer?" *Journal of the National Cancer Institute* 96, no. 20 (2004): 1560–61.

18. Global Health Council, "Women's Health: Sexual and Reproductive Health," http://www.globalhealth.org/womens_health/reproductive/ (accessed August 10, 2010).

19. Wim Van Lerberghe et al., *The World Health Report 2005—Make Every Mother and Child Count* (Geneva, Switzerland: WHO, 2005).

20. Leslie Laurence and Beth Weinhouse, *Outrageous Practices: How Gender Bias Threatens Women's Health* (New Brunswick, NJ: Rutgers University Press, 1994); Institute of Medicine (IOM), *Exploring the Biological Contributions of Human Health: Does Gender Matter?* (Washington, DC: IOM, 2001).

21. Claudia Garcia-Moreno et al., *WHO Multi-Country Study on Women's Health and Domestic Violence against Women: Summary Report of Initial Results on Prevalence, Health Outcomes and Women's Responses* (Geneva, Switzerland: WHO, 2005).

22. Feminist.com, "Facts about Violence: U.S. Statistics, Global Statistics," http://www.feminist.com/antiviolence/facts.html (accessed August 10, 2010).

23. Garcia-Moreno et al., *WHO Multi-Country Study on Women's Health and Domestic Violence against Women.*
24. Yank D. Coble et al., "Violence against Women," *Journal of the American Medical Association* 267 (1992): 3184–89.
25. Hillary Rodham Clinton, wife of former U.S. president William J. Clinton, tenure 1992–2000. She was subsequently a U.S. senator from New York and was appointed U.S. secretary of state in 2009.
26. Hillary Rodham Clinton, "Remarks to the U.N. 4th World Congress on Women Plenary Session" (delivered September 5, 1995, Beijing, China), http://www.americanrhetoric.com/speeches/hillaryclintonbeijingspeech.htm (accessed August 10, 2010):

Women's Rights are Human Rights [excerpted]
We need to understand, there is no one formula for how women should lead our lives. That is why we must respect the choices that each woman makes for herself and her family. Every woman deserves the chance to realize her own God-given potential.

But we must recognize that women will never gain full dignity until their human rights are respected and protected.

What we are learning around the world is that if women are healthy and educated, their families will flourish. If women are free from violence, their families will flourish. If women have a chance to work and earn as full and equal partners in society, their families will flourish.

It is a violation of *human rights* when babies are denied food, or drowned, or suffocated, or their spines broken, simply because they are born girls.

It is a violation of *human rights* when women and girls are sold into the slavery of prostitution for human greed.

It is a violation of *human* rights when women are doused with gasoline, set on fire and burned to death because their marriage dowries are deemed too small.

It is a violation of *human* rights when individual women are raped in their own communities and when thousands of women are subjected to rape as a tactic or prize of war.

It is a violation of *human* rights when a leading cause of death worldwide among women ages 14 to 44 is the violence they are subjected to in their own homes by their own relatives.

It is a violation of *human* rights when young girls are brutalized by the painful and degrading practice of genital mutilation.

It is a violation of *human* rights when women are denied the right to plan their own families, and that includes being forced to have abortions or being sterilized against their will.

If there is one message that echoes forth from this conference, *let it be that human rights are women's rights—and women's rights are human rights once and for all.* And among those rights are the right to speak freely and the right to be heard.

Women must enjoy the right to participate fully in the social and political lives of their countries if we want freedom and democracy to thrive and endure.

27. Irvine Loudon, "Maternal Mortality in the Past and Its Relevance to Developing Countries Today," *American Journal of Clinical Nutrition* 72, no. S1 (2000): 241S–246S.

28. Janet Carlysle Bogdan, "Childbirth in America, 1650 to 1990," in *Women, Health and Medicine in America*, ed. Rima Apple (New Brunswick, NJ: Rutgers University Press, 1990), pp. 101–20.

29. Richard W. Wertz and Dorothy C. Wertz, "Notes on the Decline of Midwives and the Rise of Medical Obstetricians," in *The Sociology of Health and Illness*, ed. Peter Conrad and Rochelle Kern (New York: Saint Martin's Press, 1994).

30. Loudon, "Maternal Mortality."

31. Bernard Guyer et al., "Annual Summary of Vital Statistics: Trends in the Health of Americans during the 20th Century," *Pediatric* 106, no. 6 (2000): 1307–17; Lee K. Frankel, "The Present Status of Maternal and Infant Hygiene in the United States," *American Journal of Public Health* 17, no. 12 (1927): 1209–17.

32. Suzanne Poirier, "Women's Reproductive Health," in *Women, Health and Medicine in America,* ed. Rima Apple (New Brunswick, NJ: Rutgers University Press, 1990), pp. 217–45.

33. Emmet L. Holt, "Infant Mortality, Ancient and Modern, An Historical Sketch," Presidential address before the American Association for the Study and Prevention of Infant Mortality, Washington D.C., November 14–17, *Archives of Pediatrics* 30 (1913): 885–915.

34. Molly Ladd-Taylor, "Women's Health and Public Policy," in *Women, Health and Medicine in America*, ed. Rima Apple (New Brunswick, NJ: Rutgers University Press, 1990), pp. 383–402.

35. This act was known as the Sheppard-Towner Act. Ladd-Taylor, "Women's Health and Public Policy."

36. U.S. Social Security Administration, "The Social Security Act of 1935," http://www.ssa.gov/history/35act.html#TITLE%20V (accessed August 17, 2010).

37. U.S. Health Resources and Services Administration, "Title V History," https://perfdata.hrsa.gov/mchb/mchreports/LEARN_More/Title_V_History/title_v_history.asp (accessed August 17, 2010).

38. U.S. Department of Agriculture, Food and Nutrition Service, "About WIC," http://www.fns.usda.gov/wic/aboutwic/mission.htm (accessed August 17, 2010).

39. Carlysle Bogdan, "Childbirth in America."

40. Jun Zhang, James F. Troendle, and Michael K. Yancey, "Reassessing the Labor Curve in Nulliparous Women," *American Journal of Obstetric Gynecology* 187, no. 4 (2002): 824–28.

41. Katherine Hartmann et al., "Outcomes of Routine Episiotomy: A Systematic Review," *Journal of the American Medical Association* 293 (2005): 2141–48.

42. BS.org, "The Pill: People and Events: Anthony Comstock's Chastity Laws," http://www.pbs.org/wgbh/amex/pill/peopleevents/e_comstock.html (accessed August 25, 2010); Carol S. Weisman, *Women's Health Care: Activist Traditions and Institutional Change* (Baltimore: Johns Hopkins University Press, 1998).

43. Poirier, "Women's Reproductive Health," pp. 223–24.

44. Ibid., pp. 223–25.

45. Ibid., pp. 225–26.

46. U.S. Centers for Disease Control, "Margaret Sanger," *MMWR Weekly*, December 3, 1999, http://www.cdc.gov/mmwr/preview/mmwrhtml/mm4847bx.htm (accessed August 18, 2010).

47. Margaret Sanger, "Comstockery in America," *Margaret Sanger Selected Writings*, http://www.nyu.edu/projects/sanger/secure/documents/speech_comstockery_in_america.html (accessed August 25, 2010).

48. Weisman, *Women's Health Care*.

49. PBS.org, "Anthony Comstock's 'Chastity' Laws," http://www.pbs.org/wgbh/amex/pill/peopleevents/e_comstock.html (accessed August 18, 2010).

50. PBS.org, "The Pill," http://www.pbs.org/wgbh/amex/pill/index.html (accessed August 18, 2010).

51. Sandra Morgen, *Into Our Own Hands: The Women's Health Movement in the United States, 1969–1990* (New Brunswick, NJ: Rutgers University Press, 2002).

52. Morgen, *Into Our Own Hands*, pp. 23–24.

53. Ibid., p. 5.

54. Boston Women's Health Book Collective, *Our Bodies, Ourselves* (New York: Simon and Schuster, 1973), http://www.ourbodiesourselves.org/about/1973cov.asp (accessed August 11, 2011). The 1979 edition of this book was banned in many U.S. high schools and public libraries, http://www.ourbodiesourselves.org/about/timeline.asp (accessed August 11, 2011). A listing of the collective's publications is available on the Our Bodies Ourselves website.

55. Morgen, *Into Our Own Hands*, pp. 5–7, 31–35.

56. U.S. Centers for Disease Control, "Unintended Pregnancy Prevention," http://www.cdc.gov/reproductivehealth/UnintendedPregnancy/index.htm (accessed August 22, 2010).

57. Women's Health Education Center, "Sterilization," http://www.womenshealthsection.com/content/gyn/gyn029.php3 (accessed August 22, 2010).

58. A. Chandra, "Surgical Sterilization in the United States: Prevalence and Characteristics, 1965–95," National Center for Health Statistics, *Vital Health Statistics* 23, no. 20 (1998): 1–33.

59. Weisman, *Women's Health Care*, p. 62.

60. Rickie Solinger, *Beggars and Choosers: How the Politics of Choice Shapes Adoption, Abortion and Welfare in the United States* (New York: Hill and Wang, 2001).

61. Global Health Council, "HIV/ AIDS: At Risk Groups—Women and Youth," http://www.globalhealth.org/hiv_aids/risk_groups1/ (accessed August 23, 2010).

62. R. Jeanne Lennane and R. John Lennane, "Alleged Psychogenic Disorders in Women: A Possible Manifestation of Sexual Prejudice," *New England Journal of Medicine* 288 (1973): 288–92.

63. Sharon Golub, *Periods: From Menarche to Menopause* (Newbury Park, CA: Sage Publications, 1992).

64. For many years in the United States, the supposed dangers of PMS (such as emotional instability) were used as justifications to restrict women from powerful positions such as the U.S. presidency or employment in jobs such as pilot.

65. Therese F. Benedek, "Sexual Functions in Women and Their Disturbance," in *American Handbook of Psychiatry*, ed. S. Arieti (New York: Basic Books, 1959).

66. N. Woods, A. Most, and G. D. Longnecker, "Major Life Events, Daily Stressors, and Perimenstrual Symptoms," *Nursing Research* 34 (1985): 263–67; Alice Dan et al., "Rationale and Evidence for the Role of Circadian Desynchrony in Premenstrual Symptoms," in *Menstrual Health in Women's Lives*, ed. Alice J. Dan and Linda L. Lewis (Chicago: University of Illinois Press, 1992), pp. 52–60.

67. Anne Figert, *Women and the Ownership of PMS: The Structuring of a Psychiatric Disorder* (Hawthorne, NY: Aldine de Gruyter, 1996).

68. Esther Rome and Jill Wolhandler, "Can Tampon Safety be Regulated?" in *Menstrual Health in Women's Lives*, ed. Alice J. Dan and Linda L. Lewis (Chicago: University of Illinois Press, 1992), pp. 261–73.

69. Lorraine Rothman, "The Development of Menstrual Extraction in the Women's Health Movement," in *The Menstrual Cycle*, vol. 1, *A Synthesis of Interdisciplinary Research*, ed. Alice J. Dan (New York: Springer Publishing, 1980), pp. 312–17.

70. Our Bodies Ourselves, http://www.ourbodiesourselves.org/book/companion.asp?id=26&compID=101 (accessed June 20, 2011).

71. Bernadine Healy, *A New Prescription for Women's Health* (New York: Penguin Books, 1995).

72. National Heart, Lung & Blood Institute, "The Women's Health Initiative (WHI)," http://www.nhlbi.nih.gov/whi/ (accessed September 15, 2010).

73. Society for Menstrual Cycle Research, "Menstrual Suppression: Menstruation Is Not a Disease," http://menstruationresearch.org/position-statements/menstrual-supression-2007/ (accessed September 8, 2010).

74. The dual responsibility that women have for work in the home and outside of the home has often been referred to as the "second shift"; see Arlie Hochschild with Anne Machung, *The Second Shift* (New York: Viking Penguin, 1989).

75. Anthony Bale, "Women's Toxic Experience," in *Women, Health and Medicine in America*, ed. Rima Apple (New Brunswick, NJ: Rutgers University Press, 1990).

76. Ibid., pp. 405–6.

77. Ibid., pp. 407–9.

78. Tesh, *Hidden Arguments;* Bird and Rieker, *Gender and Health*, p. 57.

79. Cynthia Enloe, *Bananas, Beaches and Bases: Making Feminist Sense of International Politics* (Berkeley: University of California Press, 1990).

80. Food and Agriculture Organization of the United Nations, "Women and Food Security," http://www.fao.org/FOCUS/E/Women/Sustin-e.htm (accessed August 23, 2010); Katherine Gustafson, "Why Women's Rights Matter to Our Food," http://food.change.org/blog/view/why_womens_rights_matter_to_our_food (accessed August 23, 2010).

81. Lesley Doyal, *What Makes Women Sick: Gender and the Political Economy of Health* (New Brunswick, NJ: Rutgers University Press, 1995).

82. Ibid., pp. 31–34.

83. Barbara Ehrenreich and Arlie Russell Hochschild, *Global Woman: Nannies, Maids, and Sex Workers in the New Economy* (New York: Metropolitan Publishing, 2002).

84. United Nations Global Poverty Project, "Global Poverty Info Bank: Women," http:// www.globalpovertyproject.com/infobank/women (accessed August 24, 2010).

85. United Nations Population Fund, "Gender Equality Fact Sheet: Gender Equality and Education," http://www.unfpa.org/swp/2005/presskit/factsheets/facts_gender. htm (accessed August 24, 2010).

86. Mary Daly and Katherine Rake, *Gender and the Welfare State* (Cambridge: Polity Press, 2003).

87. Judith Lorber and Lisa Jean Moore, *Gender and the Social Construction of Illness,* 2nd ed., (Walnut Creek, CA: Rowman & Littlefield, 2002).

88. Jonathan M. Metzel, "Mother's Little Helper: The Crisis of Psychoanalysis and the Miltown Revolution," *Gender & History* 15, no. 2 (2003): pp. 228–55.

89. Jonathan M. Metzl and Joni Angel, "Assessing the Impact of SSRI Antidepressants on Popular Notions of Women's Depressive Illness," *Social Science and Medicine* 58, no. 3 (2004): pp. 577–84.

90. Phyllis Chesler, *Women and Madness* (San Diego, CA: Harcourt, Brace, Jovanovich, [1972] 1989).

91. Ibid.

92. Ibid.

93. Susan E. Bell, *DES Daughters: Embodied Knowledge and the Transformation of Women's Health Politics* (Philadelphia, PA: Temple University Press, 2009).

94. Barbara Seaman, *The Doctor's Case against the Pill* (New York: Wyden, 1969); Susan C. M. Scrimshaw, "Women and the Pill: From Panacea to Catalyst," *Family Planning Perspectives* 13, no. 6 (1981): pp. 254–56, 260–62.

95. Richard B. Sobol, *Bending the Law: The Story of the Dalkon Shield Bankruptcy* (Chicago: University of Chicago Press, 1991).

96. Bale, "Women's Toxic Experience," p. 428.

97. Ciro V. Sumaya, Vivian W. Pinn, and Susan J. Blumenthal, *Women's Health in the Medical School Curriculum: Report of a Survey and Recommendations* (Rockville, MD: U.S. Health Resources and Services Administration, 1997), HRSA-A-OEA-96-1.

98. Healy, *A New Prescription for Women's Health.*

99. United Nations Population Fund, "UNFPA State of World Population 2008, Reaching Common Ground: Culture, Gender and Human Rights," http://www. unfpa.org/upload/lib_pub_file/816_filename_en-swop08-report.pdf (accessed August 10, 2010).

Chapter 5

1. Michelle Perrot, *Femmes publiques,* interviews with Jean Lebrun (Paris: Textuel, 1997).

2. Perrot, *Femmes publiques,* p. 7.

3. Jean-Jacques Rousseau, *Emile, ou de l'éducation* (1762), http://classiques.uqac.ca/ classiques/Rousseau_jj/emile/emile.html (accessed June 11, 2011). See also Susan Moller Okin, *Women in Western Political Thought* (Princeton, NJ: Princeton University Press, 1979).

4. Women had voted in local elections in Scotland and Sweden, among other places, prior to 1893, but this was the first time women were constitutionally recognized as full citizens of a nation, electors and electable.

5. The Australian Electoral Commission provides an overview of the history of indigenous voting rights in Australia at http://www.aec.gov.au/voting/indigenous_vote/aborigin.htm (accessed June 27, 2011). South Australian women were granted the vote in 1894, and seventy indigenous women were among those who voted in 1896 (http://www.parliament.sa.gov.au/Education/Students/AboutParliament/History+of+Parliament/AboriginalAustraliansandParliament/ [accessed February 15, 2010]).

6. For examples from France, see Christine Bard, *Les filles de Marianne: Histoire des féminismes 1914–1940* (Paris: Fayard, 1995) and Christine Bard, ed., *Un siècle d'antiféminisme* (Paris: Fayard, 1999).

7. Carole Pateman, *The Sexual Contract* (Cambridge: Polity, 1988); Geneviève Fraisse, *Muse de la raison* (Paris: Alinéa, 1989); Colettte Guillaumin, *Sexe, race et pratique du pouvoir: l'idée de Nature* (Paris: côté-femmes, 1992).

8. Pateman, *The Sexual Contract*.

9. Leila Ahmed, *Women and Gender in Islam: Historical Roots of a Modern Debate* (New Haven: Yale University Press, 1992); Karen Offen, "Exploring the Sexual Politics of Republican Nationalism," in *Nationhood and Nationalism in France: From Boulangism to the Great War, 1889–1918*, ed., Robert Tombs (London: Harper Collins Academic, 1991), pp. 195–209; Bronwyn Winter, *Hijab and the Republic: Uncovering the French Headscarf Debate* (Syracuse: Syracuse University Press, 2008).

10. Yesim Arat, "The Project of Modernity and Women in Turkey," and Deniz Kandiyoti, "Gendering the Modern: On Missing Dimensions in the Study of Turkish Modernity," in *Rethinking Modernity and National Identity in Turkey,* ed., Sibel Bozdogan and Reçat Kasaba (Seattle: University of Washington Press, 1997).

11. Marian Sawer and Marian Simms, *A Woman's Place: Women and Politics in Australia* (Sydney: Allen & Unwin, 1984); Margaret Reynolds, *The Last Bastion: Labor Women Working towards Equality in the Parliaments of Australia* (Chatswood: Business & Professional Publishing, 1995); Philippe Bataille and Françoise Gaspard, *Comment les femmes changent la politique, et pourquoi les hommes résistent* (Paris: La Découverte, 1999).

12. Virginia Woolf, *Three Guineas* (London: Hogarth Press, 1938).

13. Maureen Honey, *Creating Rosie the Riveter: Class, Gender, and Propaganda during World War II* (Amherst: University of Massachusetts Press, 1984). The "We Can Do It" poster is available online via Google Images.

14. Rita Thalmann, *Etre femme sous le IIIe Reich* (Paris: Robert Laffont, 1982); Claudia Koonz, *Mothers in the Fatherland: Women, the Family and Nazi Politics* (New York: St. Martin's Press, 1987); Susan Faludi, *Backlash: The Undeclared War against American Women* (New York: Crown Publishers, 1991); Robin Pickering-Iazzi, ed., *Mothers of Invention: Women, Italian Fascism, and Culture* (Minneapolis: University of Minnesota Press, 1995); Francine Muel-Dreyfus, *Vichy et l'éternel féminin: contribution à une sociologie politique de l'ordre des corps* (Paris: Le

Seuil, 1996); Aurora G. Morcillo, *True Catholic Womanhood: Gender Ideology in Franco's Spain* (DeKalb: Illinois University Press, 2000); Barbara Finlay, *George W. Bush and the War on Women: Turning Back the Clock on Progress* (London: Zed Press, 2006); Bronwyn Winter, "Pre-emptive Fridge Magnets and Other Weapons of Masculinist Destruction: The Rhetoric and Reality of 'Safeguarding Australia,'" *Signs: A Journal of Women, Culture and Society* 33, no. 1 (2007): 25–52.

15. Beatrix Campbell, *The Iron Ladies: Why Do Women Vote Tory?* (London: Virago, 1987); Bronwyn Winter, "Pauline and Other Perils: Women in Australian Right-Wing Politics," in *Right-Wing Women: From Conservatives to Extremists around the World*, ed. Paola Bacchetta and Margaret Power (New York: Routledge, 2002), pp. 197–210.

16. Gisela Bock and Pat Thane, eds., *Maternity and Gender Policies: Women and the Rise of the European Welfare States, 1880s–1950s* (London: Routledge, 1991).

17. Simone de Beauvoir, *Le Deuxième sexe* (Paris: Gallimard, 1949).

18. Susan Mitchell, *Kerryn & Jackie: The Shared Life of Kerryn Phelps and Jackie Stricker*, rev. ed. (Sydney: Allen & Unwin, 2003).

19. For example, http://www.independent.co.uk/news/world/europe/world-gets-its-first-gay-head-of-state-1519068.html; and http://www.timesonline.co.uk/tol/news/world/europe/article5607642.ece (accessed January 29, 2009).

20. See, in relation to Australia, Julia Baird, *Media Tarts: How the Australian Press Frames Female Politicians* (Melbourne: Scribe, 2004); see also Faludi, *Backlash*, in relation to the United States.

21. Beauvoir, *Le Deuxième sexe*; Sylvie Chaperon, *Les années Beauvoir (1945–1970)* (Paris: Fayard, 2000).

22. This is a line from the song "Neurotica Suburbia" by Australian singer-songwriter Robyn Archer, featured on her 1977 album *The Ladies' Choice*. The full sentence is "With satisfaction as a real housewife / I'm married to a building for the rest of my life."

23. Sohn, Anne-Marie, "Entre deux guerres: les rôles féminins en France et en Angleterre," in *Histoire des femmes en occident*, ed. Georges Duby and Michelle Perrot, vol. 5, *Le XXe siècle*, ed. Françoise Thébaud (Paris: Plon, 1992), p. 95ff.

24. Cited in Ellen Wiley Todd, *The "New Woman" Revised: Painting and Gender Politics on Fourteenth Street* (Berkley: University of California Press, 1993), note 63 to chap. 6.

25. Rebecca Kay, ed., *Gender, Equality and Difference during and after State Socialism* (Basingstoke: Palgrave Macmillan, 2007).

26. Luisa Passerini, "Société de consommation et culture de masse," in Duby and Perrot, eds., *Histoire des femmes en occident*, p. 308.

27. Elizabeth Wilson, *Adorned in Dreams: Fashion and Modernity* (Berkeley: University of California Press, 1985).

28. *The Wizard of Oz*, 1939, directed by Victor Fleming and produced by Metro-Goldwyn-Mayer, adapted from L. Frank Baum's 1900 book *The Wonderful Wizard of Oz*.

29. Benjamin Spock, *The Common Sense Book of Baby and Child Care* (New York: Pocket Books, [1946] 1957).

30. Karin A. Martin, "William Wants a Doll. Can He Have One? Feminists, Child Care Advisors, and Gender-Neutral Child Rearing," *Gender and Society* 19, no. 4 (2005): 456–79.

31. Alexandra Rutherford provides a useful, albeit brief, overview of the history of feminist critiques of masculinist psychology in "Feminist Questions, Feminist Answers: Towards a Redefinition," *Feminism & Psychology* 17, no. 4 (2007): 459–64.

32. This is the first half of a second-wave abortion rights slogan. The second half is "Women will decide our fate."

33. *The Depo-Provera Debate: Hearings before the Select Committee on Population, U.S. House of Representatives, Ninety-Fifth Congress, Second Session, August 8, 9, and 10, 1978* (Lansing: Michigan State University, 1978).

34. June Rose, *Marie Stopes and the Sexual Revolution* (London: Faber and Faber, 1993); Rickie Solinger, ed., *Abortion Wars: A Half Century of Struggle, 1950–2000* (Berkeley: University of California Press, 1998); Patricia Walsh Coates, *Margaret Sanger and the Origin of the Birth Control Movement, 1910–1930: The Concept of Women's Sexual Autonomy* (Lewiston, NY: Edwin Mellen Press, 2008).

35. Barbara B. Crane and Jennifer Dusenberry, "Power and Politics in International Funding for Reproductive Health: The US Global Gag Rule," *Reproductive Health Matters* 12, no. 24 (2004): 128–37.

36. Fiammetta Venner, *L'Opposition à l'avortement: du lobby au commando* (Paris: Berg International, 1998).

37. The "Manifeste des 343" including full list of signatories is available online at http://tempsreel.nouvelobs.com/actualites/societe/20071127.OBS7018/le_manifeste_des_343_salopes_paru_dans_le_nouvel_obs_en.html (accessed March 13, 2010). The 1974 self-published transcripts and comments by Gisèle Halimi were republished, along with testimony from Marie-Claire, in Gisèle Halimi and Simone de Beauvoir, *Le procès de Bobigny: Choisir la cause des femmes* (Paris: Gallimard, 2006).

38. Bras were not actually burned.

39. Extracts from the ad can be viewed online at Australian Screen Online: http://aso.gov.au/titles/ads/berlei-it-isnt-done (accessed December 11, 2011).

40. A brief history of Berlei, including background to the Type Indicator, can be found at the online register of Australian fashion and textile design housed by the Royal Melbourne Institute of Technology: http://www.cyberfibres.rmit.edu.au/biogs/TRC0340b.htm (accessed February 17, 2009). A visual example of a Type Indicator can be viewed on Sydney's Powerhouse Museum website: http://www.powerhousemuseum.com/collection/database/?irn=330194 (accessed February 16, 2010).

41. C. J. Boyd et al., "Why Is Virginia Slim? Women and Cigarette Advertising," *International Journal of Community Health Education* 19, no. 1 (2000): 19–32; Gloria Steinem, "Sex, Lies and Advertising," in *Gender, Race and Class in Media: A Text Reader*, ed. Gail Dines and Jean M. Humez, 2nd ed. (Thousand Oaks, CA: Sage, 2003), pp. 223–29.

42. David de Vaus, "Marriage and remarriage," chap. 13, in *Diversity and Change in Australian Families* (Canberra: Australian Institute of Family Studies, 2004).

43. Winter, *Hijab and the Republic*.
44. Ibid., p. 26.
45. Ibid., chap. 1.
46. *Shame* (1987), directed by Steve Jodrell.
47. Rebecca West, "Mr. Chesterton in Hysterics," *Clarion*, November 14, 1913.
48. The London Feminist Network website provides a very brief account of this history (http://www.ldnfeministnetwork.ik.com/p_General_RTN.ikml [accessed February 15, 2010]); see also Joan Smith, "There's Only One Yorkshire Ripper," in Joan Smith, *Misogynies* (London; Vintage, 1996), pp. 163–205.
49. Susanne Kappeler, *The Pornography of Representation* (Cambridge, UK: Polity Press, 1986); Tania Modleski, *Feminism without Women: Culture and Criticism in a "Postfeminist" Age* (New York: Routledge, 1991); Smith, *Misogynies*; Ariel Levy, *Female Chauvinist Pigs: Women and the Rise of Raunch Culture* (Melbourne: Schwartz Publishing, 2005).
50. Giovanni Lista, *Loïe Fuller, danseuse de la Belle Epoque*, 2nd ed. (Paris: Hermann Danse, 2006); Nicole G. Albert, *Saphisme et Décadence dans Paris fin-de-siècle* (Paris: La Martinière, 2005) and *Renée Vivien à rebours: études pour un centenaire* (Paris: Orizons, 2009); Colette, *Lettres à Missy* (Paris: Flammarion, 2009)
51. Simone de Beauvoir, *Le Deuxième sexe*, p. 14 (my translation).

Chapter 6

1. Karen Horney, *The Adolescent Diaries of Karen Horney* (New York: Basic Books, 1980), p. 25.
2. Vera Brittain, *Testament of Youth* (London: Penguin Books, 1993); Rose Gamble, *Chelsea Child* (London: British Broadcasting Corporation, 1979), pp. 177–93.
3. Christina Benninghaus, "In Their Own Words: Girls' Representations of Growing Up in Germany in the 1920s," in *Secret Gardens, Satanic Mills: Placing Girls in European History, 1750–1960*, ed. Mary Jo Maynes, Brigitte Søland, and Christina Benninghaus (Bloomington: Indiana University Press, 2005), p. 182.
4. Susan Foley, *Women in France since 1789* (London: Palgrave, 2004), pp. 290, 295.
5. Both quotes from Allison Steven, "Race Gender and the Politics of Segregation," *The American Prospect*, June 29, 2007, http://prospect.org/ (accessed August 23, 2010).
6. John Newsom, *The Education of Girls* (London: Faber and Faber, 1948), p. 12.
7. Foley, *Women in France*, p. 250.
8. Ibid.
9. Linda Clark, "A Battle of the Sexes in a Professional Setting: The Introduction of Inspectrices Primaires, 1899–1914," *French Historical Studies* 16 (Spring 1989): p. 116.
10. Rebecca Rogers, "Learning to Be Good Girls and Women," in *The Routledge History of Women in Europe Since 1700*, ed. Deborah Simonton (London: Routledge, 2006), p. 121.
11. Foley, *Women in France*, pp. 221–22.
12. Ute Frevert, *Women in German History, from Bourgeois Emancipation to Sexual Liberation* (Oxford: Berg Publishers, 1988), p. 263.

13. Foley, *Women in France*, p. 250.

14. Annette Mayer, *Women in Britain, 1900–2000* (London: Hodder & Stoughton, 2002), p. 107.

15. Eva Kolinsky, *Women in Contemporary Germany* (Oxford: Berg, 1989), p. 101.

16. Sheila Rowbotham, *Hidden from History* (London: Pluto Press, 1975).

17. Dale Spender, *Invisible Women: The Schooling Scandal* (London: The Women's Press, 1977).

18. Simone de Beauvoir, *Mémoires d'une jeune fille rangée* (Paris: Folio Gallimard, 1958), pp. 243–44.

19. Patricia Mazón, *Gender and the Modern Research University: The Admission of Women to German Higher Education, 1865–1914* (Palo Alto, CA: Stanford University Press, 2003).

20. European Commission, Eurydice, and Eurostat. *Key Data on Education in Europe 2005* (Luxembourg: Office for Official Publications of the European Communities, 2005); Organisation for Economic Co-operation and Development (OECD), *Education at a Glance*, http://www.oecd.org/edu/eag2008 (accessed September 24, 2012); and UNESCO, *Educational Statistics*, http://www.uis.unesco.org (accessed September 24, 2012).

21. P. Bairoch, T. Deldycke, H. Gelders, and J.M. Limbor, eds., *The Working Population and Its Structure* (Brussels: Université Libre de Bruxelles, 1968), table C3.

22. Renate Bridenthal, "Beyond 'Kinder, Küche, Kirche': Weimar Women at Work," *Central European History* 6, no. 2 (1973): p. 152.

23. João De Pina-Cabral, *Sons of Adam, Daughters of Eve, the Peasant Worldview of the Alto Minho* (Oxford: Clarendon Press, 1986), pp. 18–19.

24. Ida Blom, "'Hun er den Raadende over Husets øokonomiske Angliggender?' Changes in Women's Work and Family Responsibilities in Norway since the 1860s," in *Women's Work and the Family Economy in Historical Perspective*, ed. Pat Hudson and W. R. Lee (Manchester: Manchester University Press, 1990), p. 166.

25. Henrik Mørkeberg, "Working Conditions of Women Married to Self-Employed Farmers," *Sociologia Ruralis* 18 (1978): 95–98.

26. Alice J. Albert, "Fit Work for Women: Sweated Home-Workers in Glasgow, c. 1875–1914," in *The World Is Ill Divided: Women's Work in Scotland*, ed. Eleanor Gordon and Esther Breitenbach (Edinburgh: Edinburgh University Press, 1990), pp. 162–63.

27. Perry R. Willson, *The Clockwork Factory, Women and Work in Fascist Italy* (Oxford: Clarendon Press, 1993), p. 129.

28. Deirdre Beddoe, *Back to Home and Duty: Women between the Wars, 1919–1939* (London: Pandora, 1989), p. 51.

29. Women in Informal Employment: Globalizing and Organizing (WIEGO), *Informal Workers in Focus: Domestic Workers* (Cambridge, MA: WIEGO Secretariat, Harvard University, 2009).

30. Ellen Jordan, "The Lady Clerks at the Prudential," *Gender & History* 8, no. 1 (1996): p. 71.

31. Carole Elizabeth Adams, *Women Clerks in Wilhelmine Germany* (Cambridge: Cambridge University Press, 1988), pp. 14–15; Jordan, "Lady Clerks," p. 66.

32. Francisca de Haan, *Gender and the Politics of Office Work, the Netherlands, 1860–1940* (Amsterdam: Amsterdam University Press, 1998), p. 3.

33. Ibid., p. 228.

34. Ibid., p. 26.

35. Frevert, *Women in German History*, p. 181.

36. Sîan Reynolds, *France between the Wars: Gender and Politics* (London: Routledge, 1996), p. 95.

37. Margaret Booth, "Women as Lawyers," in *Women and Higher Education*, ed. Mary Masson and Deborah Simonton (Aberdeen: Aberdeen University Press, 2004), p. 267.

38. Sheila Rowbotham, *A Century of Women, A History of Women in Britain and the United States* (London: Viking, 1997), p. 386.

39. Deborah Simonton, *A History of European Women's Work* (London: Routledge, 1998), p. 245.

40. Susan Bachrach, "La feminization des PTT au tournand du siècle," *Mouvement Social* 140 (1987): pp. 72, 78.

41. *Hospital*, June 8, 1912, pp. 251–52.

42. Sara Burstall, "An English View of Our Schools," *New York Times*, May 1, 1909, n.p.

43. Willson, *Clockwork Factory*, p. 103.

44. Great Britain, Parliamentary Papers, *Report of the War Cabinet of Women in Industry* XXXI, 1919, p. 110.

45. Gro Hagemann, "Feminism and the Sexual Division of Labour; Female Labour in the Norwegian Telegraph Service," *Scandinavian Journal of History* 10 (1985): 146–47.

46. Gertjan DeGroot and Marlou Schrover, "Between Men and Machines: Women Workers in New Industries, 1870–1940," *Social History* 20, no. 3 (1995): p. 295.

47. Sylvie Zerner, "De la couture aux presses: l'emploi féminin entre les deux guerres," *Mouvement Social* 140 (1987): p. 22.

48. Sally Shortall, "Power Analysis and Farm Wives," *Sociologia Ruralis* 32, no. 4 (1992): p. 439.

49. Bonnie S. Anderson and Judith P. Zinsser, *A History of Their Own, Women in Europe from Prehistory to the Present* (London: Penguin, 1988), vol. 2, p. 259.

Chapter 7

1. Margaret Stacey and Marion Price, *Women, Power and Politics* (London: Routledge, 1981), p. 3.

2. Fiona A. Montgomery, *Women's Rights: Struggles and Feminism in Britain c. 1770–1970* (Manchester: Manchester University Press, 2006), p. 158. For a discussion of different ways of defining women's engagement in politics, see Kathryn Gleadle and Sarah Richardson, eds., *Women in British Politics, 1760–1860. The Power of the Petticoat* (Houndmills: Macmillan, 2000).

3. For a discussion of the different strategies women have adopted, see Virginia Sapiro, "When Are Interests Interesting? The Problem of Political Representation of Women," in *Feminism and Politics*, ed. Anne Phillips (Oxford: Oxford University Press, 1998), pp. 176–78.

4. Mary Maynard, "Beyond the 'Big Three': The Development of Feminist Theory into the 1990s," *Women's History Review* 4, no. 3 (1995) discusses the different strands of feminism (radical, liberal, and Socialist) that had been identified in earlier histories and considers the impact of postmodernism. For an overview of feminist theories in this period, see Imelda Whelehan, *Modern Feminist Thought. From the Second Wave to "Post Feminism"* (Edinburgh: Edinburgh University Press, 1995).

5. For a discussion of the complex relationship between ideas of equality and difference in the interwar years, see Harold L. Smith, ed., *British Feminism in the Twentieth Century* (Aldershot: Edward Elgar, 1990).

6. Judith Keene, "'Into the Clean Air of the Plaza': Spanish Women Achieve the Vote in 1931," in *Constructing Spanish Womanhood: Female Identity in Modern Spain*, ed. Victoria Enders and Pamela Radcliff (Albany, NY: State University of New York Press, 1999).

7. Gisela Bock, *Women in European History* (Oxford: Blackwell, 2002), pp. 179–80; Anne-Marie Sohn, "Between the Wars in Britain and France," in *A History of Women: Towards a Cultural Identity in the Twentieth Century*, ed. Georges Duby and Michelle Perrot (Cambridge, MA: Harvard University Press, 1994), pp. 93–97; Dorothy Rowe, *Representing Berlin: Sexuality and the City in Imperial and Weimar Germany* (Aldershot: Ashgate, 2003).

8. Bock, *Women in European History*, p. 146.

9. Steven C. Hause and Anne R. Kenney, *Women's Suffrage and Social Politics in the French Third Republic* (Princeton, NJ: Princeton University Press, 1984).

10. Karen Offen, *European Feminisms, 1700–1950* (Stanford, CA: Stanford University Press, 2000), p. 297.

11. Jorgen Rasmussen, "Women in Labour: The Flapper Vote and the Party System Transformation in Britain," *Electoral Studies* 3, no. 1 (1984): 47–63.

12. Martin Francis, *Ideas and Politics under Labour, 1945–51. Building a New Britain* (Manchester: Manchester University Press, 1997), pp. 200–201; Ina Zweiniger-Bargielowska, *Austerity in Britain: Rationing, Controls and Consumption, 1939–55* (Oxford: Oxford University Press, 2000), chap. 5.

13. Maurice Duverger, *The Political Role of Women* (Paris: UNESCO, 1955).

14. Karen Hagemann, "Men's Demonstrations and Women's Protest: Gender in Collective Action in the Urban Working-Class Milieu during the Weimar Republic," *Gender and History* 5, no. 1 (1993): pp. 104–5; Duncan Tanner, "Labour and Its Membership," in *Labour's First Century*, ed. Duncan Tanner, Pat Thane, and Nick Tiratsoo (Cambridge: Cambridge University Press, 2000).

15. Martin Francis, "Labour and Gender," in Tanner, Thane, and Tiratsoo, eds., *Labour's First Century*, pp. 211–15.

16. Sue Bruley, *Women in Britain since 1900* (Houndmills: Macmillan, 1999); Sheila Rowbotham, *A Century of Women* (London: Viking, 1997).

17. Barbara Caine, *English Feminism, 1780–1980* (Oxford: Oxford University Press, 1997), p. 242.

18. Ida Blom, "The Struggle for Women's Suffrage in Norway, 1885–1913," *Scandinavian Journal of History* 5 (1980): p. 21; Mariette Sineau, "Law and Democracy," in Duby and Perrot, eds., *A History of Women*, pp. 518–19.

19. Anna Rossi-Doria, "Italian Women Enter Politics," in *When the War Was Over: Women, War and Peace in Europe, 1940–1956*, ed. Claire Duchen and Irene Bandhauer-Schoffmann (London: Leicester University Press, 2000), p. 97.

20. Claudia Koonz, "Conflicting Allegiances: Political Ideology and Women Legislators in Weimar Germany," *Signs* 1, no. 3 (1976): p. 664.

21. Bock, *Women in European History*, p. 177.

22. Koonz, "Conflicting Allegiances," table 1.

23. For a discussion of the many barriers to women's political participation, see Ida Blom, "Women's Politics and Women in Politics in Norway since the End of the Nineteenth Century," *Scandinavian Journal of History* 12 (1987): pp. 30–32.

24. Brian Harrison, "Women in a Men's House. The Women MPs, 1919–1945," *Historical Journal* 29, no. 3 (1986): 623–54.

25. Gisela Kaplan, *Contemporary Western European Feminism* (London: Allen and Unwin, 1992), pp. 44–45.

26. Hugh Dalton, *Call Back Yesterday* (1953), cited in Melville Currell, *Political Woman* (London: Croom Helm, 1974), p. 63.

27. A. Garofalo, *L'Italiana in Italy* (1956), p. 105, quoted in Rossi-Doria, "Italian Women Enter Politics," p. 98.

28. Sapiro, "When Are Interests Interesting?" p. 165.

29. *Yorkshire Evening News*, December 10, 1924; interview with *Western Mail*, December 12, 1924.

30. Quoted in Koonz, "Conflicting Allegiances," p. 674.

31. Koonz, "Conflicting Allegiances," p. 674.

32. Harrison, "Women in a Men's House," pp. 34–35; see also Olive Banks, *The Politics of British Feminism* (Aldershot: Edward Elgar, 1993), chap. 4. Françoise Thébaud, "Explorations of Gender," in Duby and Perrot, eds., *A History of Women*, p. 5.

33. Koonz, "Conflicting Allegiances."

34. Caine, *English Feminism*, p. 184.

35. Johanna Alberti, *Beyond Suffrage: Feminists in War and Peace, 1914–28* (Houndmills: Macmillan, 1989); Harold L. Smith, "British Feminism in the 1920s," in *British Feminism in the Twentieth Century* (Amherst: University of Massachusetts, 1990).

36. Hagemann, "Men's Demonstrations and Women's Protest," p. 114; June Hannam, "Women as Paid Organisers and Propagandists for the British Labour Party between the Wars," *International Labour and Working-Class History* 77, no. 1 (2010): 69–88.

37. Sue Bruley, *The Women and Men of 1926* (Cardiff: University of Wales Press, 2010).

38. Offen, *European Feminisms*, pp. 299–300.

39. Hilda Romer Christensen, "Feminist Socialists in Denmark," in *Women and Socialism. Socialism and Women*, ed. Helmut Gruber and Pamela Graves (Oxford: Berghahn, 1998), p. 493.

40. Caitriona Beaumont, "Citizens Not Feminists: The Boundary Negotiated between Citizenship and Feminism by Mainstream Women's Organisations in England, 1928–1939," *Women's History Review* 9, no. 2 (2000): 411–29.

41. James Hinton, "Militant Housewives: The British Housewives' League and the Attlee Government," *History Workshop Journal* 38 (1994): 129–56.

42. Gro Hagemann, "Citizenship and Social Order: Gender Politics in Twentieth Century Norway and Sweden," *Women's History Review* 11, no. 3 (2002): 417–29.

43. Helmut Gruber, "French Women in the Crossfire of Class, Sex, Maternity and Citizenship," in Gruber and Graves, eds., *Women and Socialism*, p. 302.

44. Geoff Eley, "From Welfare Politics to Welfare States. Women and the Socialist Question," in Gruber and Graves, eds., *Women and Socialism*, p. 534.

45. Eley, "From Welfare Politics to Welfare States," p. 531.

46. Denise de Weerdt, "'Bread and Roses': Pragmatic Women in the Belgium Workers' Party," in Gruber and Graves, eds., *Women and Socialism*, p. 241.

47. Sohn, "Between the Wars," p. 118; for Germany, see Hagemann, "Men's Demonstrations and Women's Protest."

48. Pamela Graves, "An Experiment in Women-Centered Socialism: Labour Women in Britain," in Gruber and Graves, eds., *Women and Socialism*, pp. 194–98; June Hannam and Karen Hunt, *Socialist Women. Britain, 1890s–1920s* (London: Routledge, 2001).

49. Hagemann, "Citizenship and Social Order"; Barbara Hobson, "Feminist Strategies and Gendered Discourses in Welfare States; Married Women's Right to Work in the United States and Sweden," in *Mothers of a New World. Maternalist Policies and the Origins of Welfare States*, ed. Seth Koven and Sonya Michel (London: Routledge, 1993).

50. Eley, "From Welfare Politics to Welfare States," pp. 534–35.

51. Hagemann, "Citizenship and Social Order," p. 424.

52. Sheila Rowbotham, *A New World for Women: Stella Browne-Socialist Feminist* (London: Pluto Press, 1977), pp. 39–40; Lesley Hall, *The Life and Times of Stella Browne: Feminist and Free Spirit* (London: IB Tauris, 2011).

53. Graves, "An Experiment in Women-Centered Socialism," p. 202.

54. Marlene Legates, *In Their Time. A History of Feminism in Western Society* (London: Routledge, 2001), chap. 9.

55. Richard Stites, "Women and the Revolutionary Process in Russia," in *Becoming Visible: Women in European History*, 2nd ed., ed. Renate Bridenthal, Claudia Koonz, and Susan Stuard (Boston, MA: Houghton Mifflin, 1987), pp. 464–65.

56. Offen, *European Feminisms*, p. 337.

57. Caine, *English Feminism*, p. 194. For a discussion of similar conflicts in the United States, see Dorothy Sue Cobble, *The Other Women's Movement* (Princeton, NJ: Princeton University Press, 2004), chap. 2.

58. Johanna Alberti, in *Beyond Suffrage*, suggests that the involvement of women in the Labour Party strained feminist loyalties and brought them under male control. Harold L. Smith, "Sex vs. Class: British Feminists and the Labour Movement," *Historian* 47 (1984): pp. 23–24, 34–35, claims that the leadership of the Labour Party was actively hostile to feminists outside its ranks.

59. Pat Thane, "Women in the British Labour Party and the Construction of State Welfare," in Koven and Michel, eds., *Mothers of a New World*, pp. 362–72.

60. Duncan Tanner, "Gender, Civic Culture and Politics in South Wales: Explaining Labour Municipal Policy, 1918–39," in *Labour's Grass Roots: Essays on the Activities of Local Labour Parties and Members, 1918–45*, ed. Matthew Worley (Aldershot: Ashgate, 2005).

61. Carole Miller, "Geneva—The Key to Equality: Inter-War Feminists and the League of Nations," *Women's History Review* 3, no. 2 (1994): p. 238.

62. Sylvie Chaperon, "'Feminism Is Dead. Long Live Feminism!' The Women's Movement in France at the Liberation, 1944–46," in Duchen and Bandauer-Schöffman, eds., *When the War Was Over*, pp. 156–57.

63. Ida Blom, "From Communal Family Rights to Individual Rights in Women's National Citizenship in Norway," in *Women's Rights and Human Rights: International Historical Perspectives*, ed. Patricia Grimshaw, Katie Holmes, and Marilyn Lake (Houndmills: Palgrave, 2001), pp. 184–94.

64. Legates, *In Their Time*, p. 339.

65. For a detailed discussion of the legislation that was passed in different European countries, see Sineau, "Law and Democracy," pp. 498–512.

66. Legates, *In Their Time*, p. 339.

67. Barbara Schaeffer-Hegel, "Makers and Victims of Unification: German Women and the Two Germanies," *Women's Studies International Forum* 15, no. 1 (1992): pp. 103–4.

68. Mira Janova and Mariette Sineau, "Women's Participation in Political Power in Europe: An Essay in East-West Comparison," *Women's Studies International Forum* 15, no. 1 (1992): p. 117, table 1.

69. Dahlerup, ed., *The New Women's Movement: Feminism and Political Power in Europe and the USA* (London: Sage, 1987). Sheila Rowbotham, *The Past Is Before Us. Feminism in Action since the 1960s* (London: Pandora, 1989).

70. Kathie Sarachild, "Consciousness-Raising. A Radical Weapon," in *Feminist Revolution*, ed. Redstockings (New York: Random House, 1979).

71. Sheila Rowbotham, *Women in Movement: Feminism and Social Action* (London: Routledge, 1992), chaps. 24 and 25.

72. Kaplan, *Contemporary Western European Feminism*, p. 17.

73. *Women of Europe*, no. 50 (1987): p. 11, quoted in Kaplan, *Contemporary Western European Feminism*, p. 13.

74. Kaplan, *Contemporary Western European Feminism*, p. 13.

75. Janova and Sineau, "Women's Participation in Political Power," p. 117.

76. Kaplan, *Contemporary Western European Feminism*, p. 85.

77. Whelehan, *Modern Feminist Thought*.

78. Ailbhe Smyth, "The Women's Movement in the Republic of Ireland 1970–1990," in *Women's Studies Reader*, ed. Ailbhe Smyth (Dublin: Attic Press, 1993).

79. Whelehan, *Modern Feminist Thought*, chap. 10.

80. Schaeffer-Hegel, "Makers and Victims of Unification."

81. Schaeffer-Hegel, "Makers and Victims of Unification," p. 265.

82. Jill Liddington, *The Long Road to Greenham: Feminism and Anti-Militarism in Britain since 1820* (London: Virago, 1989).

83. Elizabeth Meehan, "British Feminism from the 1960s to the 1980s," in Smith, ed., *British Feminism*, p. 202.

84. See the analysis of whether the entry of more than 100 women MPs to Parliament in 1997 made a difference: Joni Lovenduski and Pippa Norris, "Westminster Women: The Politics of Presence," *Political Studies* 51 (2003): p. 100.

85. Sarah Childs, "New Labour's Women MPs: The Difference They Made," unpublished paper presented to the Economic and Social Research Council seminar series, What Difference Did the Vote Make? Seminar 1, November 2003, pp. 4–6.

86. SJFE, Antoinette Fouque, *Women's Rights and the European Union,* 1997, http://www.helsinki.fi/science/xantippa/wle/wle13.html (accessed March 10, 2011).

Chapter 8

1. Laura Mulvey, "Visual Pleasure and Narrative Cinema," *Screen* 16 (1975): 6–18 (emphasis in original).

2. Ella Shohat, "Gender and the Culture of Empire: Toward a Feminist Ethnography of the Cinema," *Quarterly Review of Film and Video* 131 (1991): 45–84.

3. Deborah Willis and Carla Williams, *The Black Female Body: A Photographic History* (Philadelphia: Temple University Press, 2002).

4. Ibid., p. 21.

5. Carla Williams, "Naked, Neutered, Noble: The Black Female Body in America and the Problem of Photographic History," in *Skin Deep, Spirit Strong: The Black Female Body in American Culture,* ed. Kimberly Wallace-Sanders (Ann Arbor: University of Michigan Press, 2002), pp. 182–200.

6. Jane Gaines, "White Privilege and Looking Relations: Race and Gender in Feminist Film Theory," *Screen* 29 (1988): 12–17.

7. Hortense Spillers, "Interstices: A Small Drama of Words," in *Pleasure and Danger: Exploring Female Sexuality,* ed. Carole Vance (London: Pandora, 1989), pp. 73–100.

8. Shohat, "Gender and the Culture of Empire," pp. 68–69.

9. Alison Griffiths, *Wondrous Difference: Cinema, Anthropology, and Turn-of-the-Century Visual Culture* (New York: Columbia University Press, 2002).

10. Pavitra Sundar, "Meri Awaaz Suno: Women, Vocality, and Nation in Hindi Cinema," *Meridians* 8 (2008): 144–79; Neepa Majumdar, "The Embodied Voice: Song Sequences and Stardom in Popular Hindi Cinema," in *Soundtrack Available: Essays on Film and Popular Music,* ed. Pamela Robertson Wojcik and Arthur Knight (Durham, NC: Duke University Press, 2001), pp. 161–81.

11. Gwendolyn Audrey Foster, *Women Filmmakers of the African and Asian Diaspora* (Carbondale: Southern Illinois University Press, 1995).

12. Trinh T. Minh-ha, *Woman, Native, Other: Writing Postcoloniality and Feminism* (Bloomington: Indiana University Press, 1990).

13. Caroline Brown, "The Representation of the Indigenous Other in *Daughters of the Dust* and *The Piano,*" *NWSA Journal* 15 (2003): 1–19.

14. Cynthia Baron, "Films by Tracey Moffatt: Reclaiming First Australians' Rights, Celebrating Women's Rites," *Women's Studies Quarterly* 30 (2002): 151–77.

15. Okwui Enwezor, *Lorna Simpson* (New York: American Federation of Arts, 2006).

16. Lorraine O'Grady, "Olympia's Maid: Reclaiming Black Female Subjectivity," *Afterimage* 20 (1992): 14–20.

17. Lisa Nakamura, "'Where Do You Want to Go Today?' Cybernetic Tourism, the Internet, and Transnationality," in *Race in Cyberspace*, ed. Beth E. Kolko, Lisa Nakamura, and Gilbert B. Rodman (New York: Routledge, 2000), pp. 15–26.

18. Willis and Williams, *The Black Female Body*, pp. 76–77.

19. Jean Baudrillard, *Simulacra and Simulation* (Ann Arbor: University of Michigan Press, [1981] 1994).

20. Coco Fusco, *The Bodies That Were Not Ours and Other Writings* (New York: Routledge, 2001).

21. Ayoka Chenzira, "Ayoka," in Ayoka Pages, http://www.ayoka.com (accessed March 31, 2009).

22. Donna Haraway, *Simians, Cyborgs, and Women: The Reinvention of Nature* (New York: Routledge, 1991).

BIBLIOGRAPHY

Abbasi-Shavazi, M. J., and P. McDonald. 2000. "Fertility and Multiculturalism: Immigrant Fertility in Australia, 1977–1991." *International Migration Review* 34 (1): 215–42.

Adams, Carole Elizabeth. 1988. *Women Clerks in Wilhelmine Germany.* Cambridge: Cambridge University Press.

Ahmed, Leila. 1992. *Women and Gender in Islam: Historical Roots of a Modern Debate.* New Haven: Yale University Press.

Albert, Alice J. 1990. "Fit Work for Women: Sweated Home-workers in Glasgow, c. 1875–1914." In *The World Is Ill Divided: Women's Work in Scotland*, ed. Eleanor Gordon and Esther Breitenbach. Edinburgh: Edinburgh University Press.

Albert, Nicole G. 2009. *Renée Vivien à rebours: études pour un centenaire.* Paris: Orizons.

Albert, Nicole G. 2005. *Saphisme et Décadence dans Paris fin-de-siècle.* Paris: La Martinière.

Alberti, Johanna. 1989. *Beyond Suffrage: Feminists in War and Peace, 1914–28.* Houndmills: Macmillan.

Allen, Judith. 1990. *Sex and Secrets: Crimes Involving Australian Women since 1880.* Oxford: Oxford University Press.

Anderson, Bonnie S., and Judith P. Zinsser. 1988. *A History of Their Own: Women in Europe from Prehistory to the Present.* 2 vols. London: Penguin.

Angier, Natalie. 2000. *Woman: An Intimate Geography.* New York: Anchor Books.

Apple, Rima, ed. 1990. *Women, Health and Medicine in America.* New Brunswick, NJ: Rutgers University Press.

Arat, Yesim. 1997. "The Project of Modernity and Women in Turkey." In *Rethinking Modernity and National Identity in Turkey*, ed. Sibel Bozdoğan and Reşat Kasaba. Seattle: University of Washington Press.

Arieti, S., ed. 1959. *American Handbook of Psychiatry.* New York: Basic Books.

Armstrong, Karen. 1996. *Jerusalem: One City, Three Faiths*. London: HarperCollins.

Armstrong, Karen. 2009. "Man vs. God." *Wall Street Journal* (September 12). Available at: http://online.wsj.com/article/SB10001424052970203440104574405030643556324.html. Accessed November 12, 2009.

Aupers, Stef, and Dick Houtman. 2006. "Beyond the Spiritual Supermarket: The Social and Public Significance of New Age Spirituality." *Journal of Contemporary Religion* 21 (2): 201–22.

Bachrach, Susan. 1987. "La feminisation des PTT au tournand du siècle." *Mouvement Social* 140: 69–87.

Bade, Klaus J. 2003. *Migration in European History*, trans. Allison Brown. Malden, MA: Wiley-Blackwell.

Baird, Julia. 2004. *Media Tarts: How the Australian Press Frames Female Politicians*. Melbourne: Scribe.

Bairoch, P., T. Deldycke, H. Gelders, and J.-M. Limbor, eds. 1968. *The Working Population and its Structure*. Brussels: Université Libre de Bruxelles.

Bale, Anthony. 1990. "Women's Toxic Experience." In *Women, Health and Medicine in America*, ed. Rima Apple. New Brunswick, NJ: Rutgers University Press.

Banks, Olive. 1993. *The Politics of British Feminism*. Aldershot: Edward Elgar.

Bard, Christine. 1995. *Les filles de Marianne: Histoire des féminismes 1914–1940*. Paris: Fayard.

Bard, Christine, ed. 1999. *Un siècle d'antiféminisme*. Paris: Fayard.

Barlow, Tani. "Buying In: Advertising and the Sexy Modern Girl Icon in Shanghai in the 1920s and 1930s." In *The Modern Girl around the World: Consumption, Modernity, and Globalization*, ed. Alys Eve Weinbaum, Lynn M. Thomas, Priti Ramamurthy, Uta G. Poiger, Madeline Yue Dong, and Tani E. Barlow. Durham, NC: Duke University Press.

Baron, Cynthia. 2002. "Films by Tracey Moffatt: Reclaiming First Australians' Rights, Celebrating Women's Rites." *Women's Studies Quarterly* 30 (1–2): 151–77.

Bataille, Philippe, and Françoise Gaspard. 1999. *Comment les femmes changent la politique, et pourquoi les hommes résistent*. Paris: La Découverte.

Baudrillard, Jean. [1981] 1994. *Simulacra and Simulation*. Ann Arbor: University of Michigan Press.

Beaumont, Caitriona. 2000. "Citizens not Feminists: The Boundary Negotiated between Citizenship and Feminism by Mainstream Women's Organisations in England, 1928–1939." *Women's History Review* 9 (2): 411–29.

Beauvoir, Simone de. 1949. *Le Deuxième sexe*. Paris: Gallimard.

Beddoe, Deirdre. 1989. *Back to Home and Duty: Women between the Wars, 1919–1939*. London: Pandora.

Bedevil. 1993. Dir. Tracey Moffatt. Women Make Movies. Available at: http://www.wmm.com/. Accessed September 28, 2010.

Bell, K. 2006. "An Overview of Assisted Reproduction in Australia and Directions for Social Research." *Australian Journal of Emerging Technologies and Society* 4 (1): 15–27.

Bell, Susan E. 2009. *DES Daughters: Embodied Knowledge and the Transformation of Women's Health Politics*. Philadelphia: Temple University Press.

Benedek, Therese F. 1959. "Sexual Functions in Women and Their Disturbance." In *American Handbook of Psychiatry,* ed. S. Arieti. New York: Basic Books.

Bennett, Paula. 1993. "Critical Clitoridectomy: Female Sexual Imagery and Feminist Psychoanalytic Theory." *Signs* 18 (2, Winter): 235–59.

Benninghaus, Christina. 2005. "In Their Own Words: Girls' Representations of Growing up in Germany in the 1920s." In *Secret Gardens, Satanic Mills: Placing Girls in European History, 1750–1960,* ed. Mary Jo Maynes, Brigitte Søland, and Christina Benninghaus. Bloomington: Indiana University Press.

"Betty Dodson: A Second Wave Feminist Liberating the World One Orgasm at a Time." n.d. Betty Dodson with Carlin Ross. Available at: http://dodsonandross.com/blogs/betty-dodson. Accessed August 23, 2009.

Bird, Chloe E., and Patricia P. Rieker. 2008. *Gender and Health: The Effects of Constrained Choices and Social Policies.* Cambridge: Cambridge University Press.

Blom, Ida. 2001. "From Communal Family Rights to Individual Rights in Women's National Citizenship in Norway." In *Women's Rights and Human Rights: International Historical Perspectives,* ed. Patricia Grimshaw, Katie Holmes, and Marilyn Lake. Houndmills: Palgrave.

Blom, Ida. 1990. "'Hun er den Raadende over Husets øokonomiske Angliggender'? Changes in Women's Work and Family Responsibilities in Norway since the 1860s." In *Women's Work and the Family Economy in Historical Perspective,* ed. Pat Hudson and W. R. Lee. Manchester: Manchester University Press.

Blom, Ida. 1980. "The Struggle for Women's Suffrage in Norway, 1885–1913." *Scandinavian Journal of History* 5: 3–22.

Blom, Ida. 1987. "Women's Politics and Women in Politics in Norway since the End of the Nineteenth Century." *Scandinavian Journal of History* 12: 17–33.

Blot, William J., and Joseph K. McLaughlin. 2004. "Response: Re: Are Women More Susceptible to Lung Cancer?" *Journal of the National Cancer Institute* 96 (20): 1560–61.

Bock, Gisela. 2002. *Women in European History.* Oxford: Blackwell.

Bock, Gisela, and Pat Thane, eds. 1991. *Maternity and Gender Policies: Women and the Rise of the European Welfare States, 1880s–1950s.* London: Routledge.

Bonaparte, Marie. 1953. *Female Sexuality.* London: Imago Publishing.

Booth, Margaret. 2004. "Women as Lawyers." In *Women and Higher Education,* ed. Mary Masson and Deborah Simonton. Aberdeen: Aberdeen University Press.

Bosanquet, Agnes. 2005. "Luce Irigaray's Sensible Transcendental: Becoming Divine in the Body." *Transformations,* no. 11. Available at: http://www.transformationsjournal.org/journal/issue_11/article_01.shtml. Accessed May 21, 2010.

Bosley, Jocelyn. 2010. "From Monkey Facts to Human Ideologies: Theorizing Female Orgasm in human And Nonhuman Primates, 1967–1983." *Signs: Journal of Women in Culture and Society* 35 (3): 647–71.

Boston Women's Health Book Collective. 1973. *Our Bodies, Ourselves.* New York: Simon and Schuster.

Boston Women's Health Book Collective. n.d. "Timeline." Available at: http://www.ourbodiesourselves.org/about/timeline.asp. Accessed September 15, 2010.

Boyd, C. J., et al. 2000. "Why is Virginia Slim? Women and Cigarette Advertising." *International Journal of Community Health Education* 19 (1): 19–32.

Braun, Virginia, Nicola Gavey, and Kathyrn McPhillips. 2003. "The 'Fair Deal'? Un-packing Accounts of Reciprocity of Heterosex." *Sexualities* 6: 237–60.

Bridenthal, Renate. 1973. "Beyond 'Kinder, Küche, Kirche': Weimar Women at Work." *Central European History* 6 (2): 148–66.

Brittain, Vera. [1933] 1993. *Testament of Youth*. London: Penguin Books.

Brockmeier, Jens. 1997. "Autobiography, Narrative, and the Freudian Concept of Life History." *Philosophy, Psychiatry, & Psychology* 4 (3): 175–99.

Brown, Callum. 2001. *The Death of Christian Britain*. London: Routledge.

Brown, Callum. 2006. *Religion and Society in Twentieth-century Britain*. Harlow: Pearson Longman.

Brown, Caroline. 2003. "The Representation of the Indigenous Other in *Daughters of the Dust* and *The Piano*." *NWSA Journal* 15 (1): 1–19.

Bruce, Steve. 2002. *God Is Dead: Secularization in the West*. Malden, MA: Blackwell.

Bruley, Sue. 2010. *The Women and Men of 1926*. Cardiff: University of Wales Press.

Bruley, Sue. 1999. *Women in Britain since 1900*. Houndmills: Macmillan.

Burstall, Sara. 1909. "An English View of Our Schools." *New York Times* (May 1): n.p.

Caine, Barbara. 1997. *English Feminism, 1780–1980*. Oxford: Oxford University Press.

Caldwell, J., Young, C., Ware, H., Levis, D., and Davis, A. 1973. "Knowledge, At-titudes and Practice of Family Planning in Melbourne, 1971." *Studies in Family Planning* 4 (3): 47–59.

Campbell, Beatrix. 1980. "A Feminist Sexual Politics: Now You See It, Now You Don't." *Feminist Review* 5: 1–18.

Campbell, Beatrix. 1987. *The Iron Ladies: Why Do Women Vote Tory?* London: Virago.

Cane, Christine, and Gunson, Niel. 1986. "Postcards: A Source for Aboriginal Biogra-phy." *Aboriginal History* 10 (1): 171–74.

Cannold, Leslie. 1998. *The Abortion Myth: Feminism, Morality and the Hard Choices Women Make*. Sydney: Allen and Unwin.

Carlysle Bogdan, Janet. 1990. "Childbirth in America, 1650 to 1990." In *Women, Health and Medicine in America*, ed. Rima Apple. New Brunswick, NJ: Rutgers University Press.

Carmichael, G. A. 1998. "Things Ain't What They Used to Be! Demography, Mental Cohorts, Morality and Values in post-war Australia." *Journal of the Australian Population Association* 15 (2): 91–113.

Carmichael, G. A., and P. McDonald. 2003. "Fertility Trends and Differentials." In *The transformation of Australia's population: 1970–2030*, ed. Siew-Ean Khoo and Peter McDonald. Sydney: UNSW Press.

Carmichael, Gordon A. 1992. "Colonial and Post-colonial Demographic Patterns." In *Gender Relations in Australia: Domination and Negotiation*, ed. Kay Saunders and Raymond Evans. Sydney: Harcourt, Brace, Jovanovich.

Chandra, A. 1998. "Surgical Sterilization in the United States: Prevalence and Charac-teristics, 1965–95." National Center for Health Statistics, *Vital Health Statistics* 23 (20): 1–33.

Chaperon, Sylvie. 2000. "'Feminism Is Dead. Long Live Feminism!' The Women's Movement in France at the Liberation, 1944–46." In *When the War Was Over:*

Women, War and Peace in Europe, 1940–1956, ed. Claire Duchen and Irene Bandhauer-Schoffmann. London: Leicester University Press.

Chaperon, Sylvie. 2000. *Les années Beauvoir (1945–1970)*. Paris: Fayard.

Chenzira, Ayoka. "Ayoka." Available at: http://www.ayoka.com. Accessed March 31, 2009.

Chesler, Phyllis. 1989 [1972]. *Women and Madness*. San Diego, CA: Harcourt, Brace, Jovanovich.

Childs, Sarah. 2003. "New Labour's Women MPs: The Difference They Made." Unpublished paper presented to the ESRC seminar series, What Difference Did the Vote Make? Seminar 1, November 2003.

Christensen, Hilda Romer. 1998. "Feminist Socialists in Denmark." In *Women and Socialism, Socialism and Women*, ed. Helmut Gruber and Pamela Graves. Oxford: Berghahn.

Clark, Anna. 2008. *Desire: A History of European Sexuality*. New York: Routledge.

Clark, Linda. 1989. "A Battle of the Sexes in a Professional Setting: The Introduction of Inspectrices Primaires, 1899–1914." *French Historical Studies* 16 (1): 96–125.

Clarke, Adele, and Virginia Oleson, eds. 1999. *Revisioning Women, Health and Healing: Feminist, Cultural and Technoscience Perspectives*. New York: Routledge.

Clinton, Hilary Rodham. 1995. "Remarks to the U.N. 4th World Congress on Women Plenary Session." Delivered September 5, 1995, Beijing, China. Available at: http://www.americanrhetoric.com/speeches/hillaryclintonbeijingspeech.htm Accessed August 10, 2010.

Coates, Patricia Walsh. 2008. *Margaret Sanger and the Origin of the Birth Control Movement, 1910–1930: The Concept of Women's Sexual Autonomy*. Lewiston, NY: Edwin Mellen Press.

Cobble, Dorothy Sue. 2004. *The Other Women's Movement*. Princeton, NJ: Princeton University Press.

Coble, Yank D., et al. 1992. "Violence against Women." *Journal of the American Medical Association* 267: 3184–89.

Colette. 2009. *Lettres à Missy*. Paris: Flammarion.

Colson, M. H. 2010. "Female Orgasm: Myths, Facts and Controversies." *Sexologies* 19: 8–14.

Conrad, Peter. 1998. *Modern Times, Modern Places: Life and Art in the Twentieth Century*. London: Thames and Hudson.

Conrad, Peter, and Rochelle Kern, eds. 1994. *The Sociology of Health and Illness*. New York: Saint Martin's Press.

Corridor. 2003. Dir. Lorna Simpson. New York: Sean Kelly Gallery.

Crane, Barbara B., and Jennifer Dusenberry. 2004. "Power and Politics in International Funding for Reproductive Health: The US Global Gag Rule." *Reproductive Health Matters* 12 (24): 128–37.

Crary, Jonathan. 1994. *Techniques of the Observer: On Vision and Modernity in the Nineteenth Century*. Cambridge: MIT Press.

Currell, Melville. 1974. *Political Woman*. London: Croom Helm.

Daly, Mary, and Katherine Rake. 2003. *Gender and the Welfare State*. Cambridge: Polity Press.

Damousi, Joy. 2005. *Freud in the Antipodes: A Cultural History of Psychoanalysis in Australia.* Sydney: UNSW Press.

Dan, Alice, ed. 1994. *Reframing Women's Health: Multidisciplinary Research and Practice.* Thousand Oaks, CA: Sage Publications.

Dan, Alice, et al. 1992. "Rationale and Evidence for the Role of Circadian Desynchrony in Premenstrual Symptoms." In *Menstrual Health in Women's Lives,* ed. Alice J. Dan and Linda L. Lewis. Chicago: University of Illinois Press.

Dan, Alice J., and Linda L. Lewis, eds. 1992. *Menstrual Health in Women's Lives.* Chicago: University of Illinois Press.

Davies, Owen. 1999. *Witchcraft, Magic and Culture 1736–1951.* Manchester: Manchester University Press.

De Beauvoir, Simone. 1958. *Mémoires d'une jeune fille rangée.* Paris: Folio Gallimard.

De Groot, Gertjan, and Marlou Schrover. 1995. "Between Men and Machines: Women Workers in New Industries, 1870–1940." *Social History* 20 (3): 279–96.

De Haan, Francisca. 1998. *Gender and the Politics of Office Work, the Netherlands, 1860–1940.* Amsterdam: Amsterdam University Press.

De Pina-Cabral, João. 1986. *Sons of Adam, Daughters of Eve: The Peasant Worldview of the Alto Minho.* Oxford: Clarendon Press.

The Depo-Provera Debate: Hearings before the Select Committee on Population, U.S. House of Representatives, Ninety-Fifth Congress, Second Session, August 8, 9, and 10, 1978. Lansing: Michigan State University, 1978.

de Weerdt, Denise. 1998. "'Bread and Roses': Pragmatic Women in the Belgium Workers' Party." In *Women and Socialism, Socialism and Women,* ed. Helmut Gruber and Pamela Graves. Oxford: Berghahn.

Dodson, Betty. 1974. "Getting to Know Me." *Ms. Magazine* (August): 106–9.

Dodson, Betty. 1974. *Liberating Masturbation: A Meditation on Self-love.* n.p.: Published by author.

Doyal, Lesley. 1995. *What Makes Women Sick: Gender and the Political Economy of Health.* New Brunswick, NJ: Rutgers University Press.

Duverger, Maurice. 1955. *The Political Role of Women.* Paris: UNESCO.

Dux, Monica. 2009. "Time to End Secrecy and Face the Anguish of Miscarriage." *Sydney Morning Herald* (January 19).

Eakin, Paul John. 1999. *How Our Lives Become Stories.* Ithaca, NY: Cornell University Press.

Ehrenreich, Barbara, and Arlie Russell Hochschild. 2002. *Global Woman: Nannies, Maids, and Sex Workers in the New Economy.* New York: Metropolitan Publishing.

Eley, Geoff. 1998. "From Welfare Politics to Welfare States. Women and the Socialist Question." In *Women and Socialism, Socialism and Women,* ed. Helmut Gruber and Pamela Graves. Oxford: Berghahn.

Enloe, Cynthia. 1990. *Bananas, Beaches and Bases: Making Feminist Sense of International Politics.* Berkeley: University of California Press.

Enwezor, Okwui. 2006. *Lorna Simpson.* New York: American Federation of Arts.

European Commission, Eurydice, and Eurostat. 2005. *Key Data on Education in Europe 2005.* Luxembourg: Office for Official Publications of the European Communities, 2005.

Evans, J., Grimshaw, P., Philips, D., and Swain, S. 2003. *Equal Subjects, Unequal Rights: Indigenous Peoples in British Settler Colonies 1830–1910.* Manchester: Manchester University Press.

Evans, Kate. 1996. "Dunckley, Dorothy Harriette (1890–1972)." In *Australian Dictionary of Biography*, vol. 14. Melbourne: Melbourne University Press.

Evans, Kate. 2009. "Miscarriage: The Loneliest Grief of All." *Independent* (January 27). Available at: http://www.independent.co.uk/life-style/health-and-families/features/miscarriage-the-loneliest-grief-of-all-1516750.html. Accessed June 10, 2009.

"Facts about Violence: U.S Statistics, Global Statistics." n.d. Feminist.com. Available at: http://www.feminist.com/antiviolence/facts.html. Accessed August 10, 2010.

Falk, Barbara. 2002. "Rosanove, Joan Mavis (1896–1974)." In *Australian Dictionary of Biography*, vol. 16. Melbourne: Melbourne University Press.

Faludi, Susan. 1991. *Backlash: The Undeclared War against American Women.* New York: Crown Publishers.

Felski, Rita. 1995. *The Gender of Modernity.* Cambridge: Harvard University Press.

Figert, Anne. 1996. *Women and the Ownership of PMS: The Structuring of a Psychiatric Disorder.* Hawthorne, NY: Aldine de Gruyter.

Finlay, Barbara. 2006. *George W. Bush and the War on Women: Turning Back the Clock on Progress.* London: Zed Press.

Foley, Susan. 2004. *Women in France since 1789.* London: Palgrave.

Foster, Gwendolyn Audrey. 1995. *Women Filmmakers of the African and Asian Diaspora.* Carbondale: Southern Illinois University Press.

Foucault, Michel. [1978] 2008. *The History of Sexuality.* Vol. 1, trans. Robert Hurley. Camberwell: Penguin.

Fouque, Antoinette. 1997. *Women's Rights and the European Union.* Available at: http://www.helsinki.fi/science/xantippa/wle/wle13.html. Accessed February 18, 2009.

Fraisse, Geneviève. 1989. *Muse de la raison.* Paris: Alinéa.

Francis, Martin. 1997. *Ideas and Politics under Labour, 1945–51. Building a New Britain.* Manchester: Manchester University Press.

Francis, Martin. 2000. "Labour and Gender." In *Labour's First Century*, ed. Duncan Tanner, Pat Thane, and Nick Tiratsoo. Cambridge: Cambridge University Press.

Frankel, Lee K. 1927. "The Present Status of Maternal and Infant Hygiene in the United States." *American Journal of Public Health* 17 (12): 1209–17.

Fraser, Nancy, and Axel Honneth. 2003. *Redistribution or Recognition? A Political-Philosophical Exchange.* London: Verso.

Freud, Sigmund. [1933] 2005. "Lecture 33: Femininity." In *The Essentials of Psychoanalysis,* ed. Anna Freud, trans. James Strachey. London: Vintage.

Freud, Sigmund. [1926] 2005. "The Question of Lay Analysis." In *The Essentials of Psychoanalysis,* ed. Anna Freud, trans. James Strachey. London: Vintage.

Freud, Sigmund. [1925] 2005. "Some Psychical Consequences of the Anatomical Distinction between the Sexes." In *The Essentials of Psychoanalysis,* ed. Anna Freud, trans. James Strachey. London: Vintage.

Frevert, Ute. 1988. *Women in German History, from Bourgeois Emancipation to Sexual Liberation.* Oxford: Berg Publishers.

Friedan, Betty. 1963. *The Feminine Mystique.* New York: W. W. Norton and Co.

Fusco, Coco. 2001. *The Bodies That Were Not Ours and Other Writings*. New York: Routledge.

Gaines, Jane. 1995. "Feminist Heterosexuality and its Politically Incorrect Pleasures." *Critical Inquiry* 1 (2, Winter): 382–410.

Gaines, Jane. 1988. "White Privilege and Looking Relations: Race and Gender in Feminist Film Theory." *Screen* 29 (4): 12–17.

Gallop, Jane. 1988. *Thinking through the Body*. New York: Columbia University Press.

Gamble, Rose. 1979. *Chelsea Child*. London: British Broadcasting Corporation.

Garcia, Francisco A. R., Karen M. Freund, Michelle Berlin, Kathleen B. Digre, Donald J. Dudley, Rose S. Fife, Geralde Gabeau, et al. 2010. "Progress and Priorities in the Health of Women and Girls: A Decade of Advances and Challenges." *Journal of Women's Health* 19 (4): 671–80.

Garcia-Moreno, Claudia, et al. 2005. *WHO Multi-country Study on Women's Health and Domestic Violence against Women: Summary Report of Initial Results on Prevalence, Health Outcomes and Women's Responses*. Geneva, Switzerland: WHO.

Garton, Stephen. 2004. *Histories of Sexuality*. London: Equinox.

Gerhard, Jane. 2002. "Revisiting 'The Myth of the Vaginal Orgasm': The Female Orgasm in American Sexual Thought and Second Wave Feminism." *Feminist Studies* 26 (Summer): 449.

Giddens, Anthony. 1992. *The Transformation of Intimacy*. Cambridge: Polity Press.

Gill, Sean. 1994. *Women and the Church of England: From the Eighteenth Century to the Present*. London: SPCK.

Gleadle, Kathryn, and Richardson, Sarah, eds. 2000. *Women in British Politics, 1760–1860. The Power of the Petticoat*. Houndmills: Macmillan.

Global Health Council. n.d. "HIV/AIDS: At Risk Groups—Women and Youth." Available at: http://www.globalhealth.org/hiv_aids/risk_groups1/. Accessed August 23, 2010.

Global Health Council. n.d. "Women's Health: Sexual and Reproductive Health." Available at: http://www.globalhealth.org/womens_health/reproductive/. Accessed August 10, 2010.

Golub, Sharon. 1992. *Periods: From Menarche to Menopause*. Newbury Park, CA: Sage Publications.

Goodall, Heather. [1996] 2008. *Invasion to Embassy: Land in Aboriginal Politics in New South Wales 1770–1792*. Sydney: Sydney University Press.

Gorman, Vanessa. 2005. *Layla's Story: A Memoir of Sex, Love, Loss and Belonging*. Camberwell: Penguin Books Australia.

Gorski, Philip S. 2003. "Historicizing the Secularization Debate: An Agenda for Research." In *Handbook of the Sociology of Religion*, ed. Michele Dillon, 110–22. Cambridge: Cambridge University Press.

Graham, Cynthia A. 2010. "The DSM Diagnostic Criteria for Female Orgasmic Disorder." *Archive of Sexual Behaviour* 39: 256–70.

Graves, Pamela. 1998. "An Experiment in Women-centered Socialism: Labour Women in Britain." In *Women and Socialism, Socialism and Women*, ed. Helmut Gruber and Pamela Graves. Oxford: Berghahn.

Griffiths, Alison. 2002. *Wondrous Difference: Cinema, Anthropology, and Turn-of-the-Century Visual Culture*. New York: Columbia University Press.

Grossman, Atina. 1984. "The New Woman and the Rationalization of Sexuality in Weimar Germany." In *Desire: The Politics of Sexuality*, ed. Ann Snitow, Christine Stansell, and Sharon Thompson. London: Virago Press.

Gruber, Helmut. 1998. "French Women in the Crossfire of Class, Sex, Maternity and Citizenship." In *Women and Socialism, Socialism and Women*, ed. Helmut Gruber and Pamela Graves. Oxford: Berghahn.

Guillaumin, Colettte. 1992. *Sexe, race et pratique du pouvoir: l'idée de Nature*. Paris: côté-femmes.

Gunn, T. Jeremy. 2003. "The Complexity of Religion and the Definition of 'Religion' in International Law." *Harvard Human Rights Journal* 16: 189–215.

Gustafson, Katherine. n.d. "Why Women's Rights Matter to our Food." Available at: http://food.change.org/blog/view/why_womens_rights_matter_to_our_food. Accessed August 23, 2010.

Guyer, Bernard, et al. 2000. "Annual Summary of Vital Statistics: Trends in the Health of Americans during the 20th Century." *Pediatrics* 106 (6): 1307–17.

Hacking, Ian. 1995. *Rewriting the Soul: Multiple Personality and the Sciences of Memory*. Princeton, NJ: Princeton University Press.

Haebich, Anna. 2000. *Broken Circles: Fragmenting Indigenous Families 1800–2000*. Fremantle, Western Australia: Fremantle Arts Centre Press.

Hagemann, Gro. 2002. "Citizenship and Social Order: Gender Politics in Twentieth Century Norway and Sweden." *Women's History Review* 11 (3): 417–29.

Hagemann, Gro. 1985. "Feminism and the Sexual Division of Labour: Female Labour in the Norwegian Telegraph Service." *Scandinavian Journal of History* 10 (2): 143–54.

Hagemann, Karen. 1993. "Men's Demonstrations and Women's Protest: Gender in Collective Action in the Urban Working-class Milieu during the Weimar Republic." *Gender and History* 5 (1): 101–19

Halimi, Gisèle, and Simone de Beauvoir. 2006. *Le procès de Bobigny: Choisir la cause des femmes*. Paris: Gallimard.

Hall, Lesley. 2011. *The Life and Times of Stella Browne: Feminist and Free Spirit*. London: IB Tauris.

Hamilton, Malcolm. 2000. "An Analysis of the Festival for Mind-Body-Spirit, London." In *Beyond the New Age: Exploring Alternative Spirituality*, ed. Steven Sutcliffe and Marion Bowman, 188–200. Edinburgh: Edinburgh University Press.

Hannam, June. 2010. "Women as Paid Organisers and Propagandists for the British Labour Party between the Wars." *International Labour and Working-Class History* 7 (1): 69–88.

Hannam, June, and Hunt, Karen. 2001. *Socialist Women. Britain, 1890s–1920s*. London: Routledge.

Haraway, Donna. 1991. *Simians, Cyborgs, and Women: The Reinvention of Nature*. New York: Routledge.

Harrison, Brian. 1986. "Women in a Men's House. The Women MPs, 1919–1945." *Historical Journal* 29 (3): 623–54.

Hartmann, Katherine, et al. 2005. "Outcomes of Routine Episiotomy: A Systematic Review." *Journal of the American Medical Association* 293: 2141–48.

Hause, Steven C., and Anne R. Kenney. 1984. *Women's Suffrage and Social Politics in the French Third Republic.* Princeton, NJ: Princeton University Press.

Hawkes, Gail, and John Scott, eds. 2005. *Perspectives in Human Sexuality.* South Melbourne: Oxford University Press.

Healy, Bernadine. 1995. *A New Prescription for Women's Health.* New York: Penguin Books.

Heelas, Paul, and Linda Woodhead, with Benjamin Seel, Bronislaw Szerszynski, and Karin Tusting. *The Spiritual Revolution: Why Religion Is Giving Way to Spirituality.* Malden, MA: Blackwell.

Hicks, Neville. 1978. *"This Sin and Scandal": Australia's Population Debate, 1891–1911.* Canberra: Australian National University Press.

Hill, Marylu. 1999. *Mothering Modernity: Feminism, Modernism, and the Maternal Muse.* Garland: New York.

Hinton, James. 1994. "Militant Housewives: The British Housewives' League and the Attlee Government." *History Workshop Journal* 38: 129–56.

Hobson, Barbara. 1993. "Feminist Strategies and Gendered Discourses in Welfare States: Married Women's Right to Work in the United States and Sweden." In *Mothers of a New World. Maternalist Policies and the Origins of Welfare States,* ed. Seth Koven and Sonya Michel. London: Routledge.

Hobson, Janell. 2005. *Venus in the Dark: Blackness and Beauty in Popular Culture.* New York: Routledge.

Hochschild, Arlie, with Anne Machung. 1989. *The Second Shift.* New York: Viking Penguin.

Hochschild, Arlie Russell. 2003. *The Commercialization of Intimate Life: Notes from Home and Work.* Berkeley: University of California Press.

Holt, Emmet L. 1913. "Infant Mortality, Ancient and Modern, an Historical Sketch." Presidential address before the American Association for the Study and Prevention of Infant Mortality, Washington, D.C., November 14–17. *Archives of Pediatrics* 30: 885–915.

Horney, Karen. 1980. *The Adolescent Diaries of Karen Horney.* New York: Basic Books.

Honey, Maureen. 1984. *Creating Rosie the Riveter: Class, Gender, and Propaganda during World War II.* Amherst: University of Massachusetts Press.

Houtman, Dick, and Stef Aupers. 2008. "The Spiritual Revolution and the New Age Gender Puzzle: The Sacralization of the Self in Late Modernity (1980–2000)." In *Women and Religion in the West: Challenging Secularization,* ed. Kristin Aune, Sonya Sharma, and Giselle Vincett, 99–118. Aldershot: Ashgate.

Hughes-D'Aeth, Tony. 2001. *Paper Nation: The Story of the Picturesque Atlas of Australasia 1886–1888.* Melbourne: Melbourne University Press.

Huntington, Samuel. 1993. "The Clash of Civilizations?" *Foreign Affairs* (Summer). Available at: http://www.foreignaffairs.com/articles/48950/samuel-p-huntington/the-clash-of-civilizations. Accessed June 3, 2010.

Hutton, Ronald. 1999. *The Triumph of the Moon: A History of Modern Pagan Witchcraft.* Oxford: Oxford University Press.

Illusions. 1983. Dir. Julie Dash. Women Make Movies. Available at: http://www.wmm.com/. Accessed September 6, 2010.

I.Mirror. 2007. Dir. China Tracy, née Cao Fei. Available at: http://www.youtube.com/user/ChinaTracy. Accessed April 3, 2009.

Institute of Medicine (IOM). 2001. *Exploring the Biological Contributions of Human Health: Does Gender Matter?* Washington, DC: IOM.

Irvine, Janice. 2005. *Disorders of Desire: Sexuality and Gender in American Psychology.* Philadelphia: Temple University Press, 2005.

Jagose, Annamarie. 2010. "Counterfeit Pleasures: Fake Orgasm and Queer Agency." *Textual Practice* 24 (3): 517–39.

Janova, Mira, and Mariette Sineau. 1992. "Women's Participation in Political Power in Europe: An Essay in East-West Comparison." *Women's Studies International Forum* 15 (1): 115–28.

Jasper, Alison. 1998. "Feminism and Religion." In *The Routledge Companion to Feminism and Postfeminism,* ed. Sarah Gamble, 158–67. London: Routledge.

Jay, Martin. 1994. *Downcast Eyes: The Denigration of Vision in Twentieth Century French Thought.* Berkeley, University of California Press.

Jayawardena, Kumari. 1995. *The White Woman's Other Burden: Western Women and South Asia during British Rule.* London: Routledge.

Jeffreys, Sheila. 1990. *Anticlimax: A Feminist Perspective on the Sexual Revolution.* London: The Women's Press.

Jonte-Pace, Diane. 1986. Review of *Freud on Femininity and Faith,* by Judith van Herik. *Theology Today* 43 (1): 123–25.

Jordan, Ellen. 1996. "The Lady Clerks at the Prudential." *Gender & History* 8 (1): 65–81.

Kandiyoti, Deniz. 1997. "Gendering the Modern: On Missing Dimensions in the Study of Turkish Modernity." In *Rethinking Modernity and National Identity in Turkey,* ed. Sibel Bozdoğan and Reşat Kasaba. Seattle: University of Washington Press.

Kaplan, Gisela. 1992. *Contemporary Western European Feminism.* London: Allen and Unwin.

Kappeler, Susanne. 1986. *The Pornography of Representation.* Cambridge, UK: Polity Press.

Katz, Jonathan Ned. 1996. *The Invention of Heterosexuality.* New York: Plume.

Kaur Singh, Nikky-Guninder. 2007. "Translating Sikh Scripture into English." *Sikh Formations* 3 (1): 33–49.

Kay, Rebecca, ed. 2007. *Gender, Equality and Difference during and after State Socialism.* Basingstoke: Palgrave Macmillan.

Keene, Judith. 1999. "'Into the Clean Air of the Plaza': Spanish Women Achieve the Vote in 1931." In *Constructing Spanish Womanhood: Female Identity in Modern Spain,* ed. Victoria Enders and Pamela Radcliff. Albany: State University of New York Press.

Kern, Stephen. 1983. *The Culture of Time and Space 1880–1918.* Cambridge: Harvard University Press.

Kevin, C. 2005. "Forming Families on the Reproductive Technology Frontier." *Griffith Review* 10: 89–102.

Kevin, C. 2011. "'I Did Not Lose My Baby…My Baby Just Died': Historicising Twenty-first Century Discourses of Early Miscarriage." In "Death Scenes," ed. David Ellison and Katrina Schlunke. *South Atlantic Quarterly* 110 (4): 849–65.

Kevin, Catherine. 2009. "Great Expectations: Episodes in a Political History of Pregnancy in Australia since 1945." In *Feminism and the Body: Interdisciplinary Perspectives,* ed. Catherine Kevin. Newcastle Upon Tyne: Cambridge Scholars Publishing.

Kidd, Rosalind. 1997. *The Way We Civilise: Aboriginal Affairs, the Untold Story.* St. Lucia: University of Queensland Press.

The Kinsey Institute website. Available at: http://www.kinseyinstitute.org. Accessed April 20, 2009.

Kociumbas, J. 1997. *Australian Childhood, a History.* Sydney: Allen and Unwin.

Koedt, Anne. [1970] 1991. "The Myth of the Vaginal Orgasm." In *A Reader in Feminist Knowledge,* ed. Sneja Gunew. London: Routledge.

Kolinsky, Eva. 1989. *Women in Contemporary Germany.* Oxford: Berg.

Koonz, Claudia. 1976. "Conflicting Allegiances: Political Ideology and Women Legislators in Weimar Germany." *Signs* 1 (3): 663–83.

Koonz, Claudia. 1987. *Mothers in the Fatherland: Women, the Family and Nazi Politics.* New York: St. Martin's Press.

Lacey, S. de. 2007. "Decisions for the Fate of Frozen Embryos: Fresh Insights into Patients' Thinking and Their Rationales for Donating or Discarding Embryos." *Human Reproduction* 22 (6): 1751–58.

Lacey, S. de. 2005. "Parent Identity and 'Virtual' Children: Why Patients Discard Rather Than Donate Unused Embryos." *Human Reproduction* 20 (6): 1661–69.

Lacey, S. de. 2006. "Patients' Attitudes to Their Embryos and Their Destiny: Social Conditioning?" *Best Practice and Research Clinical Obstetrics and Gynaecology* 21 (1): 101–12.

Lacqueur, Thomas. 2003. *Solitary Sex: A Cultural History of Masturbation.* New York: Zone Books.

Ladd-Taylor, Molly. 1990. "Women's Health and Public Policy." In *Women, Health and Medicine in America,* ed. Rima Apple. New Brunswick, NJ: Rutgers University Press.

Lake, M., and H. Reynolds. 2008. *Drawing the Global Colour Line: White Men's Countries and the Question of Racial Equality.* Melbourne: Melbourne University Press.

Lake, Marilyn. 1986. "The Politics of Respectability: Identifying the Masculinist Context." *Historical Studies* 22 (86): 116–31.

Laqueur, Thomas. 1990. *Making Sex: Body and Gender from the Greeks to Freud.* Cambridge: Harvard University Press.

Larsen, Timothy. 2002. *Christabel Pankhurst: Fundamentalism and Feminism in Coalition.* Woodbridge: The Boydell Press.

Laurence, Leslie, and Beth Weinhouse. 1994. *Outrageous Practices: How Gender Bias Threatens Women's Health.* New Brunswick, NJ: Rutgers University Press.

Leach, William. 1989. "Strategists of Display and the Production of Desire." In *Consuming Visions: Accumulation and Display of Goods in America 1830–1920,* ed. Simn J. Bronner, 99–132. New York: W. W. Norton.

Legates, Marlene. 2001. *In Their Time. A History of Feminism in Western Society*. London: Routledge.

Lennane, R. Jeanne, and R. John Lennane. 1973. "Alleged Psychogenic Disorders in Women: A Possible Manifestation of Sexual Prejudice." *New England Journal of Medicine* 288: 288–92.

Lessing, Doris. [1962] 1999. *The Golden Notebook*. New York: Harper Perennial Modern Classic.

Levin, David. *Modernity and the Hegemony of Vision*. Berkeley: University of California Press.

Levine, Alissa. 2001. "The Social Construction of Female Orgasm: A Cross-cultural Study." PhD thesis, Department of Sociology, McGill University, Montreal.

Levy, Ariel. 2005. *Female Chauvinist Pigs: Women and the Rise of Raunch Culture*. Melbourne: Schwartz Publishing.

Lewis, M. 1992. "Maternity Care and Puerperal Fever in SYDNEY." In *Women and Children First, International Maternal and Infant Welfare 1870–1945*, ed. Valerie Fildes, Lara Marks, and Hilary Marland. London: Routledge.

Liddington, Jill. 1989. *The Long Road to Greenham: Feminism and Anti-militarism in Britain since 1820*. London: Virago.

Linnell, Garry. 2001. "Too Little, Too Soon." *Good Weekend: Sydney Morning Herald* (August 11): 22–31.

Lista, Giovanni. 2006. *Loïe Fuller, danseuse de la Belle Epoque*. 2nd ed. Paris: Hermann Danse.

Loades, Ann. 2003. Review of *Sexing the Trinity: Gender, Culture and the Divine*, by Gavin d'Costa. *Theology Today* 60 (3): 413–15.

Lorber, Judith, and Lisa Jean Moore. 2002. *Gender and the Social Construction of Illness*. 2nd ed. Walnut Creek, CA: Rowman & Littlefield.

Losing Layla. 2001. Dir. Vanessa Gorman.

Loudon, Irvine. 2000. "Maternal Mortality in the Past and its Relevance to Developing Countries Today." *American Journal of Clinical Nutrition* 72 (S1): 241S–246S.

Lovenduski, Joni, and Pippa Norris. 2003. "Westminster Women: The Politics of Presence." *Political Studies* 51: 84–102.

MacKinnon, A. 1995. "From one *Fin de Siecle* to Another: The Educated Woman and Declining Birth-rate." *Australian Educational Researcher* 22 (3): 71–86.

MacKinnon, Alison. 1997. *Love and Freedom: Professional Women and the Reshaping of Personal Life*. Cambridge: Cambridge University Press.

Magarey, S. 1996. "History, Cultural Studies and Another Look at First Wave Feminism in Australia." *Australian Historical Studies* 27 (106): 96–110.

Maines, Rachel P. [1999] 2001. *The Technology of Orgasm: "Hysteria," the Vibrator, and Women's Sexual Satisfaction*. Baltimore: Johns Hopkins Press.

Majumdar, Neepa. 2001. "The Embodied Voice: Song Sequences and Stardom in Popular Hindi Cinema." In *Soundtrack Available: Essays on Film and Popular Music*, ed. Pamela Robertson Wojeik and Arthur Knight. Durham, NC: Duke University Press.

Manji, Irshad. 2004. *The Trouble with Islam: A Muslim's Call for Reform in her Faith*. New York: St. Martin's Press.

Marler, Penny Long. 2008. "Religious Change in the West: Watch the Women." In *Women and Religion in the West: Challenging Secularization,* ed. Kristin Aune, Sonya Sharma, and Giselle Vincett. Aldershot: Ashgate.

Martin, Karin A. 2005. "William Wants a Doll. Can He HAVE one? Feminists, Child Care Advisors, and Gender-neutral Child Rearing." *Gender and Society* 19 (4): 456–79.

Masters, William H., and Virginia E. Johnson. 1966. *Human Sexual Response.* Boston: Little, Brown and Company.

Mayer, Annette. 2002. *Women in Britain, 1900–2000.* London: Hodder & Stoughton.

Maynard, Mary. 1995. "Beyond the 'Big Three': The Development of Feminist Theory into the 1990s." *Women's History Review* 4 (3): 259–81.

Mazón, Patricia. 2003. *Gender and the Modern Research University: The Admission of Women to German Higher Education, 1865–1914.* Stanford: Stanford University Press.

McCalman, Janet. 1998. *Sex and Suffering: Women's Health and a Women's Hospital.* Melbourne: Melbourne University Press.

McCalman, Janet. 1984. *Struggletown. Public and Private Life in Richmond, 1900–1965.* Melbourne: Melbourne University Press.

McCalman, Janet. 2009. "To Die without Friends: Solitaries, Drifters and Failures in a New World Society." In *Body and Mind: Historical Essays in Honour of F. B. Smith,* ed. Graeme Davison, Pat Jalland, and Wilfrid Prest, 173–94. Melbourne: Melbourne University Press.

McKibbin, Ross. 2007. Review of *Religion and Society in Twentieth-Century Britain,* by Callum Brown. *English Historical Review* 122 (499, December): 1464–68.

McLaren, Angus. 1999. *Twentieth-century Sexuality: A History.* Oxford: Blackwell.

McQuire, Scott. 1997. *Visions of Modernity: Representation, Memory, Time and Space in the Age of the Camera.* Sage: London.

Meehan, Elizabeth. 1990. "British Feminism from the 1960s to the 1980s." In *British Feminism in the Twentieth Century,* ed. Harold L. Smith. Aldershot: Edward Elgar.

Mein Smith, Philippa. 1997. *Mothers and King Baby: Infant Survival and Welfare in an Imperial World: Australia, 1880–1950.* London: Macmillan.

Melody, Michael Edward, and Linda Mary Peterson. 1999. *Teaching America about Sex: Marriage Guides and Sex Manuals from the Late Victorians to Dr Ruth.* New York: NYU Press.

Metropolis. 1927. Dir. Fritz Lang. Berlin.

Metzel, Jonathan M. 2003. "Mother's Little Helper: The Crisis of Psychoanalysis and the Miltown Revolution." *Gender & History* 15 (2): 228–55.

Metzl, Jonathan M., and Joni Angel, 2004. "Assessing the Impact of SSRI Antidepressants on Popular Notions of Women's Depressive Illness." *Social Science and Medicine* 58 (3): 577–84.

Miller, Carole. 1994. "'Geneva—The Key to Equality': Inter-war Feminists and the League of Nations." *Women's History Review* 3 (2): 219–45.

Mitchell, Susan. 2003. *Kerryn & Jackie: The Shared Life of Kerryn Phelps and Jackie Stricker.* Rev. ed. Sydney: Allen & Unwin.

Modleski, Tania. 1991. *Feminism without Women: Culture and Criticism in a "Postfeminist" Age.* New York: Routledge.

Montgomery, Fiona A. 2006. *Women's Rights: Struggles and Feminism in Britain c. 1770–1970.* Manchester: Manchester University Press.

Moore, Alison. 2009. "Relocating Marie Bonaparte's Clitoris." *Australian Feminist Studies* 24 (60, June): 149–65.

Morcillo, Aurora G. 2000. *True Catholic Womanhood: Gender Ideology in Franco's Spain.* DeKalb: Illinois University Press.

Morgen, Sandra. 2002. *Into Our Own Hands: The Women's Health Movement in the United States, 1969–1990.* New Brunswick, NJ: Rutgers University Press.

Mørkeberg, Henrik. 1978. "Working Conditions of Women Married to Self-employed Farmers." *Sociologia Ruralis* 18 (2–3): 95–106.

Mottier, Veronique. 2008. *Sexuality: A Very Short Introduction.* Oxford: Oxford University Press.

Muel-Dreyfus, Francine. 1996. *Vichy et l'éternel féminin: contribution à une sociologie politique de l'ordre des corps.* Paris: Le Seuil.

Mulvey, Laura. 1975. "Visual Pleasure and Narrative Cinema." *Screen* 16 (3): 6–18.

Murthy, Prema. "Bindi Girl." Available at: http://www.thing.net/~bindigrl. Accessed July 25, 2005.

Murthy, Prema. "Mythic Hybrid Search." Available at: http://www.turbulence.org/Works/mythichybrid. Accessed July 25, 2005.

Najmabadi, Afsaneh. 2006. "Gender and Secularism of Modernity: How Can a Muslim Woman be French?" *Feminist Studies* 32 (2, Summer): 239–55.

Nakamura, Lisa. 2000. "'Where Do You Want to Go Today?' Cybernetic Tourism, the Internet, and Transnationality." In *Race in Cyberspace,* ed. Beth E. Kolko, Lisa Nakamura, and Gilbert B. Rodman. New York: Routledge.

National Heart, Lung & Blood Institute. n.d. "The Women's Health Initiative (WHI)." Available at: http://www.nhlbi.nih.gov/whi/. Accessed September 15, 2010.

National Institutes of Health, Office of Research on Women's Health. n.d. Available at: http://orwh.od.nih.gov/index.html. Accessed February 16, 2009.

National Women's Health Network. n.d. Available at: http://www.nwhn.org/. Accessed February 17, 2009.

Newport, John P. 1998. *The New Age Movement and the Biblical Worldview: Conflict and Dialogue.* Grand Rapids, MI: Eerdmans Publishing.

Newsom, John. 1948. *The Education of Girls.* London: Faber and Faber.

The New Zealand Obstetrics and Gynaecology Association. 1953. *The Expectant Mother.* Wellington: Whitcombe and Tombs Ltd.

Nice Coloured Girls. 1987. Dir. Tracey Moffatt. Women Make Movies. Available at: http://www.wmm.com/. Accessed February 12, 2010.

Nowaira, Amira Hassan. 2001. "Arabic Autobiography." In *The Encyclopaedia of Life Writing,* ed. Margaretta Jolly, 45–47. Chicago: Fitzroy Dearborn.

Offen, Karen. 2000. *European Feminisms, 1700–1950.* Stanford, CA: Stanford University Press.

Offen, Karen. 1991. "Exploring the Sexual Politics of Republican Nationalism." In *Nationhood and Nationalism in France: From Boulangism to the Great War, 1889–1918,* ed. Robert Tombs, 195–209. London: Harper Collins Academic.

Office for Research on Women's Health. 2006. *Women of Color Data Book.* 3rd ed. Bethesda, MD: National Institutes of Health.

O'Grady, Lorraine. 1992. "Olympia's Maid: Reclaiming Black Female Subjectivity." *Afterimage* 20 (1): 14–20.

Okin, Susan Moller. 1979. *Women in Western Political Thought.* Princeton, NJ: Princeton University Press.

Organisation for Economic Co-operation and Development (OECD). 2008. *Education at a Glance 2008.* Available at: http://www.oecd.org/edu/eag2008. Accessed March 3, 2009.

OurBodiesOurselves.org. n.d. Available at: http://www.ourbodiesourselves.org/book/companion.asp?id = 26&compID = 101. Accessed June 20, 2011.

Paisley, Fiona. 2009. *Glamour in the Pacific: Cultural Internationalism and Race Politics in the Women's Pan-Pacific.* Honolulu: Hawai'i University Press.

Passerini, Luisa. 1992. "Société de consommation et culture de masse." In *Histoire des femmes en occident Histoire des femmes en occident,* ed. Georges Duby and Michelle Perrot. Vol. 5, *Le XXe siècle,* ed. Françoise Thébaud, 297–313. Paris: Plon.

Pateman, Carole. 1988. *The Sexual Contract.* Cambridge: Polity.

Patton, Cindy. 1989. "Hegemony and Orgasm—Or, The Instability of Heterosexual Pornography." *Screen* 30 (Winter–Spring): 100–110.

PBS.org. n.d. "Anthony Comstock's 'Chastity' laws." Available at: http://www.pbs.org/wgbh/amex/pill/peopleevents/e_comstock.html. Accessed August 18, 2010.

PBS.org. n.d. "The Pill." Available at: http://www.pbs.org/wgbh/amex/pill/index.html. Accessed August 18, 2010.

PBS.org. n.d. "The Pill: People and Events: Anthony Comstock's Chastity Laws." Available at: http://www.pbs.org/wgbh/amex/pill/peopleevents/e_comstock.html. Accessed August 25, 2010.

Peiss, Kathy. 1986. *Cheap Amusements: Leisure in Turn-of-the-Century New York.* Philadelphia: Temple University Press.

Perrot, Michelle. 1997. *Femmes publiques,* interviews with Jean Lebrun. Paris: Textuel.

Petro, Patrice. 1989. *Joyless Streets: Women and Melodramatic Representation in Weimar Germany.* Princeton, NJ: Princeton University Press.

Pickering-Iazzi, Robin, ed. 1995. *Mothers of Invention: Women, Italian Fascism, and Culture.* Minneapolis: University of Minnesota Press.

Piess, Kathy. "Girls Lean Back Everywhere." In *The Modern Girl around the World: Consumption, Modernity, and Globalization,* ed. Alys Eve Weinbaum, Lynn M. Thomas, Priti Ramamurthy, Uta G. Poiger, Madeline Yue Dong, and Tani E. Barlow, 347–53. Durham, NC: Duke University Press.

Poirier, Suzanne. 1990. "Women's Reproductive Health." In *Women, Health and Medicine in America,* ed. Rima Apple. New Brunswick, NJ: Rutgers University Press.

Potts, Annie. 2000. "Coming, Coming, Gone: A Feminist Deconstruction of Heterosexual Orgasm." *Sexualities* 3: 55–76.

Potts, Annie. 2002. *The Science/Fiction of Sex: Feminist Deconstruction and the Vocabularies of Hetero-sex.* London: Routledge.

Pregnancy Outcome Unit, Epidemiology Branch. 2008. *Pregnancy Outcomes in South Australia, 2008.* Adelaide: SA Health.

Prentice, Thompson. 2006. "Health, History and Hard Choices: Funding Dilemmas in a Fast-changing World." Presented at "Health and Philanthropy: Leveraging

Change," University of Indiana, August 2006. Available at: http://www.who.int/ global_health_histories/seminars/presentation07.pdf. Accessed August 10, 2010.

Purvis, June. 2002. *Emmeline Pankhurst: A Biography.* London: Routledge.

Ram, Kalpana, and Margaret Jolly, eds. 1998. *Maternities and Modernities: Colonial and Postcolonial Experiences in Asia and the Pacific.* New York: Cambridge University Press.

Rasmussen, Jorgen. 1984. "Women in Labour: The Flapper Vote and the Party System Transformation in Britain." *Electoral Studies* 3 (1): 47–63.

Reagan, L. 2003. "From Hazard to Blessing to Tragedy: Representations of Miscarriage in Twentieth-century America." *Feminist Studies* 29 (2): 356–78.

Reassemblage. 1982. Dir. Trinh T. Minh-ha. Women Make Movies. Available at: http:// www.wmm.com/. Accessed February 12, 2010.

Reiger, Kerreen. 1985. *The Disenchantment of the Home: Modernizing the Australian Family, 1880–1940.* Melbourne: Oxford University Press.

Reiger, Kerreen. 2001. *Our Bodies, Our Babies: The Forgotten Woman's Movement.* Melbourne: Melbourne University Press.

Reilly, James C. 2005. *Poverty and Life Expectancy: The Jamaica Paradox.* Cambridge: Cambridge University Press.

Reilly, James C. 2001. *Rising Life Expectancy: A Global History.* Cambridge: Cambridge University Press.

Reynolds, Margaret. 1995. *The Last Bastion: Labor Women Working Towards Equality in the Parliaments of Australia.* Chatswood: Business & Professional Publishing.

Reynolds, Sîan. 1996. *France between the Wars: Gender and Politics.* London: Routledge.

Rich, Adrienne. 1980. "Compulsory Heterosexuality." In *Sexualities: Critical Concepts in Sociology,* ed. Ken Plummer. London: Routledge.

Robinson, John. 1963. *Honest to God.* SCM Press: London.

Rogers, Rebecca. 2006. "Learning to be Good Girls and Women." In *The Routledge History of Women in Europe since 1700,* ed. Deborah Simonton. London: Routledge.

Rome, Esther, and Jill Wolhandler. 1992. "Can Tampon Safety be Regulated?" In *Menstrual Health in Women's Lives,* ed. Alice J. Dan and Linda L. Lewis. Chicago: University of Illinois Press.

Rose, Jacqueline. 2005. "Femininity and its Discontents." *Feminist Review* 80: 24–43.

Rose, June. 1993. *Marie Stopes and the Sexual Revolution.* London: Faber and Faber.

Rosen, George. 1993. *A history of Public Health.* Baltimore, MD: Johns Hopkins University Press.

Rossi-Doria, Anna. 2000. "Italian Women Enter Politics." In *When the War Was Over: Women, War and Peace in Europe, 1940–1956,* ed. Claire Duchen and Irene Bandhauer-Schoffmann. London: Leicester University Press.

Rothman, Lorraine. 1980. "The Development of Menstrual Extraction in the Women's Health Movement." In *The Menstrual Cycle,* ed. Alice J. Dan. Vol. 1, *A Synthesis of Interdisciplinary Research.* New York: Springer Publishing.

Rousseau, Jean-Jacques. 1762. *Emile, ou de l'éducation.* Available at: http://classiques. uqac.ca/classiques/Rousseau_jj/emile/emile.html. Accessed July 14, 2009.

Rowbotham, Sheila. 1997. *A Century of Women: A History of Women in Britain and the United States*. London: Viking.

Rowbotham, Sheila. 1974. *Hidden from History*. London: Pluto Press.

Rowbotham, Sheila. 1977. *A NEW world for Women: Stella Browne, Socialist Feminist*. London: Pluto Press.

Rowbotham, Sheila. 1989. *The Past Is before Us. Feminism in Action since the 1960s*. London: Pandora.

Rowbotham, Sheila. 1992. *Women in Movement: Feminism and Social Action*. London: Routledge.

Rowe, Dorothy. 2003. *Representing Berlin: Sexuality and the City in Imperial and Weimar Germany*. Aldershot: Ashgate.

Rutherford, Alexandra. 2007. "Feminist Questions, Feminist Answers: Towards a Redefinition." *Feminism & Psychology* 17 (4): 459–64.

Rutherford, Paul. 2007. *A World Made Sexy: Freud to Madonna*. Toronto: University of Toronto Press.

Safran, William, ed. 2003. *The Secular and the Sacred: Nation, Religion and Politics*. London: Frank Cass.

Sanger, Margaret. n.d. "Comstockery in America." Margaret Sanger Papers Project. Available at: http://www.nyu.edu/projects/sanger/secure/documents/speech_com stockery_in_america.html. Accessed August 25, 2010.

Sapiro, Virginia. 1998. "When are Interests Interesting? The Problem of Political Representation of Women." In *Feminism and Politics*, ed. Anne Phillips. Oxford: Oxford University Press.

Sarachild, Kathie. 1979. "Consciousness-raising. A Radical Weapon." In *Feminist Revolution*, ed. Redstockings. New York: Random House.

Sawer, Marian, and Marian Simms. 1984. *A Woman's Place: Women and Politics in Australia*. Sydney: Allen & Unwin.

Schaeffer-Hegel, Barbara. 1992. "Makers and Victims of Unification: German Women and the Two Germanies." *Women's Studies International Forum* 15 (1): 101–10.

Schivelbusch, Wolfgang. 1980. *The Railway Journey: Trains and Travel in the Nineteenth Century*, trans. Anselm Hollo. Oxford: Basil Blackwell.

Scott, Joan Wallach. 2007. *The Politics of the Veil*. Princeton, NJ: Princeton University Press.

Scrimshaw, Susan C. M. 1981. "Women and the Pill: From Panacea to Catalyst." *Family Planning Perspectives* 13 (6): 254–56, 260–62.

Seaman, Barbara. [1969] 1981. *The Doctor's Case against the Pill*. New York: Wyden.

Segal, Lynne. 1983. "Sensual Uncertainty, or Why the Clitoris Is Not Enough." In *Sex and Love: New Thoughts on Old Contradictions*, ed. Sue Cartledge and Joanna Ryan. London: Women's Press.

Segal, Lynne. 1994. *Straight Sex: Rethinking the Politics of Pleasure*. Irvine: University of California Press.

Shohat, Ella. 1991. "Gender and the Culture of Empire: Toward a Feminist Ethnography of the Cinema." *Quarterly Review of Film and Video* 131: 45–84.

Shortall, Sally. 1992. "Power Analysis and Farm Wives, an Empirical Study of the Power Relationships Affecting Women on Irish Farms." *Sociologia Ruralis* 32 (4): 431–51.

Shulman, Alix. 1971. "Organs and Orgasms." In *Woman in Sexist Society: Studies in Power and Powerlessness,* ed. Vivian Gornick and Barbara K. Moran. New York: New American Library.

Simonton, Deborah. 1998. *A History of European Women's Work.* London: Routledge.

Simonton, Deborah, ed. 2006. *The Routledge History of Women in Europe since 1700.* London: Routledge.

Simonton, Deborah. 2011. *Women in European Culture and Society, Gender, Skill and Identity, from 1700.* London: Routledge.

Sineau, Mariette. 1994. "Law and Democracy." In *A History of Women. Towards a Cultural Identity in the Twentieth Century,* ed. Georges Duby and Michelle Perrot. Cambridge, MA: Harvard University Press.

Singer, Josephine, and Irving Singer. 1972. "Types of Female Orgasm." *The Journal of Sex* 8 (4, November): 255–67.

Smith, Harold L., ed. 1990. *British Feminism in the Twentieth Century.* Aldershot: Edward Elgar.

Smith, Harold L. 1984. "Sex vs. Class: British Feminists and the Labour Movement." *Historian* 47: 19–37.

Smith, Joan. 1996. *Misogynies.* London: Vintage.

Smyth, Ailbhe. 1993. "The Women's Movement in the Republic of Ireland 1970–1990." In *Women's Studies Reader,* ed. Ailbhe Smyth. Dublin: Attic Press.

Sobol, Richard B. 1991. *Bending the Law: The Story of the Dalkon Shield Bankruptcy.* Chicago: University of Chicago Press.

Society for Menstrual Cycle Research. n.d. "Menstrual Suppression: Menstruation Is Not a Disease." Available at: http://menstruationresearch.org/position-statements/menstrual-supression-2007/. Accessed September 8, 2010.

Society for Women's Health Research. n.d. Available at: http://www.womenshealth research.org/site/PageServer. Accessed February 12, 2009.

Sohn, Anne-Marie. 1994. "Between the Wars in Britain and France." In *A History of Women. Towards a Cultural Identity in the Twentieth Century,* ed. Georges Duby and Michelle Perrot. Cambridge, MA: Harvard University Press.

Sohn, Anne-Marie. 1992. "Entre deux guerres: les rôles féminins en France et en Angleterre." In *Histoire des femmes en occident Histoire des femmes en occident,* ed. Georges Duby and Michelle Perrot. Vol. 5, *Le XXe siècle,* ed. Françoise Thébaud, 91–114. Paris: Plon.

Sointu, Eeva, and Linda Woodhead. 2008. "Spirituality, Gender, and Expressive Selfhood." *Journal for the Scientific Study of Religion* 47 (2, May): 259–76.

Solinger, Rickie, ed. 1998. *Abortion Wars: A Half Century of Struggle, 1950–2000.* Berkeley: University of California Press.

Solinger, Rickie. 2001. *Beggars and Choosers: How the Politics of Choice Shapes Adoption, Abortion and Welfare in the United States.* New York: Hill and Wang.

Spender, Dale. 1977. *Invisible Women: The Schooling Scandal.* London: The Women's Press.

Spillers, Hortense. 1989. "Interstices: A Small Drama of Words." In *Pleasure and Danger: Exploring Female Sexuality,* ed. Carole Vance. London: Pandora.

Spock, Benjamin. [1946] 1957. *The Common Sense Book of Baby and Child Care.* New York: Pocket Books.

Spohn, Willfried. 2003. "Multiple Modernity, Nationalism and Religion: A Global Perspective." *Current Sociology* 51 (4): 265–86.

Stacey, Margaret, and Marion Price. 1981. *Women, Power and Politics*. London: Routledge.

Starr, Paul. 1982. *The Social Transformation of American Medicine*. New York: Basic Books.

Steinem, Gloria. 2003. "Sex, Lies and Advertising." In *Gender, Race and Class in Media: A Text Reader,* ed. Gail Dines and Jean M. Humez, 223–29. 2nd ed. Thousand Oaks, CA: Sage.

Steven, Allison. 2007. "Race, Gender and the Politics of Segregation." *American Prospect* (June 29). Available at: http://prospect.org/. Accessed August 23, 2010.

Stites, Richard. 1987. "Women and the Revolutionary Process in Russia." In *Becoming Visible: Women in European History,* ed. Renate Bridenthal, Claudia Koonz, and Susan Stuard. 2nd ed. Boston, MA: Houghton Mifflin.

Sumaya, Ciro V., Vivian W. Pinn, and Susan J. Blumenthal. 1997. *Women's Health in the Medical School Curriculum: Report of a Survey and Recommendations.* Rockville, MD: U.S. Health Resources and Services Administration. HRSA-A-OEA-96–1.

Sundar, Pavitra. 2008. "Meri Awaaz Suno: Women, Vocality, and Nation in Hindi Cinema." *Meridians* 8 (1): 144–79.

Tanner, Duncan. 2005. "Gender, Civic Culture and Politics in South Wales: Explaining Labour Municipal Policy, 1918–39." In *Labour's Grass Roots: Essays on the Activities of Local Labour Parties and Members, 1918–45,* ed. Matthew Worley. Aldershot: Ashgate.

Tanner, Duncan. 2000. "Labour and its Membership." In *Labour's First Century,* ed. Duncan Tanner, Pat Thane, and Nick Tiratsoo. Cambridge: Cambridge University Press.

Taylor, Charles. 1991. *The Ethics of Authenticity*. Cambridge, MA: Harvard University Press.

Tesh, Sylvia Noble. 1988. *Hidden Arguments: Political Ideology and Disease Prevention Policy*. New Brunswick, NJ: Rutgers University Press.

Thalmann, Rita. 1982. *Etre femme sous le IIIe Reich*. Paris: Robert Laffont.

Thane, Pat. 1993. "Women in the British Labour Party and the Construction of State Welfare." In *Mothers of a New World. Maternalist Policies and the Origins of Welfare States,* ed. Seth Koven and Sonya Michel. London: Routledge.

Thébaud, Françoise. 1994. "Explorations of Gender." In *A History of Women. Towards a Cultural Identity in the Twentieth Century,* ed. Georges Duby and Michelle Perrot. Cambridge, MA: Harvard University Press.

Thompson, S. 2007. "'Awakened by Angels': Personal Narratives of Perinatal Death in Late Twentieth-century Western Australia and Their Effects on Hospital Policies and Programmes." *Studies in Western Australian History* 25: 166–80.

Todd, Ellen Wiley. 1993. *The "New Woman" Revised: Painting and Gender Politics on Fourteenth Street*. Berkley: University of California Press.

Trinh T. Minh-ha. 1990. *Woman, Native, Other: Writing Postcoloniality and Feminism*. Bloomington: Indiana University Press.

Tuana, Nancy. 2004. "Coming to Understand: Orgasm and the Epistemology of Ignorance." *Hypatia* 19 (1, Winter): 194–232.

Twomey, C. 1997. "'Without Natural Protectors': Responses to Wife Desertion in Gold-rush Victoria." *Australian Historical Studies* 28 (108): 22–46.

U.S. Centers for Disease Control. 1999. "Achievements in Public Health, 1900–1999: Control of Infectious Diseases." *MMWR Weekly* 48 (29, July 30): 621–29. Available at: http://www.cdc.gov/mmwr/preview/mmwrhtml/mm4829a1.htm. Accessed July 13, 2010.

U.S. Centers for Disease Control. 1999. "Achievements in Public Health, 1900–1999: Healthier Mothers and Babies." *MMWR Weekly* 48 (38, October 1): 849–58. Available at: http://www.cdc.gov/mmwr/preview/mmwrhtml/mm4838a2.htm. Accessed July 13, 2010.

U.S. Centers for Disease Control. n.d. "Leading Causes of Death in Females, United States." Available at: http://www.cdc.gov/Women/lcod/. Accessed August 10, 2010.

U.S. Centers for Disease Control. 1999. "Margaret Sanger." *MMWR Weekly* (December 3). Available at: http://www.cdc.gov/mmwr/preview/mmwrhtml/mm4847bx.htm. Accessed August 18, 2010.

U.S. Centers for Disease Control. 2003. "Public Health and Aging: Trends in Aging—United States and Worldwide." *MMWR Weekly* 52 (6, February 14): 101–6. Available at: http://www.cdc.gov/mmwr/preview/mmwrhtml/mm5206a2.htm. Accessed July 13, 2010.

U.S. Centers for Disease Control. n.d. "Unintended Pregnancy Prevention." Available at: http://www.cdc.gov/reproductivehealth/UnintendedPregnancy/index.htm. Accessed August 22, 2010.

U.S. Department of Agriculture, Food and Nutrition Service. n.d. "About WIC." Available at: http://www.fns.usda.gov/wic/aboutwic/mission.htm. Accessed August 17, 2010.

U.S. Department of Health and Human Services, Office on Women's Health. Available at: http://www.womenshealth.gov/owh/. Accessed February 21, 2009.

U.S. Department of Health and Human Services, Public Health Service, National Institutes of Health. 1999. *Agenda for Research on Women's Health for the 21st Century. A Report of the Task Force on the NIH Women's Health Research Agenda for the 21st Century.* Vol. 1, *Executive Summary.* Bethesda, MD: NIH, Publication No. 99–4385.

U.S. Health Resources and Services Administration. n.d. "Title V History." Available at: https://perfdata.hrsa.gov/mchb/mchreports/LEARN_More/Title_V_History/title_v_history.asp. Accessed August 17, 2010.

U.S. Social Security Administration. n.d. "The Social Security Act of 1935." Available at: http://www.ssa.gov/history/35act.html#TITLE%20V. Accessed August 17, 2010.

United Nations Educational, Scientific, and Cultural Organization (UNESCO). n.d. *Educational Statistics.* Available at: http://www.uis.unesco.org. Accessed March 2, 2009.

United Nations Food and Agriculture Organization. n.d. "Women and Food Security." Available at: http://www.fao.org/FOCUS/E/Women/Sustin-e.htm. Accessed August 23, 2010.

United Nations Global Poverty Project. n.d. "Global Poverty Info Bank: Women."
    Available at: http://www.globalpovertyproject.com/infobank/women. Accessed
    August 24, 2010.
United Nations Population Fund. n.d. "Gender Equality Fact Sheet: Gender Equality
    and Education." Available at: http://www.unfpa.org/swp/2005/presskit/factsheets/
    facts_gender.htm. Accessed August 24, 2010.
United Nations Population Fund. n.d. "UNFPA State of World Population 2008,
    Reaching Common Ground: Culture, Gender and Human Rights." Available at:
    http://www.unfpa.org/upload/lib_pub_file/816_filename_en-swop08-report.pdf.
    Accessed August 10, 2010.
Van der Veer, Peter. 2001. *Imperial Encounters: Religion and Modernity in India and
    Britain*. Princeton, NJ: Princeton University Press.
Van de Velde, Th. H. [1928] 1971. *Ideal Marriage: Its Physiology and Technique*. Lon-
    don: William Heinemann.
Van Lerberghe, Wim, et al. 2005. *The World Health Report 2005—Make Every Mother
    and Child Count*. Geneva, Switzerland: WHO.
Vaus, David de. 2004. *Diversity and Change in Australian Families*. Canberra: Austra-
    lian Institute of Family Studies.
Venner, Fiammetta. 1998. *L'Opposition à l'avortement: du lobby au commando*. Paris:
    Berg International.
Verbrugge, Lois M. 1990. "Pathways of Health and Death." In *Women, Health and
    Medicine in America: A Historical Handbook,* ed. Rima D. Apple. New Bruns-
    wick, NJ: Rutgers University Press.
Vincett, Giselle, Sonya Sharma, and Kristin Aune. 2008. "Introduction: Women, Re-
    ligion and Secularization: One Size Does Not Fit All." In *Women and Religion in
    the West: Challenging Secularization,* ed. Kristin Aune, Sonya Sharma, and Giselle
    Vincett. Aldershot: Ashgate.
Walkowitz, Judith. 1992. *City of Dreadful Delights: Narratives of Sexual Danger in
    Late-Victorian London*. Chicago: University of Chicago Press.
Wallis, Lila A., and Marian Betancourt. 1999. *The Whole Woman: Take Charge of
    Your Health in Every Phase of Your Life*. New York: Avon Books.
Wang, Y. A., G. M. Chambers, M. Dieng, and E. A. Sullivan. 2009. *Assisted Reproduc-
    tive Technology in Australia and New Zealand 2007*. Assisted Reproductive Tech-
    nology Series 13. Canberra: Australian Institute of Health and Welfare.
Ward, Graham. 2000. *Theology and Contemporary Critical Theory*. Basingstoke:
    Macmillan.
Ware, Vron. 1992. *Beyond the Pale: White Women, Racism & History*. London: Verso.
Waterhouse, Jill. n.d. "Holt, Beatrice (Bea) (1900–1988)." *Australian Dictionary of
    Biography,* vol. 17. Melbourne: Melbourne University Press.
Weeks, Jeffrey. 2010. *Sexuality*. 3rd ed. London: Routledge.
Weisman, Carol S. 1998. *Women's Health Care: Activist Traditions and Institutional
    Change*. Baltimore: Johns Hopkins University Press.
Wertz, Richard W., and Dorothy C. Wertz. 1994. "Notes on the Decline of Midwives
    and the Rise of Medical Obstetricians." In *The Sociology of Health and Illness,* ed.
    Peter Conrad and Rochelle Kern. New York: Saint Martin's Press.

West, Rebecca. 1913. "Mr. Chesterton in Hysterics." *Clarion* (November 14).

Whelehan, Imelda. 1995. *Modern Feminist Thought. From the Second Wave to "Post Feminism."* Edinburgh: Edinburgh University Press.

Williams, Carla. 2002. "Naked, Neutered, Noble: The Black Female BODY in America and the Problem of Photographic History." In *Skin Deep, Spirit Strong: The Black Female Body in American Culture,* ed. Kimberly Wallace-Sanders. Ann Arbor: University of Michigan Press.

Willis, Deborah, and Carla Williams. 2002. *The Black Female Body: A Photographic History.* Philadelphia: Temple University Press.

Willson, Perry R. 1993. *The Clockwork Factory: Women and Work in Fascist Italy.* Oxford: Clarendon Press, 1993.

Wilson, Elizabeth. 1985. *Adorned in Dreams: Fashion and Modernity.* Berkeley: University of California Press.

Wilson, Elizabeth. 1991. *The Sphinx in the City: Urban Life, the Control of Disorder and Women.* London: Virago Press.

Winter, Bronwyn. 2008. *Hijab and the Republic: Uncovering the French Headscarf Debate.* Syracuse, NY: Syracuse University Press.

Winter, Bronwyn. 2002. "Pauline and Other Perils: Women in Australian Right-wing Politics." In *Right-wing Women: From Conservatives to Extremists around the World,* ed. Paola Bacchetta and Margaret Power, 197–210. New York: Routledge.

Winter, Bronwyn. 2007. "Pre-emptive Fridge Magnets and Other Weapons of Masculinist Destruction: The Rhetoric and Reality of 'Safeguarding Australia.'" *Signs: A Journal of Women, Culture and Society* 33 (1): 25–52.

Woollacott, Angela. 1999. "White Colonialism and Sexual Modernity: Australian Women in the Early Twentieth Century Metropolis." In *Gender, Sexuality and Colonial Modernities,* ed. Antoinette Burton. London: Routledge.

Women's Health Education Center. n.d. "Sterilization." Available at: http://www.womenshealthsection.com/content/gyn/gyn029.php3. Accessed August 22, 2010.

Women in Informal Employment: Globalizing and Organizing (WIEGO). 2009. *Informal Workers in Focus: Domestic Workers.* Cambridge, MA: WIEGO Secretariat, Harvard University.

Woodhead, Linda. 2008. "'Because I'm Worth It': Religion and Women's Changing Lives in the West." In *Women and Religion in the West: Challenging Secularization,* ed. Kristin Aune, Sonya Sharma, and Giselle Vincett. Aldershot: Ashgate.

Woods, N., A. Most, and G. D. Longnecker. 1985. "Major Life Events, Daily Stressors, and Perimenstrual Symptoms." *Nursing Research* 34: 263–67.

Woolf, Virginia. 1938. *Three Guineas.* London: Hogarth Press.

World Health Organization. n.d. Gender, Women and Health. Available at: http://www.who.int/gender/en/. Accessed February 26, 2009.

World Health Organization. 2009. *Women and Health: Today's Evidence Tomorrow's Agenda.* Geneva, Switzerland: WHO.

World Health Organization. n.d. "The World Health Report 2003—Shaping the Future." Available at: http://www.who.int/whr/2003/overview/en/print.html. Accessed August 10, 2010.

Zerner, Sylvie. 1987. "De la couture aux presses: l'emploi féminin entre les deux guerres." *Mouvement Social* 140: 9–26.

Zhang, Jun, James F. Troendle, and Michael K. Yancey. 2002. "Reassessing the Labor Curve in Nulliparous Women." *American Journal of Obstetric Gynecology* 187 (4): 824–28.

Zweiniger-Bargielowska, Ina. *Austerity in Britain: Rationing, Controls and Consumption, 1939–55*. Oxford: Oxford University Press.

CONTRIBUTORS

Liz Conor lectures in Australian studies at the National Centre for Australian Studies, School of Journalism, Australian and Indigenous Studies, Monash University. She is the author of *The Spectacular Modern Woman: Feminine Visibility in the 1920s* (2004) and co-editor (with Jane Lydon) of *Double Take: Colonial Visualities*, a special edition of *Journal of Australian Studies* 35, no. 2 (June 2011). She is currently working on a second monograph, *Skin Deep: The Aboriginal Woman in the White Imagination*.

Alice J. Dan is Professor Emerita, University of Illinois at Chicago, Center for Research on Women and Gender. She edited *Reframing Women's Health: Multidisciplinary Research and Practice* and *Menstrual Health in Women's Lives*.

June Hannam is Emeritus Professor of Modern History at the University of the West of England, Bristol. Her publications include *Isabella Ford, 1855–1924* (1989); with Karen Hunt, *Socialist Women, Britain 1880s–1920s* (2001); and *Feminism* (2007). Her current research interests are in Labour women MPs and propagandists between the wars and women's politics in Bristol after enfranchisement. She is a member of the steering committee of the Women's History Network.

Janell Hobson is Associate Professor of Women's Studies at the State University of New York at Albany. She is the author of *Venus in the Dark: Blackness and Beauty in Popular Culture* (2005) and *Body as Evidence: Mediating Race, Globalizing Gender* (2012).

Catherine Kevin is a lecturer in history at Flinders University in Adelaide, South Australia. She is the editor of *Feminism and the Body* (2009) and co-editor of *Branding Cities, Cosmopolitanism, Parochialism and Social Change* (2009).

Mary Rojek Kleinman, MA, is a doctoral student in sociology at Loyola University Chicago. She previously developed many curricular programs in women's health for medical students and practicing physicians. She serves on the executive board of the Sex and Gender Women's Health Collaborative, a group whose goal is to integrate sex and gender medicine into medical education.

Maureen Perkins is Associate Professor in the School of Social Sciences and Asian Languages at Curtin University, Western Australia. Her publications include *Visions of the Future* (1996), *The Reform of Time* (2001), and *Visibly Different* (2007). She is editor of the journal *Life Writing*.

Zora Simic is Lecturer in History and convener of Women's and Gender Studies at the University of New South Wales, Sydney. She is coauthor of *The Great Feminist Denial* (2008).

Deborah Simonton is Associate Professor of British History at the University of Southern Denmark and author of *Women in European Culture and Society, Gender, Skill and Identity from 1700* (2010) and *A History of European Women's Work, 1700 to the Present* (1998). She is currently leading an international network on "Gender in the European Town," funded by the Danish Research Council.

Bronwyn Winter is Associate Professor in the Department of French Studies at the University of Sydney. She is author of *Hijab and the Republic: Uncovering the French Headscarf Debate* and contributing co-editor of *September 11, 2001: Feminist Perspectives* (republished in North America as *After Shock: September 11, 2001: Global Feminist Perspectives*). She is currently working on her next book, *9/11 Emergency: Has September 11, 2001 Changed the World for Women?*

INDEX

Note: Page numbers in **bold** refer to images.